C000174603

Alcohol Recove

The Complete Problem Drinking Solution

By Lewis David

WINS Health & Wellbeing Publishing

2019

Legal & Disclaimer

The information contained in this book is not designed to replace or take the place of any form of medicine or professional medical advice. The information contained in this book has been compiled from sources deemed reliable, and it is accurate to the best of the Author's knowledge; however, the Author cannot guarantee its accuracy and validity and cannot be held liable for any errors or omissions. Changes are periodically made to this book. You must consult your doctor or get professional medical advice before using any of the suggested remedies, techniques, or information in this book. Upon using the information contained in this book, you agree to hold harmless the Author from and against any damages, costs, and expenses, including any legal fees potentially resulting from the application of any of the information provided by this guide. This disclaimer applies to any damages or injury caused by the use and application, whether directly or indirectly, of any advice or information presented, whether for breach of contract, tort, negligence, personal injury, criminal intent, or under any other cause of action. You agree to accept all risks of using the information presented inside this book. You need to consult a professional medical practitioner before embarking on any program or information in this book.

About the Author

I am an Addictions Therapist and member of the Federation of Drug and Alcohol Practitioners. I was trained in government-sponsored services and have diplomas in Cognitive Behaviour Therapy and Addictions Therapy.

I work in treatment facilities and hospitals, carrying out clinical assessments and working on recovery plans with clients. Thousands of drinkers and other drug users have attended my therapeutic groups, workshops, and seminars. I have also trained treatment practitioners, police, and paramedics regarding alcohol issues.

A Note on Spellings in this Book

I am aware that this book will be read throughout the English-speaking world. Therefore, I have chosen spellings that I believe to be used in the majority of English-speaking countries. So, I have, for example, used program rather than programme, colour rather than color, counsellor rather than counselor, and realize rather than realise.

Dedications:

To my inspirational wife, Antonia.

To all the remarkable clients I have met working in addiction services.

Contents

Introduction 12

Book 1: Alcohol and You

Alcohol and You 15

Making a Decision 23

Seeing through the Alcohol Scam 32

Understanding Alcohol Use Disorder 42

Exploding the Myths of Drinking 48

Choosing Your Path: Moderation or Sobriety 60

Choosing Your Method: Reduction or Detox 69

Drugs That Can Help: Naltrexone and Nalmefene 76

Understanding Your Withdrawal Cycle 83

Using the Power of Time 89

Your Timeline for Change 99

Building Motivation 107

Crushing those Cravings 123

Winning the Head Game 129

Solution Focused Thinking 142

Stopping those Spinning Wheels 156

Recruiting Your Cheerleaders 164

AA and the 12 Steps 174

Smart Recovery and the 4-Point Program 186

Cognitive Behavioural Therapy (CBT) 194

Relapse Prevention 203

Now the Nightmare is Over, What Do You Want the Dream to Be? 212

Book 2: Reversing Alcoholism

Preamble 219

Reversing Alcoholism 231

The Research 241

But Isn't It A Disease? 246

Case Study – Patricia 255

Case Study – Mike 262

Book 3: Change Your Life Today

A User Guide to A Fabulous Life 274

Change Your Life Today 276

It All Begins with Desire 283

But I Don't Know What I Want 291

The Path 298

Following the Instructions 305

Don't Wait Until You're Ready 311

Motivation on Demand 318

Open-Minded Outcomes 323

Recording the Stats 328

Finding Your People 334

Achievement Stacking 339

Super Empowerment 347

Living with a Lighter Touch 355

Serving Up Success 366

Something Out of Nothing 372

Taking Off the Filter 383

This Time Will Be Different 389

Obsessed with Addiction 399

A Taste to Die For 409

Weighing Up Success 415

Healthy Ever After 434

Happiness by Design 443

Dreams by Choice 450

Thank You 452

Introduction

"Alcohol Recovery" is a collection of three books, written by Addiction Therapist, Lewis David. When read together, these books provide a complete solution to problem drinking issues and creating a better life. They are as follows:

Book 1: Alcohol and You – How to Control & Stop Drinking.

Having been on Amazon's Best Seller lists since 2017, "Alcohol and You" has already helped thousands of drinkers and their families. The book includes everything you need to know to self-diagnose the extent of your alcohol problem, decide what is the best solution for you, and gives you all the tools you need to achieve a successful result.

Book 2: Reversing Alcoholism – Real Recovery from Alcohol Addiction.

Using world-class research, "Reversing Alcoholism" reveals the truth about what really happens to problem drinkers – and it's much different to what most people believe. A must-read for all heavy drinkers and their families. Can alcoholism really be reversed? Find out.

Book 3: Change Your Life Today- The Ultimate Guide to Motivation, Success and Happiness.

Most problem drinkers find that putting down the drink is just the start of the process of rebuilding their lives after alcohol. A whole new world awaits you. "Success and Happiness in a Random World" shows you how to find your true path and then turn your deepest desires into reality. Get ready to live your dream.

Book 1:

Alcohol and You:

How to Control and Stop Drinking.

Alcohol and You

You know you need to do something about your drinking. But where do you start? Indeed, you might be asking yourself, can you really change something that has become so central to your life, something that maybe, deep down, you love? You might be confused about whether to cut down or stop drinking, and the thought of stopping forever is terrifying.

Your motivation might be a health warning from your doctor. Maybe you are getting into trouble at work because hangovers are making you call in sick too often. Perhaps alcohol is threatening your relationships, you are having arguments with loved ones and although you are defending your drinking, you secretly suspect that they are right. Maybe you have legal problems, a driving ban or worse. Perhaps your finances are in ruins because you spend so much money on alcohol. Or maybe you have simply reached a point where the problems alcohol brings to your life have exhausted you and you want to call time, you have had enough.

Don't worry. Whatever has brought you to this point, and whatever kind of drinker you are, you have found the right book.

I am an Addictions Therapist working every day with people who, like you, have alcohol issues. I work in one-to-one consultations with drinkers, run workshops, retreats and seminars about drinking and addiction.

More and more, I see my clients achieving great results using insights that you can't pick up from existing books on the market. This is why I wrote this book, to share my knowledge and the experiences of my clients with you in the following pages.

This book is packed with winning ideas that my clients have tried and tested. Everything you will read is based on solid therapeutic science. There is no ideology or dogma here, just loads of practical advice that you can put to work right away.

It doesn't matter whether you are here to reduce your drinking, to stop, or don't know which way to go. This book will help to clarify which option is best for you.

What this book will do is lay out the best ideas and leave you to decide which ones you want to pick up and use. I have no particular philosophy to push because I believe that not everything works for everyone. So I invite you to try out the techniques in this book, some may work for you and others may not. It is not necessary for everything to work for you. The important thing is that you find what you need to achieve your drinking goals. You might find that you use most of the ideas or maybe just a few. It doesn't matter. It's the results you achieve that count.

There are a number of programs for people who want to deal with their alcohol difficulties. You might have heard about "12 Step" or "CBT". You might have read books by former problem drinkers who have found a way to stop that has worked for them and now want you to follow their ideas.

All of these different philosophies are well-intentioned and have varying amounts of success for different drinkers. But they are often contradictory and can be baffling for the person who just wants to get out of their problem, who just wants results. This is made worse by the fact that some people promoting certain solutions might have commercial interests at heart.

Also, people who overcome their own alcohol problems often feel compelled to promote their chosen solution with the zeal of the converted. This is understandable. Overcoming addiction is life-changing and the newly-minted sober person wants to share their insight with the world. But sometimes this leads to tunnel-vision and totally dismissing other approaches that might be equally valid, just different.

The effects of alcohol cause mental confusion, so if we add on top of that varying claims about the effectiveness of different programs, then it's not surprising that the drinker who is seeking help can get totally bewildered, and a bewildered person is unlikely to overcome an addiction. So let me be clear about what the program is in this book. The program is the one that works for you. This book is about finding what that is, putting it to work, and getting the outcome you desire.

Drinkers in crisis feel out of control, they don't understand why they are being compelled to drink so much and behave in ways that hurt themselves. They don't understand why they can start the day feeling awful, swearing in total sincerity never to drink again, yet a few hours later find themselves steaming drunk once more. They don't understand why having a drink, instead of getting rid of the craving, just sets up a new craving to want another drink right away. They don't understand why, even though they can see the damage drinking is doing, they can't stop themselves. Alcohol seems like some huge overpowering dark force that always gets the upper hand with them.

But it doesn't have to be that way.

To this end, we will be demystifying the whole business of drinking. I have found from spending thousands of hours working with drinkers that this works. If you understand what is going on, it cuts alcohol down to size. You start to see it for what it is, simply an addiction, and people are constantly conquering addictions.

Tens of millions of people have broken their addiction to nicotine, which is every bit as addictive as alcohol, probably more so. Similarly, people are giving up notoriously addictive substances like heroin and cocaine all the time. And people around you are moderating or stopping their alcohol use all the time.

A dependence on alcohol is simply an addiction, and an addiction is just a habit gone wrong. That's all it is; nothing more. It's nothing unusual, and it's certainly nothing to be ashamed of.

As is often said, we humans are creatures of habit. This is just as well, as we would find it hard to get through the day without habits. If every time you woke up in the morning, you had to invent your morning routine afresh, your days would have a slow start. Driving to work would be painful if every morning you had to decide your route again. Indeed, driving your car would be impossible, as driving is made up of many small habits that you worked on when you were in the process of learning to drive. If you had to learn all those little habits again every time you wanted to drive your car, you wouldn't go anywhere. Habits can be helpful.

Your drinking probably started off as a small habit, and in those days it may have been helpful. A little alcohol can help people overcome social anxiety, probably the most common reason why people start drinking. It can help them feel more confident. It can help them when life gets difficult and they need to switch off. But that little alcohol can become a lot. Then the habit turns ugly and becomes more of a problem than the problems it originally overcame. It has morphed into being a powerful addiction.

Demystifying alcohol changes that. My clients find that when they understand what happens when they drink, alcohol suddenly becomes robbed of its power. Knowledge puts the power in your relationship with alcohol back in your hands. The knowledge you will get from reading this book will start to give you control.

There are 21 chapters following this, and each one offers a fresh concept and a new way of dealing with alcohol problems. Look upon these 21 chapters as being a menu. You don't have to order every dish. Select the ones that appeal most to you, as they are the ways that are most likely to work.

The rewards are huge. You will become less fearful and anxious. You will learn much about yourself and techniques that will help you in all aspects of your life. You will become richer. You will find it easier to control your weight. You will be able to wake up with a clear head and a clear conscience, not worried about what you might have done the night before. You will be able to tell your doctor the truth when he asks you those awkward questions about your drinking. Your career will benefit. Your relationships will be better. Your mental faculties will be sharper. Your overall happiness will improve. And you might add an extra 10 or more years to your life to enjoy all these benefits.

With so much to look forward to, therefore, I would like to invite you to start thinking about controlling your drinking as something to get excited about, rather than something to fear; as an adventure, not a chore; as a glittering prize within your grasp.

Free PDF Download: How to Self-Diagnose Alcohol Dependency in Minutes.

Before getting into the main body of this book, you might find it useful to answer a questionnaire that will show you where you are on the scale of alcohol dependency. To get a copy, all you have to do is send a blank email (it doesn't need a subject or anything) to alcoholfix@gmail.com, and an autoresponder will send you what you need immediately.

The questionnaire is widely used by clinical staff in addiction services. I use it as part of the assessment process when I see a new client. The PDF explains how it works. I hope you find it useful.

Making a Decision

Sometimes you might feel that there are two voices in your head, and these voices are having a constant argument. One is saying that you really should change your drinking, there is an urgent need. The other voice is reassuring you that despite obvious evidence to the contrary, despite your life starting to come apart at the seams, that you can carry on drinking. It is saying things like: "Well, maybe I don't really have a problem. I don't need to worry. Maybe, I can just leave it as it is." But before you leave it, ask yourself a few questions to diagnose whether you really have a problem.

Here are a few common pointers that alcohol might be a problem. Do any of the following sound like you?

Do you plan your day around your drinking?

If you work, do you go to the bar as soon as the work day is done? Or do you open a bottle as soon as you get in the house? Do you find reasons to fit in a little drink during the day? If you are not working, are you looking at your watch, trying to decide when would be a decent hour to have your first drink? If you are going to eat with family or colleagues, do you suggest places where you can be sure of getting a drink?

Do you know all the best places to get a drink?

If you are buying a bottle on the way home, do you have an encyclopaedic knowledge of all the places that sell your favourite brand? Do you know how much it costs in different stores? If you like a cold drink, do you know which stores keep your brand chilled, so you don't have to waste time chilling your drink when you get home? Do you know all the places that have Happy Hours? Do you know the bars where the owner is most likely to offer you a free drink on the house?

Does a delay in getting your first drink of the day put you in a panic?

Be honest with yourself. Do you start to feel a rising tide of panic when something happens to threaten your regular drink? Maybe you need to work late, but all you can think about is when you will be able to get your usual drink. Maybe a family commitment comes up. You are expected to be somewhere, all smiles for the family photos, but in your head, you are desperately trying to figure out how you can excuse yourself and get to that drink.

Are your friends mostly drinking buddies?

You tell your family what great friends you have, they are always there for you, at the bar. You regard non-drinkers with deep suspicion. Even some of your friends irritate you if they don't drink fast enough. In fact, you are the fastest drinker in your group. You find excuses to squeeze in extra drinks.

You pride yourself on your reputation for always being the first to arrive and the last to leave. You boast about having a high tolerance for alcohol. You joke that vodka and orange is a health drink. You love telling drinking stories.

Do you drink to escape problems?

Whenever life throws difficulty at you, then you drink. In fact, you say, drink is your friend. Without it, you would be really miserable, you tell anyone who will lend you a sympathetic ear. Just look at the bills you have to pay, you say, ignoring the thousands you spend every year on booze. Look at your health problems, another reason to reach for a drink. You can't get a decent job, and your boss is complaining about all the days you have off with mysterious stomach complaints. In fact, life is just so unfair, you deserve to have a little drink, you say.

If that wasn't bad enough, then there are the miserable people in your family who say that if you didn't drink, then your health would improve. You would have the money to pay your bills and you wouldn't have to buy the weekly groceries on a credit card. You would be better thought of at your job. What do they know? They don't understand how tough it is being you.

Does your drinking embarrass you?

You're worried that the guys who collect your recycling think that you're an alcoholic because of how many empties you have every week, so you sneak a few bottles into your neighbour's recycling at night when no one's looking.

When you go to the supermarket to buy booze, you buy a bag of salad as well as the litre of vodka, so the woman on the checkout won't think you're an alcoholic. Also, you don't buy drink from the same store two days in a row, as you are worried that the personnel talk about the amount of alcohol that you buy.

When you are awake half the night throwing up, you try to convince your partner it must have been because of something not cooked right in your dinner earlier. It couldn't have been anything to do with all the wine you drank, you say, because it was a good vintage.

When the doctor asks you how much you drink, you cringe and lie outrageously. You don't want to get a lecture on how drink damages your health because deep down you fear what you are doing to your body.

Do you drink when you don't want to?

Sometimes it seems like too much hard work, but you go for a drink anyway. You don't really feel like it, but you know you have to. You tolerate having to listen to your drinking friends telling the same old boring stories over and over again because you haven't drunk enough yet. Sometimes you drink when you are unwell. You still manage to get to the store, even though you feel like you are dying.

Have you tried to moderate or stop your drinking but found it too hard?

You have woken up a hundred times swearing that you will do something about your drinking. Usually, your resolve is short lived and by evening you have completely forgotten and are back at the booze. Maybe now and again you have managed a few days without drink, maybe even a dry January. But as soon as you started again, it was like a dam bursting. You might have even gone to an AA meeting or two, but then convinced yourself that they are a bunch of cranks and it was not for you.

Do you wake up in fear of what you might have done the night before?

Some mornings you wake up in a sweat, reaching for your mobile phone, worried you have sent someone an inappropriate text or sent your boss an email saying what you really think about his management skills. Worse, you worry you might have been in a fight or driven your car to get a take away while you were blind drunk.

Do you blame other people for your drinking?

When you drink heavily because someone has upset you, you believe it is their fault that you drank. You believe that your driving ban was the police's fault, they should have been busy catching crooks, not good citizens like you who had just had one too many.

When you drink because something goes wrong in your life, you believe it is the fault of life, or fate, or the universe that you drank. You believe that you drink because life is unfair, other people are unfair, and that you just need a good break in life, then things would be OK, and you wouldn't need a drink.

If any of the above sound familiar, then now is the right time to make a decision. In the past, you might have made a decision to do something about your drinking many times and then a few hours later your commitment has drifted off like so much confetti in the wind. It is easy to make a decision at four o'clock in the morning when you are hugging the toilet and feeling like you are dying after a big night on the booze, and then later in the day to have forgotten all about that decision.

So this decision needs to be like no other. It is a commitment to embrace change. This goes against the instinct of an addicted person. Addiction wants to keep you in the same self-destructive loop, day after day, year after year, until it destroys you. That is what addictions do.

The drinkers I work with usually have very entrenched routines. Frequently, they are daily drinkers who often start drinking at the same time of the day with such regularity that you could set your watch by them. Then there are the binge drinkers, who usually have entrenched routines but over longer time frames. (We will be talking more about this in the chapter about withdrawal cycles.)

Even when drinkers realise what is happening, they find it hard to go against that instinct and break out of that loop. Sometimes I hear clients saying they can't get out of their "comfort zone", but it is not comfortable at all, it is painful, it is a "discomfort zone". There is nothing comfortable about having your career destroyed by drinking. There is nothing comfortable about being told you have liver disease. There is nothing comfortable about your partner leaving you because you fall into bed every night in a sweaty, drunken heap. There is nothing comfortable about being worried sick about the debts that are piling up. There is nothing comfortable about becoming incontinent. There is nothing comfortable about waking up in a hospital or police cell, not knowing what happened. Yet the discomfort zone drags people back with a magnetic force.

Until they make a decision to embrace change.

I want you to make that decision now. Don't worry about how you are going to do it. That's what the rest of this book is about. But if you feel ready to make that decision, there is something I would like you to do to mark the occasion. I want you to take a small action because decision without action goes nowhere. You have fallen into this trap before. You have decided to do something about your drinking but ended up drinking again within hours, because the decision wasn't backed up by action.

I want you to tell someone important in your life that you have made this decision. Say that you have decided to get a grip on your drinking and this time and you are going to give it everything you've got. Say you're not sure how you are going to do it yet, but you have a book written by a professional to guide you, and you are going to follow it.

You don't have to stop at telling just one person. Tell more. Tell the world. Research shows that people who make a public pronouncement of their intention are vastly more likely to succeed than people who keep it to themselves.

Does that make you feel anxious? That's okay because embracing change will make you feel anxious at first. But it's also exciting. Think about it: anxiety and excitement are quite similar feelings, are they not? And when you have done it, you will feel good.

Do you remember at the start of this chapter we were talking about those two voices arguing in your head? Well, after you read the last couple of paragraphs, I expect the argument erupted again. One voice will be telling you that what I am saying makes sense. That is the voice that wants the best for you, the one that wants you to have a healthier, richer, and happier life. The other voice, the one telling you to ignore what you are reading and stay in your discomfort zone, is the voice of your addiction, which is starting to panic because it feels under threat, and you now know what addictions want to do, they want to destroy you.

You don't need me to tell you which voice to listen to. It's time to make that decision.

Seeing Through the Alcohol Scam

I was recently sitting in a hotel restaurant waiting for my meal and my attention began to drift to the other guests. The wine waiter was busy attending to his clients. I watched the same ritual as he moved from table to table. He would pour a little wine into a glass for the guest to taste and then stand motionless displaying the bottle's label towards the guest. After swishing round the wine and trying to look like a connoisseur, the guest would then nod and the wine waiter would fill the glasses of the guests on the table. The waiter then moved on to the next table, where the same ritual would play out.

I wondered how many times that same ritual was happening at dinner tables around the world that evening – probably millions. I've taken part in that ritual myself, and if other people want to drink, that's up to them; it's none of my business. But I'm quite happy not to be involved in the silly wine ritual any more.

Frankly, I used to find it embarrassing. I would swish the wine around and try to look like I knew something about it, and then accept the bottle. I had an agreement with the wine waiters of the world. I always knew I would accept the wine and they always knew I would, too. I was a compliant customer who would willingly pay three times the price that the same bottle would cost in a supermarket, and then pretend I knew something about wine. How crazy is that? Sometimes, to break this deadlock and make myself feel better about it, I fantasized about the idea of spitting the wine out in a disgusted fashion and sending the bottle back, just for the hell of it, but I never did.

I used to know a man who owned a vineyard in the Borba region of Portugal, where wine production is an important part of the local economy. I was invited to visit, which I did. It was impressive. The place was a model of shining high tech manufacturing, a finely-tuned machine for churning out the Borba region's wine to the consumer.

The owner proudly presented me with a selection of the wine, including a few bottles of the "good stuff", the expensive wine that the Portuguese who picked the grapes would probably not be able to afford to buy themselves. I tried some of this wine when I got home. I didn't like it. I tried a bit more, thinking I must be missing something. I had seen since I was a child all those food and drink programs on TV where wine buffs droned on about wine being witty, elegant, cheeky, complex, and so on. But I didn't seem to have that ability. I thought there was something wrong with me.

I consulted a friend who had a reputation for being a wine-lover. He was the sort of guy who would drive across a continent just to visit a vineyard with a good reputation. I explained my predicament. I told him that I had been given some good wine, but I just didn't know whether it was witty, elegant, cheeky, or complex. He gave me the sort of superior but understanding look that my old Latin teacher used to give me when I confessed to being completely baffled.

He told me that he knew the wine I was talking about and that it was excellent. The problem wasn't the wine, it was me. I had drunk too much plonk, my palate needing educating. The remedy was for me to study wine, spend huge amounts of money on expensive vintages and then one day I too would be able to stick my nose knowingly into one of those huge glistening wine glasses and confidently give my verdict on the witty, elegant, cheeky, or complex conundrum.

This illustrates something that sets alcohol apart from other drugs. I have worked with users of many drugs, from tobacco to cocaine to heroin, and most of them realise that they are using a substance that is harmful. They understand that they are in the grip of a nasty drug that could kill them. I've worked in the needle exchange at a drug project where heroin users would come in to get clean needles and dispose of their old equipment. I've talked to hundreds of users, and I have never met one who glamourized their heroin use. They knew heroin was bad news. Similarly, crack cocaine users know that the drug is bad, even if they love it. Tobacco smokers mostly want to stop. Research shows that 40% of smokers try to stop every year. They know it's a bad drug. If someone gives up one of these drugs, they are usually congratulated, even by people who continue to use the same drug.

With alcohol, however, it's completely different. As my story about the wine illustrates, alcohol is beyond reproach and seemingly it was me that was the problem. I wasn't trying hard enough to understand wine! Alcohol is not to blame. You are to blame.

And because alcohol has this exalted status, if you have a problem with alcohol because you drink too much and it damages your life, then society believes that it is you that is the problem, not the drug.

Surely this cannot be right.

Why does alcohol have this special place among drugs? I know when I gave up tobacco, people said well done, including other smokers, because they too would like to quit. But if you tell people you have given up drinking, you are challenged. People want to know why, or they try to break your resolve by cajoling you into having a drink. People assume there is something wrong with you because you have decided not to use the most socially destructive drug on the planet.

One reason for this is that in the western world drinkers are in the majority, and what the majority do is considered normal. Therefore, if you stop drinking you must be abnormal. But that doesn't mean you are wrong.

I was congratulated on giving up smoking, but if I had given up smoking back in the 1950s when 80% of the population smoked, it would have been different. Back then smoking was considered normal. Nowadays, if you light up a cigarette in the office, you could be sacked. But back then, offices were full of smoke and employers had an obligation to provide ashtrays for staff and let them smoke all they wanted. Doctors prescribed cigarettes for stress, and indeed in the United States, doctors endorsed tobacco advertising. If I had given up smoking back then, I would in all likelihood have been regarded as odd, just as someone who stops drinking might be nowadays. But that doesn't mean I would have been wrong to stop smoking, as history has shown, I would have been right.

But with alcohol, use is hyped up and glamourized, and we believe the hype and the glamour. From early childhood, we are indoctrinated into the idea that alcohol is good. When I was small, my father worked as a manager for a transport company. At Christmas time the sales people from truck companies would visit him and give him presents to try to buy his favour. Frequently the gift would be alcohol. I remember him coming home with presentation boxes of wine. It sent to me the clear message that if you wanted to please someone, you gave them alcohol; therefore alcohol must be a good thing.

Even from an early age, I was aware of glitzy and persuasive advertising for alcohol. I was invited to "try a taste of Martini, the most beautiful drink in the world" according to the song on the TV ad. "Guinness is good for you", I was told by the ad agency.

Successful people all seemed to drink. As a small boy watching those glittering shows from Hollywood on TV, I thought Frank Sinatra and Dean Martin seemed to float through life on a sea of Bourbon. I didn't really know what Bourbon was, but it seemed to be the thing to drink if you wanted a Hollywood lifestyle. And if my father took me to the cinema, I would see James Bond drinking vodka before saving the world and winning over the attractive woman.

No wonder people of my generation grew up with a positive image of alcohol.

It is still the case nowadays that the information we see in the media is heavily biased towards making profits, not promoting healthcare. Mind-numbing sums of money are spent every year on promoting the sale of alcohol compared to what is spent on educating people about alcohol. The drinks company Diageo, for example, spent an eye-watering 2.64 billion U.S. Dollars on marketing in 2014. That's just one company.

With access to these immense marketing budgets, the drinks companies sell us a totally fictional image of what drinking is like. The image is one of style, sophistication, relaxation, reward, of being among smiling friends, of ideal summers with a cool beer, and perfect Christmases with a glass of port.

The drinker is happy to buy these images as it affirms your drinking, validating your addiction. Alcohol companies don't tell you that buying their brand puts you at risk of permanent brain damage, life-threatening seizures, cancers, stroke and heart attack.

Drink companies trade in human misery. Take for example manufacturing beer and cider with 9% alcohol content. The only people who will buy beer that strong will be drinkers who have lost control, only someone with an addiction would want to drink that. The brewers must realize that the market for such drinks is made up of drinkers in crisis. They are cynically pedalling this stuff to vulnerable people who are hopelessly in alcohol's grip, whose health is being seriously damaged.

Likewise supermarkets that pile up drink promotions right at the entrance of the store, where you have to go past rows of bottles to get to the things you came in to buy. What the retailer wants is for you to make an impulse buy, and this preys on the drinkers who have a problem. In the past, there would be a drinks section that you could avoid. Now drink pops up everywhere. I recently found a random beer promotion in the stationery section of a supermarket – you could go in for a pencil and come out with a pack of Budweiser instead!

It's you, the drinker, who is the target of this marketing. Forget the image of the cosy drinks company that's your friend. It's just not true. All they want is your dollar (or pound or euro or rupee). If you can see through this and see that you are just being exploited, you can use this to start building some motivation. Get angry with these companies for what they have done to you. Some clients I have worked with have found a lot of motivation in getting angry when they realise that the big drinks companies are just using them as pawns, that shareholders profits are valid reasons to destroy people's lives.

I also want you to get past the idea that there is something wrong with you if you cut down or stop drinking. There is nothing wrong with being sober. It's actually rather pleasant waking up feeling happy and well and looking forward to your day, rather than waking up feeling like a freight train ran over you in the night. True, your drinking buddies wouldn't agree, but that's why they're your drinking buddies.

Attitudes are starting to change now. In many countries we are starting to see health information on adverts and on cans and bottles. Admittedly, it's a bit lame at the moment. In the UK, we are encouraged to "Drink responsibly". Frankly, that isn't going to make someone who is drinking a litre of vodka a day suddenly cut back. But it is a sign of things to come. Pressure is growing for better health warnings, and maybe eventually a move to plain packaging, as we have seen with tobacco in some countries.

While the majority of people drink, it will take time for this to happen. In all probability, many people in government who can make these decisions are drinkers themselves, so they are hardly likely to be motivated to push for change. But once drinkers become the minority, change will happen much quicker. And this could be on the way. In the United States in 2015, only 56% of people reported they drank within the last month, just a small majority.

Increasingly, we see publicity for having sober breaks. Dry January has been around a long time. But more and more we see people taking time off from alcohol, and the more this happens, the more it will become more socially normal not to drink. This seems to be particularly taking hold with young people. The Office of National Statistics in the UK reports that one person in five between the ages of 16-24 is teetotal.

Many people simply need advice and information about alcohol. Drinkers usually know surprisingly little about what they're drinking. Sure, they might know the best place in town to buy a Cabernet Sauvignon at a discount, or which store always keeps their favourite brand of beer in the chiller, but they don't know much about how alcohol works and what it does to their minds and bodies. Few drinkers know how to come off alcohol safely.

This book is about to transform what you know about alcohol and how to moderate or stop drinking. I am not going to lecture you and tell you what to do. But I am going to give you the knowledge you need to be able to take a more informed, adult decision about your drinking. You are about to break alcohol's hold over you.

Understanding Alcohol Use Disorder

Alcohol Use Disorder - which healthcare professionals use in assessments – gives us a range to assess the extent of problematic alcohol use in different people, a spectrum of drinking severity, if you like. This is very helpful, because drinkers are not the same. What defines heavy drinking will vary from one person to another, and what defines a problem will vary depending on the type of damage that drinking is doing to a person's life.

Physiologically we are all different and the way our bodies process alcohol varies greatly. I have worked with drinkers who can drink relatively large amounts of alcohol without much downside and stop whenever they like. At the other extreme, I had one client once whose problem drinking level was just two glasses of wine, a quantity that most drinkers reading this book would regard as trivial. But because of the inefficient way her body processed alcohol, those two glasses of wine were enough to get her very drunk and give her a three-day hangover.

In this chapter you will be able to self-diagnose Alcohol Use Disorder (AUD). There is no shame in getting a positive diagnosis. AUD can strike anyone, regardless of age, race, upbringing, education or genetics. And it's very widespread. According to the American government agency the National Institute of Alcohol Abuse and Alcoholism, 17 million adults in the United States had AUD in 2012 alone, that's 7.2% of the population over 18 years old.

I find that talking about AUD is more helpful than talking about alcoholism. There are good reasons for this. Firstly, calling someone an alcoholic has very negative connotations, as it is most often used as an insult. It's an unhelpful label to put on someone and it's also a sticky label that people find hard to lose once it has been put on them.

If you call a child an idiot, there is a danger that she will grow up believing that to be true and she will underachieve as a result. Similarly, if you call someone an alcoholic there's a danger that he will then start acting out in the way he believes an alcoholic would, and it will become self-fulfilling.

Secondly, using the word alcoholic is very black and white and gives rise to the idea that you are either an alcoholic or you are not. A lot of people believe that if you are an alcoholic, you must stop drinking; whereas if you are not an alcoholic, it's okay to drink.

As the result of this, there are a lot of drinkers out there drinking dangerously high amounts of alcohol, but think it's okay because they believe they are not alcoholic. There are also a lot of drinkers who have been driving themselves crazy for years because they have a constant debate going on in their head about whether they are alcoholic, which gets them nowhere.

AUD has different categories: mild, moderate and severe. It's really useful in my job for me to understand which category a client falls into, because the sort of advice I might give to someone with severe AUD would be inappropriate for someone with mild AUD. It helps us to be able to treat drinkers as individuals. It gets us away from using a one-size-fits-all approach to excessive drinking.

From your point of view being a drinker, it is also useful because it gives you a realistic idea of where you are in terms of the severity of your problem. It is common amongst drinkers that they are unrealistically optimistic in terms of how well they are doing, or sometimes they might be unrealistically gloomy.

What's more, AUD opens the door for making progress. Because in diagnosing AUD we look at drinking in the last 12 months, it is not a fixed diagnosis for ever and a day. If you are diagnosed as having severe AUD, for example, that doesn't mean you will always have severe AUD. Over time, as your drinking patterns change, the severity of your diagnosis can change.

I don't want to give rise to false hope that if you have severe AUD that you can somehow suddenly and miraculously become a moderate drinker. But you can, with professional help, lessen the severity and make your drinking issues much more manageable.

You can self-assess whether you have AUD very simply. Here are some questions to ask yourself, which come from the National Institute of Alcohol Abuse and Alcoholism.

In the past year, have you:

1. Had times when you ended up drinking more, or longer than you intended?

2. More than once wanted to cut down or stop drinking, or tried to, but couldn't?

3. Spent a lot of time drinking? Or being sick or getting over the after-effects?

4. Experienced craving – a strong need, or urge, to drink?

5. Found that drinking – or being sick from drinking – often interfered with taking care of your home or family? Or caused job troubles? Or school problems?

6. Continued to drink even though it was causing trouble with your family or friends?

7. Given up or cut back on activities that were important to you, or gave you pleasure, in order to drink?

8. More than once gotten into situations while or after drinking that increased your chances of getting hurt (such as driving, swimming, using machinery, walking in a dangerous area, or having unsafe sex)?

9. Continued to drink even though it was making you feel depressed or anxious or adding to another health problem? Or after having had a memory blackout?

10. Had to drink much more than you once did to get the effect you want? Or found that your usual number of drinks had much less effect than before?

11. Found that when the effects of alcohol were wearing off, you had withdrawal symptoms, such as trouble sleeping,

shakiness, irritability, anxiety, depression, restlessness, nausea, or sweating? Or sensed things that were not there?

You need to answer yes to at least two of the above symptoms for an assessment of AUD.

If you have answered yes to two or three symptoms, your assessment is: mild.

If you have answered yes to four or five symptoms, your assessment is: moderate.

If you have answered yes to six or more symptoms, your assessment is: severe.

Remember, this is not a diagnosis that is written in stone for all time. Understanding where you are at this moment with AUD gives you a starting point. Reading and implementing the information in this book will be a great way to improve your AUD assessment.

Exploding the Myths of Drinking

You remember in an earlier chapter, we were talking about those voices in your head having an argument? Well, before we go any further, I think it's time to disarm the voice of your addiction. As you read this book, that voice is going to do a lot of shouting, it feels under threat, it won't be happy until you are back in the discomfort zone that will destroy you. The main weapon that voice has is repeating myths around alcohol until you believe them. So let's take a look at some of these ideas and see if they are really true or simply myths.

Life would be boring without a drink

In the workshops I run with drinkers, this is probably the problem that people raise the most, the question of boredom. People just cannot imagine getting through an evening without a drink. Life would just be so boring. Is this really true?

Here is an extract from a conversation with a client:

Kevin: "It's all been going really well with keeping off the booze. I'm really pleased. I've been focusing on work and doing stuff with the family in the evening. My partner is really happy. But obviously I am going to have a few drinks on Sunday."

Me: "Sunday? You've lost me on that one. Why do you say it's obvious that you will have a drink on Sunday?"

Kevin: "It's the football, of course! My team are playing. It's a big game. I'm going to watch it on satellite, on the big screen. It'll be great, I can't wait. Obviously I'll have a drink."

Me: "That word 'obviously' again...I still don't understand what is obvious about drinking because football is on TV. Can you explain?"

Kevin (looking at me in total surprise): "Well, it would be boring without a drink. Obviously!"

Me: "So, let me see if I understand this. Your favourite team are playing?"

Kevin: "Yes."

Me: "It's a big game?"

Kevin: "Yes."

Me: "You've got a big satellite TV to watch it on?"

Kevin: "Yes."

Me: "But you would find all that boring without a drink. Is that correct?"

Kevin (starting to hesitate): "Yes. Well, no. I'm not sure now. Maybe."

Me: "You find football boring without a drink?"

Kevin: "No, I love it."

Me: "If you love it, why do you need the drink?"

Kevin: "I suppose I've always had a drink when I watch football. I suppose it's just a habit."

Me: "So watching the football wouldn't be boring without a drink, then?"

Kevin: "Now that I think about it, I suppose it wouldn't be. And my partner would be pleased."

Me: "Why's that?"

Kevin: "Well the last time there was a big game on TV, I had a few too many and fell asleep on the sofa. She had spent ages getting Sunday dinner ready and she was really angry. We had a hell of an argument after. Perhaps it would be better just to get some Pepsi in the fridge this time."

You can see what happened here. Kevin had simply assumed that watching the football without a drink would be boring because it was his habit to drink while watching the game, nothing more. It was just a myth that had grown up in his mind. All it really took to dispel this myth was to question whether it was really true. If Kevin had concluded that football really would be boring without a drink, then he would have been better finding a new sport to follow rather than getting drunk.

It's not surprising that if you have been turning to alcohol as your go-to action in most situations that you would think that life without it is boring. But next time you are in that situation, consider whether it is lack of alcohol that is boring or is it what you are doing? Should you be looking to replace the activity with something more entertaining or absorbing, rather than simply reaching for the bottle?

It is also the case that there is nothing intrinsically exciting about alcohol. If you are sitting alone, doing nothing and bored, all that will happen if you drink is that you will be sitting alone, doing nothing, bored and drunk - hardly a great improvement.

In complete contrast to the drinker who thinks that being sober is unremittingly boring, people who are habitually sober regard drinking as boring. You can see what they mean if you go to a bar and listen to drunken people talking to each other. Short-term memory becomes affected very quickly when people drink, with the result that people keep repeating themselves, and usually louder as well. Not great entertainment.

I run workshops on boredom. I brainstorm with a group of drinkers, who think that life without drinking is boring, all the things they could do without having a drink. On one occasion, the group came up with over 200 ideas in a few minutes. Not bad going for a group of people who said they couldn't think of anything to do! Try it yourself next time you are bored, see how close you can get to our 200, then pick one from your list and go do it.

Alcohol helps me deal with anxiety and depression

This is widely-held belief, certainly among people who come to me for help. I would estimate that 80% of drinkers I see are on prescription anti-depressants when they first arrive for treatment and think that alcohol helps them with anxiety and depression. The irony is that alcohol makes anxiety worse and is a depressant. Using it to combat these things is like putting gasoline on a fire in the hope of putting it out. So why is it that most people don't realize that?

I think it is because the first thing alcohol depresses when it goes into the brain is our self-control, we feel a bit like a dog let off the leash, it's exciting, which gives the illusion that alcohol is giving us a lift. However, it's very short-lived. After a couple more drinks, your mood will be on the way down. But as your memory will be starting to fail, the following day you are much more likely to remember the pleasant bit at the beginning, rather than the nasty stuff that happened later in the night.

It is a characteristic of all drugs - whether you are talking about crack cocaine, nicotine, heroin, ecstasy, or alcohol – that it tends to be the bit at the beginning that is the good part. Also with alcohol, you might not realise it, but if it has been a while since you had a drink, you will be in withdrawal. That "I really need a drink" feeling is telling you that you are in withdrawal. Consequently, that first drink gives you a lift because that feeling of withdrawal gets washed away, which feels good for a short time.

Heavy alcohol use in fact increases the chances of developing depression, increases the severity of symptoms of depression and makes recovery from depression more difficult. One bit of good news for people suffering with depression and heavy alcohol use, however, is that if alcohol is taken out of equation, things can improve quickly, with a substantial reduction in depressive symptoms only five weeks after drinking stops, according to NHS information.

There are much better ways to deal with anxiety and depression than drinking. Although these conditions are not the topic of this book, the later chapter about Spinning Wheels, which includes links to Mindfulness-Based Relapse Prevention, may be helpful.

Alcohol helps me relax

Most people, including non-drinkers, would take it as a given that alcohol is relaxing. But is that really true? We are told that alcohol is relaxing, and most advertising for alcohol reinforces this idea. You will have seen countless adverts showing people enjoying a drink in exotic, vacation locations or at the end of the working day with friends. The link between alcohol and relaxation is drummed into us from early childhood, so it's not surprising that when we first pick up a drink, we expect it to relax us.

But is it more the case that drinking alcohol is something we do when we are relaxing already? If you are having a drink after work, you were relaxing already. If you have a drink on vacation, you were relaxing already. And that little lift that alcohol gives you, as discussed a few paragraphs ago, adds to the illusion that it is the alcohol which is responsible for relaxing you, not that you were simply relaxing already.

If alcohol is relaxing, then people would become more and more relaxed the more they drink. Yet if we look at people's behaviour when they have a lot to drink, we see people getting very excited, upset, crying, getting into fights, domestic violence, breaking up the city centre on Saturday night. Is that really the behaviour of people who are relaxed?

One person was referred to me because, after a night of drinking lots of alcohol, which is allegedly relaxing, he had poured gasoline all over himself and tried to set fire to himself. When I asked him about this, he said he had no recollection of the incident at all and he had no idea why he tried to turn himself into a human torch. Whatever the reason, I doubt it was because he was feeling relaxed.

Alcohol helps me sleep

Here is a short extract from a typical conversation I have had with many drinkers when they have seen me for an assessment:

Client: "I couldn't get to sleep without alcohol."

Me: "Alcohol gets you to sleep."

Client: "That's absolutely right."

Me: "What do you think about then you wake up at 4 a.m.?"

Client: "Oh, I just think about what's going on, what I need to do, my mind goes round and round in circles and I can't get back to sleep..........Hang on a minute, how did you know I wake up at four in the morning?"

Everyone is amazed that I know they wake up at four in the morning. But it isn't difficult. The majority of daily drinkers wake up around that time.

The reason is the Law of Rebound, which states that every drug has the opposite effect when it wears off. So in the case a stimulant, such as crack cocaine, it makes you energised and happy for a short time when you take it, but the user will be tired and in a low mood for a long time when it wears off. When it comes to opiates, they make you constipated when you use them, so you had better be near a bathroom when they wear off.

In the case of alcohol, it wears off pretty quickly. So if you start drinking after work or when the kids go to bed and then alcohol makes you sleepy, overnight it will wear off and around four in the morning your system will wake up and, before you know it, you are wide awake.

I have a high tolerance to alcohol, so I can get away with it

The ability to drink lots is often held up as something to admire. You know the sort of thing:

"He drinks like he's got hollow legs."

"She can drink all the men under the table."

"He drinks like a fish, but he never seems drunk."

Quite why we have this admiration for people who can drink till they're senseless is hard to say. But it isn't a quality to be admired - it's one to be feared. Developing a high tolerance means is that the body's natural defence system to keep you safe from harm, namely being sick, is bypassed.

If you can drink and drink all night, you are in real danger, because you are able to keep drinking until you reach life-threatening levels of intoxication. You can also get brain damage from alcohol-related dehydration, have a seizure as a result of lower blood sugar levels, or have a heart attack or a stroke.

You will be at risk of alcohol poisoning, which is a killer. As we have discussed, alcohol is a depressant, and in alcohol poisoning, the respiratory system becomes so depressed that you simply stop breathing, and then it's game over.

The risk of respiratory failure becomes even higher for people who take medication called benzodiazepines, which includes common prescription drugs like Valium, Librium, Tamazepam and Xanax. Benzos, as they are commonly known, also depress the respiratory system, so if you are taking benzos and drinking, it increases the risk that your breathing could fail.

Ironically, people with high tolerance to alcohol are at risk of developing a condition known as reverse tolerance, which means that tolerance levels drop dramatically. It can happen quickly and the same person who the week before could drink a blue whale under the table suddenly starts getting crazily drunk on tiny amounts of alcohol. What is happening is that the liver has become so damaged that it can no longer process alcohol efficiently, a potentially fatal condition.

Drinking makes me happy

My clients all with have one thing in common when I first meet them, they are all heavy drinkers. Some of them drink astounding amounts of alcohol when they first refer to me.

So if drinking alcohol makes people happy, then the people I meet in my job would surely be the happiest people in the world, because they drink loads.

But they are not happy - far from it. Most are taking anti-depressants. Most have serious life issues, often as a direct result of their drinking. I have also found that the more people drink, the unhappier they are.

This has led me to formulate my First Law of Recovery from Alcohol Addiction:

"Misery increases in direct proportion to the amount of alcohol taken."

I feel I'm missing out if I don't drink

I can't argue with this. If you don't drink, or drink in moderation, you are indeed missing out. Here are some of the things you could potentially be missing out on: stroke, heart attack, cancer, sclerosis of the liver, impotence, job loss, brain damage, embarrassing yourself at social events, anxiety, hangovers, debts, memory loss, incontinence, poor eye-sight, shakes, arguments, free overnight accommodation in prison, seizures, depression, saying things you regret, heavy sweating, wet brain, jaundice, inappropriate texting, divorce, blackouts, early death.

Wouldn't you like to miss out on that lot?

Choosing your Path:
Moderation or Sobriety

After dealing with so many drinkers who arrive at my consulting room in search of help, it seems obvious to me that there are many kinds of drinkers, with varying levels of problems. It logically follows, therefore, that there may be various solutions.

Drinkers come in a wide range, a spectrum of alcohol use. At one end there is the occasional drinker who just has a drink on special occasions and then only a small quantity. At the other extreme is the person who drinks several litres of spirits every day. Everyone else who ever lifts a glass is at some point on the spectrum between those extremes.

There are different theories about where you draw a line across the spectrum and say that those on one side don't have a problem and those on the other side do. In reality, the line is probably fairly wide and vague. As we saw in chapter three and diagnosing AUD, it is a wide spectrum.

This is because what alcohol does in one person's body may be quite different from someone else's. Your size, sex, and age all play a part.

What's more, it's not just the effect on the body that indicates problem levels of drinking. When I am assessing someone who has come to me with drink issues, I will be looking at the effect on relationships, career, finances, criminal record, social standing, self-esteem, mental faculties, happiness and general quality of life. Then I will start putting together a plan with the drinker.

In order to start making a plan to overcome the alcohol issues that have brought you to this book, however, we will need to consider a fundamental question. Which is right for you, moderation or sobriety? In order to start to answer this question, take a look at the statements below. Which of these are true for you?

1. If you can't get a drink, you show signs of physical dependence, such as shaking hands, heavy sweating, and feelings of panic.

2. Previous attempts at controlled drinking have quickly ended in failure.

3. You have needed an alcohol detox under medical supervision in the past.

4. You have a strong desire for sobriety or a commitment to AA.

5. There are a lot of heavy drinkers in your family and social group.

6. You have been in hospital because of drinking.

7. You have lost a job because of your drinking.

8. You get verbally abusive or physically violent when drunk.

9. You put yourself at risk when drunk.

10. You have a criminal record because of drinking.

If you answered "yes" to any of the above, I suggest you have an honest heart-to-heart with yourself about whether moderation is really going to work for you. If you answered "yes" to several of the above, then really the chances of you sustaining moderation over a period of time are not promising. I am not saying impossible. I have sometimes seen my clients produce surprising results. But I don't want to give you false hope, and you may need to explore some other options as well, which you will be looking at as you read through this book.

Now take a look at the following list and again consider which are true for you:

1. You have in the recent past had periods of time when you have drunk at non-problem levels.

2. If you were unable to get a drink, it would not cause you any serious distress.

3. You have a strong preference for normal drinking.

4. You have been able to show self-control in other parts of your life, such as giving up smoking, successfully dieting, or having a training program.

5. You are not receiving treatment for serious mental health issues.

6. You do not have addiction problems with other drugs.

7. You get few bad physical reactions to a night's drinking.

8. Drinking doesn't have a detrimental effect on your work.

9. Your family and friends are supportive of your drinking moderately.

10. You are not violent or abusive when you drink.

If you can agree with most of the above 10 statements, then moderate drinking might work for you. That said, just because you can drink moderately doesn't mean you should not become sober. But it does mean you have a choice.

What research shows us

The biggest piece of research into moderation was a controlled drinking program run at the University of New Mexico in the United States over 20 years. The results of the program, as shown in follow ups after 3 or more years, make interesting reading for anyone wanting to moderate.

What the researchers found in their follow up studies was that 15% of participants in the program were drinking at stable levels of moderation, which was defined as 10 American standard drinks per week (equivalent to 17.5 British Units or 14 Australian standard drinks).

Another 23% were described as achieving "pretty good moderation", defined as up to 14 American standard drinks per week (equivalent to 24.5 British Units or 19.6 Australian standard drinks).

In addition, 24% were abstaining from drinking alcohol altogether, while the remaining participants in the program had returned to drinking at harmful levels.

It is encouraging that in total 38% were still drinking at either stable or pretty good moderation. But what I find particularly interesting is the 24% who were abstaining, because remember this was a controlled drinking program; people hadn't joined in order to abstain. So why had such a high percentage stopped drinking entirely?

The answer for some people was that, as they had been used to drinking to get drunk, they found that moderate drinking seemed pointless and they might as well not drink at all. For others, they found that moderate drinking was just too hard. Either they simply couldn't do it, or couldn't sustain it. They found that not drinking at all was in fact easier for them than trying to control it.

Most drinkers when they come for professional help are hoping they can become moderate drinkers. They simply can't face the idea of giving up drinking, it's just too frightening. So people will often say things like "I'd just like to be able to have a few drinks with my friends at the weekend" or "I'd like to be able to have a drink on special occasions" or "I'd like to be able just to stop after a couple of drinks".

Some drinkers can moderate without too much difficulty and can achieve these aims. Some can moderate, but it's hard work and great effort is required. A significant number, however, are unrealistically optimistic about their ability to moderate, and are sadly doomed to failure. If you fall into this last category, you can save yourself time and heartache by facing up to the fact now.

Some people, however, even after a significant period of heavy drinking, can become moderate drinkers. In fact, this is a much more common phenomenon than is often acknowledged. We see it all the time with young people.

There is nothing unusual about single people without responsibilities drinking heavily for several years in their early twenties as part of an alcohol-centred social life. But they don't become dependent, and when life takes a new turn and something more interesting comes along, they simply reduce their drinking or stop.

There is no drama about this. Most of them will not need to enter treatment. All that is happening is that their life priorities have changed and being out with their friends drinking large amounts of alcohol is of no interest anymore.

They have found something more important, more absorbing: falling in love, starting a family, or launching a career. It doesn't even occur to most of these people that they have escaped the grip of an addictive drug. They just feel that they have moved on.

Another type of drinker I sometimes see in my practice is the person who has been a moderate drinker for years, but has suddenly entered a period of heavy drinking and can't seem to get out of it. Usually we find that there has been a life event that caused this: the loss of a loved one or the loss of a job is the most common.

My role is then to provide support until the person has been able to deal with the underlying issue, at which point they can usually make an adult decision about whether to resume moderate drinking or take a break from alcohol.

On the other hand, some people have by necessity a very black and white relationship with alcohol. They either drink heavily or not at all. They cannot find a happy middle-ground. They become addicted really easily. After perhaps just a few encounters with alcohol in their youth, they become dependent, and there is no such thing as safe drinking for them. In this situation, they may need to go to a medically supported detox, a subject we will be covering later in this book.

Quite why some people become dependent drinkers and others don't is unknown. Some people can give up drinking and go for years without a drink, but it only takes one encounter with alcohol for them to become re-addicted all over again. It's instantaneous. Yet other people can drink like a parched horse for years and then suddenly stop with no apparent ill effects, as if nothing had happened.

There are various ideas on why people vary so much in their reaction to alcohol. There are theories around genetics, trauma, and upbringing. But no one really knows. It seems to be an example of human diversity. The important thing for you is to see which type you are, and work from there.

If you are still unsure about which category you fall in to, there is good news. You can defer your choice of path. You can try reducing in stages and see how you feel about it as you go. You might find that it is too difficult. But you might find that you can achieve a plateau at a level of drinking that doesn't cause you problems. Or you might find that you can keep reducing right down to zero.

Later in this book, we will be exploring all this further and constructing your plan for success.

Choosing Your Method:
Reduction or Detox

In this chapter we will be looking at choosing a method to get to your goal of moderation or sobriety, and I need to right away up-front make a warning: if you have been drinking heavily, you should not suddenly stop completely. There is a very real danger of seizure. Anyone who has a history of fitting is particularly at risk, but it could happen to anyone. If in any doubt, you should consult a physician.

What happens is that your brain and central nervous system become used to the suppressant effect of alcohol. If the alcohol is suddenly removed, this causes a rebound effect called hyper-excitability, which can trigger a seizure. The risk of seizure should not be taken lightly as it can have very serious consequences.

For this reason, I recommend to clients either to reduce in stages or, if they want to stop drinking completely and find reduction is too difficult, to consider a medically supervised detox. Cessation, suddenly stopping, is something I would only suggest to people who frequently stop already for several days at a time without any sign of withdrawal.

Reduction

You can use reduction as a method whether you want to go for moderation or sobriety - it's just a question of how far you reduce. With sobriety as a goal, clearly this is simple, your goal is zero. But how about if you want to moderate, what does moderation look like?

Without an international standard, it looks confusing, with different countries giving slightly different recommendations. But to give us a benchmark to work with, let's look at the United States, as this book will probably be read there more than anywhere else.

In the United States, the recommended limit for low risk drinking is 14 standard drinks per week for men, and 7 standard drinks per week for women. That's equivalent in the UK about 24 British units for men and 12 for women, or in Australia that would work out to about 20 Australian standard drinks and 10 for women. You can Google the exact recommendations for your country. In any event, I hope that will give you a guideline to work with for an eventual goal.

I use the phrase "eventual goal" because, if you are drinking five or ten times that amount per week at the moment, these levels of drinking will seem so far below what you are used to that they might well seem ridiculous to you. You probably can't get your head around drinking amounts that seem so vanishingly small.

The solution to this is simply not to worry about it right now - just focus on the first step of a reduction plan. There is no point in obsessing about the later stages of your reduction if you can't achieve the first step.

A good reduction plan would look like this:

1. To start off, you need to know exactly what you are reducing from. What exactly is your starting point? If you are the sort of drinker who drinks the same every day, this is easy. But if your drinking varies, I suggest you download a drinks diary app onto your phone. Choose one that looks fun, as there is no reason why dealing with your alcohol issue should be some sort of mournful time.

2. Carry on drinking normally for a week. Use your drinks diary app every time you have a drink. You don't need to tell people what you are doing. They will probably assume you are just checking your messages.

3. After the week, work out exactly what your average consumption is.

4. Reduce the amount you drink by 20%, so if for example you drink 10 beers a day, reduce to eight.

5. Stay at this level for a week, so your system gets used to this being normal consumption for you.

6. After a week, if you are feeling stable, reduce by a further 20% for a week.

7. Repeat until you reach your goal.

So to sum up, you establish exactly what you are drinking now, and then reduce by 20% per week. Do not exceed the 20% weekly reduction in order to avoid getting an adverse reaction. If at any time you get a bad reaction, such as substantial shaking or hallucinations, get medical assistance. And don't over-think what you're doing, don't start projecting into the future, just focus on this week's goal.

Detox

The word detox gets thrown around in magazines and blogs to describe all sorts of reduction, people talk about detoxing to purge the body. It is also used in a figurative sense, I heard someone talking about detoxing from social media, by which I guess they meant purging your mind.

When it comes to alcohol, however, detox is a much more serious matter. It's not like detoxing from, let's say, sugar, which you can safely do at home. When we talk about detoxing off alcohol, we mean a medically supervised treatment plan. You should not try to detox without professional help.

The only people who should be considering a detox are:

a) Drinkers who are committed to quitting altogether. Detox is not for people who want to cut down.

b) Drinkers who need to be detoxed so other medical procedures can be performed. For instance, you might be admitted to hospital for something totally unrelated to alcohol, but the hospital will have to detox you to work with you.

c) Drinkers who are physically dependant. Signs of dependency include drinking to stop the shakes in the morning, heavy sweating after drinking, and having the reflex to vomit but with nothing coming up, which is commonly known as the dry heaves. You might feel itchy, like something is crawling across your skin. Hallucinations can occur, especially about insects – you might imagine swarms of wasps are after you.

Another thing to consider about detox is that it is not a miracle cure. I meet many people in my work who have been through numerous detoxes. It's heart-breaking to see drinkers desperately pinning their hopes on a detox, only to relapse within days. The actual detox itself is just the start. Staying sober afterwards takes dedication. The techniques in this book will help.

The usual way to detox is by taking a drug under medical supervision that replaces alcohol, so your body doesn't go into seizure and you are not plagued by cravings. A drug which is commonly prescribed is chlordiazepoxide, also known as Librium. Your condition will be regularly checked by a nurse, and you will probably be given relapse prevention counselling.

A typical detox will take about a week. After that, you will come off the chlordiazepoxide. You may then be prescribed another drug called acamprosate, also known under the brand name Campral, which you can take for several months if necessary, to reduce cravings.

Another drug you might come across is called disulfiram, also known as Antabuse. This can be prescribed to people when the initial detox period is over. It works in quite a different way, it's a deterrent. It works by blocking an enzyme in your gut which processes alcohol. The upshot of this is that if you drink with disulfiram in your system, you will probably be very sick.

Disulfiram isn't used much in my part of the world. I don't think medical prescribers are keen to recommend something that can make you sick - it goes against the prescriber's instinct. In fact, I have only worked with one client who used disulfiram. He had been happily sober for over a year, but said he liked to take it as a deterrent against him having a sudden moment of madness and picking up a drink. It made him think twice.

Most detoxes are in-patient detoxes in a hospital or private detox facility. However, in some areas home detoxes are available to people who have good support from family at home. A nurse visits every day to check the patient's blood pressure and general well-being. I often attend people on home detoxes to deliver relapse prevention counselling.

You might find that detox in your part of the world is a bit different, so check with your local drug and alcohol agency what's normal where you live.

Drugs That Can Help:
Naltrexone and Nalmefene

In the chapter on detox, we were discussing drugs that are used to help drinkers stop drinking. But what if you don't want to detox? What if you're not even sure if you want to stop drinking entirely?

In this chapter we are going to take a look at a different type of drug, the opioid antagonist, and in particular two drugs in this class, Naltrexone and Nalmefene. Naltrexone is a generic drug that has been around for decades. Nalmefene is manufactured under the brand name Selincro by the drug company Lundbeck.

The idea of the opioid antagonists is that they block the pleasurable effects of alcohol, so although they don't stop you from having a drink, they take away the desire to carry on drinking. This looks like great news for the drinker who wants to achieve moderation. It also looks like great news for the drinker who wants to stop, as using an opioid antagonist makes it easier for the drinker to reduce safely as a prelude to stopping entirely, without having to go through a detox.

How the opioid antagonist works is that it blocks the receptors in the brain that produce the feeling of well-being and sedation that comes with alcohol, especially that first drink or two. The usual rush of endorphins, the feel-good hormones that alcohol releases in your brain, is effectively switched off. Consequently, the drinker who has taken a drink is less interested in picking up another as the reward system is not active.

One of the main differences between normal drinkers and heavy drinkers is that normal drinkers find that having a drink or two will meet their desire to have a drink - they reach a point where they have simply had enough and want to stop, rather as normal eaters will stop eating when they feel full. But the heavy drinker doesn't have that same sense of having enough, because having a drink, rather than meeting that desire to have a drink, will instead set off a craving for another, which in turn set off a craving for another, and so on until something stops them from drinking or they pass out. However, this should cease to be a problem if using the opioid antagonist.

This way of controlling your drinking was pioneered by Dr John Sinclair, who studied at the University of Cincinnati but went on to practice in Finland. Sinclair believed that drinking to problematic levels was in fact a learned behaviour to which some people were more susceptible than others. His research indicated that in certain people the reward, which he called reinforcement, was caused by endorphins being released that bind with the opiate receptors in the brain. This sets up a very powerful addictive cycle. His theory was that if you could block the receptors while alcohol was present in the brain, you could break this cycle. The opioid antagonists do this.

He used Naltrexone on experiments with rats while he was still an undergraduate at Cincinnati. Rats were exposed to alcohol over a period of time. Sinclair then took the alcohol away for several weeks, so the rats were forced to go cold-turkey. He then re-introduced alcohol to the rats to see if they had lost interest in alcohol during their period of abstinence. On the contrary, he found that they binged when they had the opportunity to drink again. He theorised that alcohol deprivation, rather than reducing the desire to drink, actually increased it. Sinclair went on to confirm his ideas in tests with people. In order to avoid the alcohol-deprivation effect, he used Naltrexone with drinkers to help them reduce and claimed a 78% success rate.

What happens in practice is that the drinker takes the opioid antagonist, Naltrexone or Nalmefene, approximately an hour before drinking. They will then need to do nothing unusual. They are free to drink as normal. There is no need to employ any special moderate drinking techniques.

The drinker should, if the medication works, not drink so much as the drug is blocking the feeling of reward. This is then repeated over time. The desire to drink is then reduced a little every time. So this method could work either for someone wanting to moderate or as a slow detox technique for someone who wants to become alcohol-free. Sinclair called this gradual reduction in the desire to drink "extinction", so the less you drank, the less you wanted to drink, until you didn't want to drink at all. This has become known as the Sinclair Method.

The Sinclair Method has obvious attractions for the drinker. It sounds great. All gain and no pain. You just keep drinking until you naturally lose the desire for it – as Sinclair puts it, you drink yourself sober. It sounds fantastic.

My reaction to the Sinclair Method as an Addiction Therapist was a little more sceptical when I first heard of it. Would it actually work in practice? It's one thing for something to have a 78% success rate is clinical trials. It's a little different when you are dealing with real people out in the world.

I have now had the opportunity to work with a number of clients who have been taking an opioid antagonist. In the UK where I work, Nalmefene was introduced by the NHS in 2014. You obtain a prescription from your GP. However, it comes with strings attached. You need to have alcohol counselling alongside taking the drug. That's where people like me come in, providing the counselling.

What I have observed is promising but not conclusive. I stress that I am just talking about my observations of how it has worked with people I have been working with; I have not conducted a scientific study. But the conclusion I am coming to is that Nalmefene can indeed help drinkers, but it is not a magic solution to everyone's drinking problems, because it seems a lot depends on how the person taking the drug gets on with the side effects.

Some people get along fine with Nalmefene from the start and have no side effects. Others have had side effects the first once or twice they have used it, but it then settled down. Still others have had side effects, in particular dizziness or sickness, which has been sufficiently severe for them to terminate taking the drug.

In those that can tolerate the drug, most report that it does help. I have often heard reports from clients on Nalmefene saying that they have poured a drink, had a few sips, but then forgotten about it, only to notice much later that they still have half their drink left. It also helps if the person has something mentally-absorbing to do.

In the case of a client I have been working with recently, he found that his alcohol usage dropped to such trivial amounts that he decided to stop drinking altogether. His GP then changed his prescription from Nalmefene to Acamprosate, a drug which helps to reduce cravings for people who have stopped drinking (we discussed Acamprosate in Chapter 5).

Interestingly, this client had not started taking Nalmefene with the aim of stopping drinking. He just wanted to cut down. But when his drinking fell to the equivalent of less than a bottle of wine per week, he decided he might as well drop the drink entirely, as he was so close to zero anyway.

His experience shows that Nalmefene can indeed provide a pathway to abstinence, if that is what you want. Sinclair's research showed that 25% ended up becoming abstinent of alcohol. The remainder would have to continue taking the drug.

This method gives an extra option for the drinker wanting to moderate or stop. If you think that Nalmefene or Naltrexone could help you, the first step is to talk to your GP and ask his or her advice. If the GP feels it would be suitable for you, the doctor can then signpost you to a suitable alcohol counsellor to support you.

However, I have found that there is a lack of knowledge among doctors – at least in my part of the world – about using opioid antagonists with drinkers. It's surprising that it isn't better known, since Sinclair published his "Method for Treating Alcohol-Drinking Response" back in 1989.

If you run into difficulty, there is a non-profit organization that can help. The C3 Foundation, who can be found via their web site www.cthreefoundation.org, was created to promote the Sinclair Method, and they can help in finding a physician in your area who is familiar with the method. The web site includes a link to a TED Talk by actor Claudia Christian and more information including a description of the method by Sinclair himself.

Understanding Your Withdrawal Cycle

Understanding your withdrawal cycle can be a key tool in sorting out your drinking difficulties. To explain what a withdrawal cycle is, let's look at a scenario that is very common, as described by one of my clients, Alex.

The Creation of a Daily Drinker

Alex said: "When I first started drinking, it was just on a Saturday night. I had left school and started working, so I had some money in my pocket and I started going out for a sociable drink.

I didn't really think there was anything wrong with it. After all, it was what my friends did, it was normal. In fact, it would have seemed a bit odd if I hadn't gone for a drink.

It was fun. I had a laugh with my friends, we played pool, and we tried to pull girls. And we drank. Sometimes we drank a lot. Maybe I would make a bit of an idiot of myself. Maybe I would throw up when I got home. But I didn't think anything of it. I was just behaving like any number of men my age.

Pretty soon, the weekend drink started on a Friday night after work and stretched until the early hours of Sunday morning. Again, I didn't think much about this. After all, millions of people have a drink after work on Friday, and lots of them will carry on into the weekend. Why not? You've worked all week – surely you deserve a drink and relax.

No one commented on my behaviour. I was still living at home. My parents didn't drink much, but I know my Dad had been a bit of a boozer when he was younger. So I think they just regarded me as being normal, even on the nights when I got home really steaming drunk.

This went on as my weekly ritual for months. Then it changed slightly. I started popping out for a few drinks around Tuesday. It just seemed such a long wait to get to Friday. I didn't drink loads on Tuesdays because I had to get to work the next day.

Again no one commented on my behaviour. Why not pop out for a few beers and shoot a few frames of Pool on a Tuesday? I wasn't getting into trouble. There wasn't any harm in it.

Then after a while I started to notice something. I began to start missing alcohol after a couple of days. Waiting three days for Tuesday or Friday to roll around started to seem like quite a pain. For example, at work on Friday morning, I would just be thinking about when I could get out of work and go straight down the pub.

So I had a great idea: If waiting three days for a drink was getting hard, why wait? Have a drink before the cravings set in. Brilliant! Problem solved! And so I started drinking every couple of days. Then I found that waiting two days felt too long. So I became a daily drinker.

For the next few years, the highlight of my day was getting that first drink immediately after work, and the time frame between drinks got even shorter. I was having a drink at lunchtime, just to keep me going.

What followed was years of hell: a broken marriage, heavy debts, a lost driving licence and job losses. I had become - as I heard it described years later at my first AA meeting - a functioning alcoholic. But I wasn't functioning very well."

What had happened with Alex was that his withdrawal cycle had shortened more and more. To start off, he had a weekly cycle. Then when he started drinking on Tuesdays, his withdrawal cycle shortened to 72 hours.

This 72 hour withdrawal cycle is common with many drinkers. Often these are people whose drinking doesn't cause many problems. They are drinkers who don't realise they are in a cycle. They would probably be surprised, even outraged, if someone used the word withdrawal in connection with their drinking. Drinkers mostly think it is just drug users who experience withdrawal, forgetting that alcohol is a drug, too.

Some drinkers never go past the 72 hour cycle. But for many it is just a stage on the way to becoming the daily drinker.

The Binge Drinker

In my experience of working with drinkers, daily drinkers greatly outnumber binge drinkers. But the binger's problems are just as valid. At first, it seems that the binge drinker is an exception to the rule of the cyclical drinker. But on closer investigation, the cycle can still be found. It is just a bigger cycle.

A common binger's cycle is where they will drink heavily at the weekend, but then not drink at all in the week. They will say "I don't have a problem. I can go for days without a drink." They will be convinced that this is true, even if someone looking from the outside can see that their life is falling apart.

However, the reality usually is that they don't drink for several days simply because they feel so hammered from the weekend session that they just can't face a drink. But when, after a few days, they feel better, the urge to drink returns.

It is ironic that recovery from feeling sick because of alcohol brings on the urge to drink again, which is guaranteed to lead to feeling sick all over again. It makes no sense that someone would want to behave in this way. After all, if eating peanuts made you feel sick for days, you would simply stop eating peanuts. But when alcohol is involved, common sense goes out of the window.

Another fairly common bingeing scenario is the binger who will drink heavily for a couple of weeks or more, then take at least a week off. This is just an even longer cycle.

A few binge drinkers are impossible to categorise, their drinking is so unpredictable. In some instances, bingers can even go months between drinks, then for a few days or weeks they just go off the rails.

I believe that in this last case, what we are seeing are not binge drinkers at all, although they might think they are. What we are seeing is drinkers going through periods of drinking and sobriety. They don't recognise this to be the case, however, because the period of sobriety isn't intended to be for ever.

Using Your Withdrawal Cycle

When you become aware of what your withdrawal cycle is, you can use this information to start to reduce. What you do is to start to push the boundaries of the cycle back.

So let's say for example that you are the sort of daily drinker who always starts drinking after work at 6 p.m. You can push back your starting time to 6.30, stay with that for a few days to get used to it, then move to 7 p.m.

It's important that you don't just drink your normal amount in a shorter time, and don't finish later than normal either. If you keep to this plan, logically you would end up with evenings where you don't drink at all, and then you will be making real progress.

Try adapting this idea to your cycle of drinking. For example, if you are a binger, try taking a day longer than normal between binges, then two days, and so on.

Using the Power of Time

Here is a story related by a former drinker called Karen. She has now been happily past her alcohol problems for several years. She doesn't struggle with it anymore. She has a very simple attitude to alcohol nowadays. She can take it or leave it, so she just leaves it.

But it hasn't always been this way. She was a heavy daily drinker from her early twenties until giving up over two decades later. Her life had been a mad roller coaster ride of dramatic up and downs. Finally, she realised that her life was heading into another dramatic downward phase from which she was afraid she might not survive. She realised that the drinking had to stop. This is the story of the first few months.

"I knew I needed to stop drinking as a matter of urgency. I had all sorts of problems: work, money, relationships, and on top of that my body was giving me a few warnings that I couldn't ignore anymore.

I wasn't even enjoying my drinking. It was just a pain. It was something I had to do, it was just pure addiction. I would find myself going out in the rain or snow to get a drink. I knew I would rather be at home in the dry and the warm, but I didn't have a choice. My addiction was demanding that I go out and get a drink.

It had to stop.

I started by forcing myself to cut down. This wasn't easy. It's amazing how if you just cut down by one drink a day – which doesn't sound like much – just how much you miss even that small amount of alcohol. But I was motivated.

Fear of what would happen if I didn't stop was forcing me on. Over a few weeks I gradually started to cut down. I managed to get down to a bottle of wine a day, or equivalent in other drinks. I hovered around that level for a week. Because I had been used to drinking a lot more than that for years, drinking just a bottle of wine in the evening felt like such a small amount to drink that it didn't hit the spot. The cravings were with me all day long, and that bottle of wine in the evening wasn't satisfying them. It was sending me crazy.

Then one morning something fantastic happened, I think that because of all my efforts to cut down, a switch must have just flipped in my head, and out of nowhere I woke and thought to myself: I'm not going to drink today, and I didn't. It felt very weird but okay. I spent much of the day wondering in the countryside, starting to come to terms with my first few hours of sobriety. It felt delicate but good at the same time. That was my first alcohol-free day in years.

The following day I woke up feeling okay, somehow cleaner both physically and mentally, and I liked that feeling. But I suddenly realised that I didn't have a plan. I had been so focused on cutting down that I hadn't thought about what I would do when I actually stopped. I started to panic because I didn't know what to do next.

I didn't know anything about getting help and what support services were out there. I knew nothing about CBT, Mindfulness, government-run drug and alcohol services and other things that people use to help them. But I did have a friend who I knew was in AA. So I asked her if I could go with her to one of her meetings, and that night I toddled off to my first meeting.

It was a surreal evening, but that was just because of where my head was. The meeting was nice, the people were friendly, the room was comfy and the biscuits were good, so that ticked a lot of boxes for me. I didn't have much idea what people were talking about. I remember people kept talking about having a program. I had no idea what they meant, but it seemed that having a program was a good thing. I wondered if I could order one off Amazon!

The first few weeks of my sobriety were, as you can imagine, up and down, but actually not as difficult as I had imagined. I kept going to the AA meetings. I still didn't have much idea what people were talking about, but the great thing was that the meetings were in the evening, and as I used to do my drinking in the evening, it was wonderful to have something to do during my usual drinking hours.

My head was still very floaty as I got used to this strange new world. But I was getting to like being sober. It was starting to be fun, which was something I hadn't expected I would say in my last days of drinking.

One thing I really enjoyed was driving. I would drive into town at 10 o'clock at night, simply because I could. I wasn't worried about the police, in fact I wanted to get pulled over and be breath-tested just so I could feel smug.

But after about a month of sobriety, things started going downhill. I had heard someone at a meeting say that stopping drinking was like making an emergency stop in a delivery van – it was great to stop, but then everything in the back flies forward and hits you in the back of the head. I started to understand what he meant.

That floaty feeling was replaced by a grim realization that dealing with my drinking was only the start. My years of drunkenness had left me with some heavyweight practical issues to deal with which were piling up. As far as the issues that I had brought on myself were concerned, I thought that, well, it was my own fault and I just had to clear up my own mess. But I was also learning that just because you have become sober, life doesn't become fair, and you have to be willing to clear up the unfair stuff as well. The going was getting tough.

I was also starting to worry that I had given myself brain damage with my drinking. I remember being at a meeting after about three months of sobriety and feeling the left side of my brain buzzing. I thought 'Oh my God, is it going to be like this for the rest of my life?'

On top of this, things weren't going so smoothly with AA. I was still going to the meetings, five or six a week. But I had also started on the 12 Step Program (yes, I had discovered what they meant by having a program) and I was struggling with it. Sure, there was lots of good stuff in it. The lessons I learnt about resentments and self-pity, for example, were great lessons that have benefitted me hugely to this day. But other aspects really didn't sit well with me.

I never felt comfortable with being sponsored by another AA member (which is a pre-requisite for doing the Steps). I just couldn't get comfortable with having someone know so much about me whose only qualification for doing the job was being a self-confessed alcoholic. I'm sure the two sponsors I tried were very genuine people, and I am equally sure that there are thousands of wonderful sponsors out there doing fabulous work, but I just couldn't get on with it.

During those first six months, I even started to have suicidal thoughts for the first time in my life. This wasn't because of the lack of alcohol. It was because my years of drinking had left me with so many problems. I started to wonder if I had left it too late in life to get sober, that my life was permanently screwed up. It did get easier though.

Firstly, I heard people at meetings talk about how they had done AA in their own way and it had been okay. This reassured me that I didn't have to be a 12-Step fundamentalist. I know some people really need to do the AA program rigidly by the letter of the book, and if that's what works for them, I wish them well. But it wasn't my way, and I was relieved to find out that was okay too.

Secondly, I started to read up on Cognitive Behavioural Therapy which I started to find really beneficial. It started to answer a lot of questions that I had about my own thinking that the 12 Steps hadn't answered. Also, I had begun trying mindful relaxation, which was starting to help.

Then after about six months of sobriety, something really marvellous and unexpected happened. I began experiencing short periods, just a few minutes, at random times without warning, when my head just felt great. I can best describe it as being like when a beam of sunlight breaks through a dark grey sky and lights up the landscape. Then it would go away again. I began looking forward to these random happenings. I had no idea what was going on, but I wasn't complaining.

Over the next few weeks, it started happening more often and lasting longer. Then I realised what was happening. My brain was regenerating. I was experiencing what it was like to have a lucid mind for the first time in decades, and it was great!

In the years that have followed, I have moved on amazingly in my life. I have studied and forged a new career, which would have been impossible with my old drunken brain. AA, CBT and Mindfulness have all played a part. More recently, working with a qualified recovery therapist has helped draw it all together. Alcohol is no longer a big, scary addiction that I don't understand. I don't have to hide from it. I don't care if alcohol is around. It has been put firmly in its place."

Taking a sober break

We can see from Karen's story what can happen if we just give the brain time to repair itself. In getting into recovery from Alcohol Use Disorder, sometimes the best thing we can do is just relax and let time perform its miracles as the body and mind regenerates.

Alcohol is often associated with liver damage, and for good reason. But whereas liver damage can take a long time to develop and does not affect every drinker, damage to the brain happens much quicker and to some extent affects all heavy drinkers. It shows up in memory loss, moodiness, anxiety, depression, and poor decision making.

Brain damage in some extreme cases can be permanent. There is a condition with the grand name of Wernicke–Korsakoff Syndrome - more commonly known simply as wet brain – which is brain damage caused by a catastrophic loss of Thiamine (vitamin B1) in your body as a result of drinking. If you get this, there is no way back, the damage is permanent. This is why, if your GP is aware you are a heavy drinker, you might have been prescribed Thiamine capsules.

Happily, only a small minority of drinkers develop wet brain. For the rest, the damage can mostly be reversed if the brain is given time without alcohol to repair itself – a sober break.

For this reason, I recommend to drinkers who are seeking moderation rather than abstinence that they too consider taking some time out away from the booze altogether. It gives the brain time to repair itself and crucially it also breaks that addictive cycle.

I have seen many times that trying to achieve moderation simply by cutting down and without a period of total sobriety usually ends in failure. It is like trying to put out a fire by putting less gasoline on it – sooner or later the fire will flare up. If you take a sober break, the fire (the addiction) will have chance to go out. So having a sober break makes sense, even if you are intending to drink again. And who knows, you might like the experience of being sober so much that you might not go back to drinking.

If you are unsure about whether to moderate or stop, then taking a sober break makes total sense. You already know what heavy drinking is like. If you give sobriety a trial period, you can then compare the two and make an informed choice about what you want to do.

So how long should your sober break last for? Well, there is no maximum time, as long as you like, in fact, the longer the better. You know from Karen's story the benefits really kicked in after six months, and six months is a common period to really start feeling big benefits.

If the idea of going six months without a drink scares you witless, then just pick a shorter time frame, a couple of weeks is better than nothing, and a month is better than a couple of weeks, and so on. When you reach your chosen target, you can then choose whether to extend it or not.

It is entirely up to you. No one is taking alcohol away from you. It is not a punishment. Alcohol will still be at the store if you want it. Just remember, however, that when you pick up that drink, you are potentially also picking up the problems that led you to buy this book, all over again.

Your Timeline for Change

In the past there were many theories about how people in addiction made changes. But the model that has proved to have stood the test of time, and is now near universally accepted, is known as the Stages of Change.

This was created by two researchers from the University of Rhode Island - James Prochaska and Carlo di Clemente - who had a great idea. Instead of theorising about how change occurred, they went out and asked lots of people who had actually done it. This was in the 1970s and at that time the dangers of smoking had been known for over a decade, resulting in many people giving up. They interviewed people who had stopped and asked them what had happened. The results of this research were published in 1982.

The Stages of Change has since been found to apply to other addictions, not the least being alcohol, and people like myself who work in the field are all familiar with the theory. I have found that clients have also benefited from understanding the stages of change, because it gives them a framework to understand where they are in terms of their recovery from addiction. It also helps to give you a timeline to work with, so you can plot your progress.

Pre-contemplation

This is the first stage. Contemplation means thinking about something, so someone in pre-contemplation hasn't yet started. They haven't realised that the problem exists. They have no interest in change. The penny has yet to drop.

Drinkers can be in pre-contemplation for years, even though the evidence is stacking up and everyone around them can see quite clearly that the problem is there. One quite remarkable example of someone who had spent years in pre-contemplation, even though alcohol was like a wrecking ball in his life, was Mike. He came to me unwillingly (drinkers in pre-contemplation are always unwilling) sent by family who were concerned he could be facing another term in jail if he didn't stop drinking.

Mike presented as a nice guy in his thirties, a bit confused as to why his family had sent him to talk to me. The conversation went like this:

Me: "Tell me about your drinking, Mike."

Mike: "Well, I like a drink. But there's nothing more to it than that."

Me: "So why do your family think it's a problem?"

Mike: "The last time I was arrested, I had had a drink."

Me: "What happened?"

Mike: "I was just down the pub at lunchtime with my brother, and you know how things can get a bit out of hand...."

Me: "Go on."

Mike: "It was silly really. It was his idea. We decided to go and rob the post office across the road. It wasn't serious. We were only after some beer money."

Me: "Were you drunk at the time?"

Mike: (laughing) "Drunk as a skunk, mate!"

Me: "Mike, how many times have you been to prison?"

Mike: "Nine times. I'm sick of it. I don't think I'm cut out to be a criminal. I keep getting nicked"

Me: "You've been to prison nine times. How many of those times did you go to prison for offences you committed while drunk?"

Mike: (long pause, he was thinking hard) "Well, now that you mention it, all of them."

Me: "Alcohol has put you in prison nine times?"

Mike: (another long pause) "I see what you're getting at."

That really was Mike's moment of insight. In all the times he had been to prison, he had always though it was his fault, because he wasn't cut out to be a criminal. It had genuinely never occurred to him that it was the alcohol all the time. This isn't a judgement on Mike - it is truly amazing how alcohol can blind people to the obvious.

Contemplation

When the penny has dropped, we move on to the next stage of change, contemplation. This is where you know there is a problem, but you're struggling to change. This is a painful place to be. I always know when I am talking to someone in contemplation, because they tell stories of often daily struggles to manage their problem. They will refer to waking up in the morning, feeling sick and remorseful, not wanting to drink again. But by the evening they are once again roaring drunk. They often don't understand why.

People can spend years in this painful place, knowing that they need to do something, but seemingly incapable of taking any meaningful action. Sometimes they never get out, they die in contemplation.

Decision

This isn't actually a stage, it's an event. Life becomes so painful that a serious decision to change takes place and the drinker is finally propelled forward from the pain of contemplation. Decision can take place suddenly and unexpectedly after a long period of contemplation.

Preparation

Now things are happening. You, the reader of this book, could be in preparation right now. Buying this book is part of your preparation. This stage need not take long, not longer than a month, and maybe only a few hours.

It could involve ringing up your local drug and alcohol service to make an appointment for an assessment. It could involve you researching when your local AA meetings are on. It could be that you register with a recovery web site, like Smart Recovery or Hello Sunday Morning (we'll be talking about all these later in the book). You are making plans.

Action

This is a very busy time. When you are in the action phase you are typically going to lots of recovery meetings or spending evenings on recovery web sites. You are reading lots of recovery-based material and learning new skills. You may be signed up to a CBT course. You could have enlisted one-to-one support from an addictions therapist like me. You may be in AA and studying the 12 Steps, or you could have discovered Smart Recovery and are doing the 4-Point Program (more about AA and Smart later in the book). You are making friends with other people who are doing the same thing. You might be in a rehab, or doing a medically supervised detox.

A typical time frame for this period is 3 to 6 months. As you can see, there are different ways of doing the action phase. The right way is the one that is right for you. If you are still not sure what your plan should be, later chapters in this book will show you a way that works for you.

Maintenance

The action phase is very busy and too busy to sustain over a long period. But after a few months it should be possible to slow things down a bit and get into the maintenance stage. This stage will see you becoming less obsessed with recovery and getting back into normal life.

If you have been drinking heavily for years, normal life is something that will take some getting used to, so you will still need to be very vigilant for trigger events that could cause you to relapse. You will still be taking an active interest in recovery and still attending meetings, or using online support, and maybe even seeing an addictions therapist like me. But you won't be doing so much and with less intensity. You might have even started doing some mentoring with people who are trying to get into recovery.

The time frame of the maintenance stage is controversial. AA believes that the maintenance stage is for life, as AA theory is that once an alcoholic, always an alcoholic - even if you don't drink anymore and haven't touched a drop for years - so you always need to stay in maintenance and work on your recovery. On the other hand, Smart Recovery believes that after a year or two, you should be ready to get on with normal life and leave recovery. Smart calls this "graduation".

So which is right? I think that it depends on the person. Some people can indeed just move on, they leave their old behaviour in the past and that's where it stays. But other people cannot do that and they need to stay vigilant for good. I think a lot depends on how severe their drinking was to start off with and how long they had been drinking at harmful levels.

Lapse or relapse

Like decision, this is not a stage, it is an event, and I hope it's an event that you don't have to deal with. But realistically, not everyone gets it right first time. Some people will need to have several attempts to reach their goal. So what's the difference between lapse and relapse?

I would call a lapse just a quick slip that might only involve one or two unplanned drinks, and which is over in a day or so. It doesn't do much damage to your plan and you can pick up again at the stage you were at before.

A relapse is a full-blown return to your old levels of drinking over a period of several days. This is likely to mean you go backwards through the stages, quite possibly all the way back to the contemplation stage.

If this does happen, it isn't the end of the world, and all being well, you can learn from what went wrong and quickly get back on track. The important thing is to act quickly. The longer you stay in relapse, the harder it is to get out.

Don't think, "It's okay, I have stopped before so I know I can stop again next week." The actor Robin Williams relapsed after twenty years of sobriety while on location for a movie in Alaska. In a later interview he said that he thought he would stop after a week, but in the event it was three years before he could stop again. His experience is not uncommon.

Building Motivation

If you search You Tube for the word motivation, you will see lots of videos of people getting pumped up. If you search Google Images, you will see lots of motivating slogans. And maybe this sort of thing will work for a short period of time.

If you watch a team sport like football, before the game you will often see the players huddled together, going through some sort of ritual bonding to help get them motivated for the game. That's great when you just need to get motivated for a short while to play football.

Getting motivated to address an alcohol problem is a different matter. You need to find a different kind of motivation, one that can be sustained, and one that works all round the clock, every day, not just for an hour or two. I often hear clients say they can't get motivated, but then after learning a few simple techniques, they find that they can after all. In fact anyone can get motivated, it's just a question of how, it's a learned behaviour.

In this chapter I am going to share with you some motivational techniques that I have seen my clients use time and again. There is nothing complicated about these techniques. There is no need to get into any deep psychology. In fact, when it comes to motivation, it's the simple techniques that work the best. So let's look at a few:

The pros and cons tool

It's really important to write things down. I know it sounds like a pain. Why should you write things down, when they are in your head already? But please trust me on this one - writing things down makes a big difference. And write it big. Make it bold. Put is where you can see it.

A good place to start your writing is with the reasons why you want to control your drinking. Here is a simple way of brainstorming this with yourself. This technique has been used countless times, and it works. Simply take a piece of paper and put a line down the middle. At the top of the first column, write "Advantages of Drinking" and at the top of the second column write "Disadvantages of Drinking".

Now get writing. Your advantages of drinking column might contain things like "I like getting high", "I feel more confident socially" that sort of thing. You decide, it's your life, write down what is important to you.

In the disadvantages column, you might write things like: hangovers, driving bans, arguments with my partner, early death, throat cancer, incontinence, financial worries, weight gain, diabetes, heart attack, all sorts of fun stuff like that. But again, this is your list, put down what is important to you. Take your time about this exercise. Put aside an hour when you will not be disturbed. Get as many thoughts on paper as you can. You might surprise yourself with what comes out of your head.

What you will probably end up with is a short list in the advantages of drinking column, and a very long list in the disadvantages of drinking column. I have done this exercise many times with people in workshops. Sometimes we brainstorm a group version on a flipchart. It can be a moment of major insight for people. You might have thought you knew why you want to take action on your drinking, but doing this exercise can really bring it home.

There's a guy I met called Pete who told me a great story about how he had used just such a list. He said he worked in South America as a surveyor for a multinational company. The area he lived in was pretty remote. There was a small English-speaking ex-pat community and as often seems to be the case in the ex-pat world, alcohol was central to much of the socialising.

Pete realised one day that he had managed to get himself addicted to alcohol. He was having difficulties getting up for work, he was sneaking drinks at lunch time, he had had a couple of warning signs from his body that he might be getting incontinent (I won't share the details in case you are eating), he was having embarrassing memory lapses, and most of the time he felt lacking in energy and in a low mood.

In the remote area where he lived, there were no recovery meetings he could attend and no local drug and alcohol services he could access. But he did find some useful advice on the internet including a suggestion to do a pros and cons list as I have recommended here. So he did that. He looked at it and he found the arguments against drinking really compelling. He told me that he framed that piece of paper and put it up on the wall of his bedroom where he would see it every morning when he woke up, and that piece of paper had kept him sober ever since, which is a few years ago now.

Pete's story is a powerful example of how just writing things down can have a big impact. You can also see how powerful your own thinking can be when you see it in front of you. No one had told Pete what to put on the paper. No one had tried to persuade him to stop drinking. The simple two-column exercise had been a way for him to download his thoughts on to paper so he could see them.

Keeping a journal

Another way of finding motivation through writing is keeping a journal of your recovery from your alcohol issues. You are doing an amazing thing, it deserves to be recorded. It will be a history of your achievement that you will be able to look back on with pride at a future date.

You can use it to record whatever you want, but here are some suggestions:

Your target in terms of alcohol consumption (or lack of) for the day and what you actually achieved in practice.

Your feelings, whether good or bad or just neutral

Any trigger events and how you handled them, for example if a friend unexpectedly turned up at your place with a bottle

How you slept and how you felt when you woke up

If you are taking a sober break, how many days so far

How people are reacting to you now and changes in your relationships

How much money you have saved

Your hopes for the future

Your plan to keep you on track for the following day

List the people you met and whether they were helpful to your aims

Keep a record of the recovery meetings you attend

And so on....

I suggest also being creative with how you use your journal. Drinking dulls down your creativity, so crank up your creative side by using colour in your journal, maybe include a few drawings, maybe some mind maps. Let your self-expression free. This will actually help to keep you sober, because the part of your brain you use being creative is a different part to where your addictive urges live. Make it lively, make it fun.

As you get going with your journal and begin recording achievements, it becomes self-motivating. You might find, for example, that you can resist that extra drink simply because you want to record in your journal that you hit your target for the day.

Don't try harder, make a plan

I have a pet hate: people saying they are going to try to do something, particularly the drinkers I work with. You might think this is odd, you might think I want people to say they are going to try. But I don't. That statement is usually followed by failure. What I want to hear is that they have a plan.

Compare these two conversations.

Conversation A

Me: "So how are you going to achieve your alcohol goal this week?"

Larry: "I'm going to try really hard."

Conversation B

Me: "So how are you going to achieve your alcohol goal this week?"

Sally: "I have made a plan for where I'm going to be all week. I don't want to have any time where I've got time with nothing to do but think about drinking. I'm going to recovery meetings on alternate nights, and on the other nights I've arranged to meet non-drinking friends. I want to lose weight, so I am recording my weight every morning as a motivator to keep off the booze, because there are so many calories in alcohol. I'm also putting all the money I used to spend on drink in a big jar where I can see the money pile up, and on Saturday I'm going to take some money out and buy myself some new shoes."

Who do you think is likely to succeed? If I was a betting man, my money would be on Sally every time. She has a plan, and plans are motivating.

Take an action

People think that you need to be motivated to get into action. But try it the other way round. Instead of waiting to get motivated, do something, anything, just to get rolling. You will find that your motivation starts to wake up and you get some momentum going. It's really important, though, not to over-think it. If you start to give it too much consideration, prevarication is likely to set in.

A great way to get rolling is to do something in the next 60 seconds. That's too short a period of time in which to over-think. It's also such a short period of time that you don't need to think too much about what you are going to do anyway, because there isn't that much you can do in 60 seconds.

Here's an example. Let's say you normally start drinking at five o'clock in the afternoon. To break that habit you've decided that at five you're going to take your dog for a walk instead. Great idea, but when five o'clock rolls around, you look out the window, you think it might rain, you start thinking - perhaps I ought to leave it a few minutes. Then you leave it a few minutes more. Over-thinking has led to prevarication. Before you know it, you've cracked open a beer, and you've lost the game.

Now let's do it with a 60 second action. Same scenario, it's five o'clock, weather looks a bit dodgy, but instead of thinking about that, you do your 60 second action that you've decided in advance. That 60 second action is simply to put the lead on the dog. Nothing more, you have 60 seconds to put the lead on your dog. In all probability, before you have time to think about it, you and your furry friend are off down the road and you've won the game.

Another example: as part of your efforts to get sober, you've decided to start exercising in the morning. Prioritising looking after yourself is a great way to cut down the importance of alcohol in your life. So you set your alarm for early. When the alarm goes off, your mind starts telling you to roll over for a few more minutes. Next thing you know, you've slept in and lost the game.

Now imagine the same scenario, but this time you've decided your 60 second action is to put the coffee on - nothing more, because you can't do more in 60 seconds. So the alarm goes off, and before your mind can start to convince you to stay in bed, you've got the coffee pot in your hand and you're feeling ready to roll.

Make a chart

This is another idea that is so simple but incredibly effective.

You need two things. A goal to aim for and a wall planner, which you can get from a stationery store – even a big calendar will do.

I can give you an example of how this has worked to crack an addiction in my own life. In my case, it doesn't involve drinking, it involves smoking, but you will easily be able to use the same idea for drinking.

I was a smoker for many years. I was so addicted to nicotine, it was crazy. I had tried all sorts of things to stop, patches, nicotine chewing gum – nothing worked - until I got a calendar with a month displayed on it. I also got a packet of stickers. Some stickers had sunshine symbols on them and others had rainy symbols on them. I put the chart up on the wall in the kitchen where I would see it numerous times every day.

The strategy was simply this: at the end of the day, if I had not smoked, I would put a sticker on the calendar for that day. If I had had an easy day without smoking, I would put up a sunny symbol. If it had been a difficult day being without tobacco, I would put up a stormy symbol. But the most important thing was that I was going to get to the end of the day and put up a sticker.

I made this the most important thing in my day. In fact, for a month, it was the most important thing in my life. Come hell or high water, I would get through the day without smoking so I could put up that sticker. If I had to crawl across hot coals to get to the end of the day and put up that sticker, I would do it. No patches, no nicotine gum, and above all no excuses.

By the end of the first week, I had seven stickers up on my chart – and they were all rainy symbols! It had been hell. But I was really proud of my achievement. Every time I saw the calendar – which was many times every day – I felt proud and I was motivated even more to keep going. The fact that it had been hell was also motivating – I never wanted to go through that again, so this time had to be it. No turning back.

I got to the end of the month, and admired my chart. I didn't carry on with the chart technique after the month, because by then I had cracked it. I think there were three elements in the success of this strategy:

1) It was simple, over-thinking couldn't come into it

2) I had turned quitting into a game, and games are very motivating

3) It was very visual. Every time I went into the kitchen, the calendar was in my face

So use this with your drinking goal. You can use it for days without drinking, or days without going over a moderation level, whatever your goal happens to be.

Make your autopilot work for you

Have you ever been intending to drive somewhere you don't normally go, and suddenly realised that you have instead taken a more familiar route without thinking about it? How did that happen?

Your on-board navigation system has overridden your intended route. I am not talking about the navigation system in your GPS, I am talking about the autopilot in your head.

Every time you took that familiar route in the past, perhaps it was the way you drive to work every day, the neural pathway in your head got more and more entrenched, and unless you are trying to override it, it will take control and take you on the route it thinks you want to go.

Heavy drinkers are usually people with deeply entrenched routines. Take for instance the phenomenon of the most common problem drinker – the daily drinker. The daily routine will usually start with a ritual of getting over the night before. It might include coffee, showering, an emergency trip to the bathroom, trying to get some food inside you. In the case of more dependent drinkers, it might involve having a drink to stop the shakes.

There might also be a mental routine, beating yourself up for getting drunk again, thinking up excuses for why you can't perform your duties like going to work or getting the kids to school, without admitting it's just because you are too hung over. The routine will then follow a familiar pattern that ensures the drinker gets drunk again at some point in the day.

But even entrenched habits can change if you really want them to. I have seen instances where this has happened very suddenly, much to the surprise of everyone and especially the drinker concerned. I have seen examples where the drinker has had a sudden deeply moving moment of insight that has completely changed their view of their drinking. This is often triggered by a negative event, such as an arrest, an accident, a doctor's diagnosis, or a loved one leaving because of the drinker's level of alcohol use. Or sometimes it might be that one day the drinker just reaches a tipping point, one day they wake up and think, I can't do this anymore, and they never drink again.

Such events are remarkable and inspiring, but they are the minority. I would not advise a drinker to wait for this moment of insight before taking action, they might die waiting. In the vast majority of cases, it comes down to taking determined action to change the routine. This can take a while, and it might need a few attempts to get it right. But if you can start to flip your negative routine to a positive routine, and use the power of habit to work for you instead of against you, this becomes self-motivating. You will want more, because success is addictive too.

But how do you perform the miracle of turning round this deeply entrenched habit? Breaking out can seem hopelessly difficult. After all, even changing simple habits like biting your nails takes work. So what hope is there when the problem is compounded by having a hugely addictive substance like alcohol involved?

The answer might lie in the analogy we made earlier with driving, and overcoming the autopilot in your head. Consider this: if I want to take a different route, there might only be one key adjustment I need to make. There might be one key road junction where, if you turn left you will find yourself on your usual route and will inevitably end up at your usual destination (drunk). But if you turn right, you will, with no further effort, find yourself following a whole new route. It all came down to what action you took at that key junction.

Now we can look at that in a real life example. Let's take the example of a drinker who is out of work and finds himself drinking in the morning, leading to a drunken day and all sorts of self-defeating chaos. The key moment – arriving at that important junction – will arrive early on. It might be for example when he takes the decision to go to the local store and get his first drink of the day. So the key to taking a different route and avoiding the day of chaos is in that single moment.

If the drinker can put a different action into his routine at that point and make that the most important action of the day, a totally changed day can flow from there. There can be any number of things he could put in place. There might be a support meeting at his local drug and alcohol service he could go to. He could sign up for Thai Chi at his local leisure centre. There could be a sober friend he could meet for coffee. He could do some voluntary work that would take his attention. There are any number of things he could do that could totally transform the route his day takes.

Now take a look at your routine. Is there a critical junction in the day that leads you to a drink? What could you do at that junction to change the direction of your day? For instance, if like most drinkers, you like to have your first drink on an empty stomach, then changing direction could be something as simple as having a sandwich half an hour before your normal drinking time. Now find your junction and decide how you can take a different direction at that moment.

Crushing Those Cravings

Having a technique to deal with alcohol cravings is a fundamental skill to develop in order to control your drinking. Over the past few years, my clients have tried many techniques, and here are a few of the ones that they have found work particularly well. You don't need to use all of them. Just having one that works for you consistently is enough. These are visualisation techniques that help demystify alcohol.

The Screaming Kid

Imagine you walk into a supermarket and along one of the rows you see the following scene. There is a two year old child, rolling around the floor, crying and screaming at the top of its voice, face turning bright red. The child has seen a little sugary snack that it wants. In the child's mind, this little snack is now the centre of its universe, getting it is all the kid cares about.

Standing by the child is the parent, looking very uncomfortable, concerned for the child but also very embarrassed at what is going on in a public place, with a crowd of onlookers starting to gather. The parent is trying to comfort the child with reassuring stories about having dinner when they get home.

But the kid is having none of it, because it wants that snack, nothing else will do, and it wants it now, right now, this very second. It doesn't care about its parent. It doesn't even care about its own safety. It rolls around, banging its fists on the floor, in an uncontrolled fit of self-pity (because it doesn't have what it wants) mixed with outrage (because the parent is not giving it what it wants).

If you were the parent, what you would do?

When I put this question to drinkers who attend my workshops, responses vary. Some say they would give the kid the snack just to get some peace, and get out of the store as soon as they could.

But most people say they wouldn't give in, because if they were to give in, it would only encourage the child to behave in the same way again in the future, maybe worse. They are right.

Next time you have an alcohol craving, try imagining the craving is that screaming kid. It's all about wanting something right now, to the exclusion of all else, with that same mix of self-pity and outrage because you haven't got a drink. Now imagine that you are the parent (the person trying to control your drinking) looking down on that screaming kid (your craving).

What are you going to do?

You have a choice. On one hand, you could just give in. Give the screaming kid (the craving) what it wants (a drink) to shut it up. The problem with this, however, is that by giving in, you guarantee that the screaming kid (craving) will soon be back, and next time it will be even more demanding, because it knows it has the measure of you. What's more, that kid is going to grow up and become an even bigger problem every year.

On the other hand, you can be firm. You will have to tolerate a lot of screaming, but that isn't going to kill you, and in the long run, you will be the responsible parent with a well-behaved child.

Play the Movie through to the End

This is a technique that is a big favourite with a lot of my clients.

I want you to imagine that the craving for a drink is like the trailer for a movie. Trailers always show the best bits to entice you to go see the whole movie.

In the same way, when you get a craving, your mind plays a "trailer" of how it would like you to believe the experience of having a drink is going to be. For example, it might conjure up an image of you sitting contentedly in a comfortable bar as the waiter pours your favourite drink. Or it might show you an image in your mind of you having a laugh with your friends, with you the centre of attention. Maybe it might even show you a scene of you being witty and attractive to someone you want to impress.

But now play this movie through to the end. How does the movie of you giving in to a craving normally end, what are the final scenes usually like?

Is the final scene usually you having a blistering row with your partner? Is the final scene usually you on your knees in the bathroom, your head down the toilet? Or is it the traffic police pulling you over to the side of the road, and telling you to breathe into the breathalyser? Or is it you waking up to the realisation that you made inappropriate comments to everyone you know on Facebook? Or is it your boss telling you you're fired? Or is it you looking in the mirror and being disgusted by what you see looking back at you in the morning?

When you get a craving, don't just judge it on the basis of the trailer, play the movie to the end.

The Box of Cravings

This is a game. It comes as a surprise to drinkers who attend my workshops that I talk about playing games. Surely, they say, with something as serious as alcohol dependency, you can't play a game with it?

I disagree, and this is why: games are energising, games are motivating. Take for example a teenager who feels that he (it's more likely a boy) is just too tired to get up, can't be bothered to get out of bed. If you are a parent to a teenager, you will know what I mean. But give that same teenager a new game for his X-Box, and that teenager who moments earlier could hardly stay awake will suddenly become totally energised and won't need sleep for days. That's the power of a game.

So this is how we play the game called Box of Cravings:

Imagine there is a box that contains all the cravings you have for alcohol. Standing by the box is your opponent (addiction). The idea of the game is that your opponent is going to throw the cravings at you, one by one. What you have to do is to dodge the cravings.

If you let one of the cravings hit you - which happens when you pick up a drink - you lose the game, the box of cravings becomes full again and your opponent is restored to maximum energy. But if you can keep dodging them until the box is empty, you win.

This is a game that gets easier for you the longer you can keep going, because the biggest cravings are at the top of the box, and the more the box empties, the more your opponent has to use smaller cravings that are less likely to hit you. Also, your opponent gets weaker as the game goes on and starts throwing the cravings less often and with less force.

This game is a good indication for what happens with cravings in reality. When you first stop taking alcohol or any addictive substance, the cravings will be big and they will be frequent. But the longer you go on, the easier it gets, until eventually you win.

A nice thing about this game is that you can actually get to a point where you welcome the cravings, because you know each time you have one thrown at you, the box gets a bit emptier and you are closer to victory.

Winning the Head Game

When it comes to normal drinkers - by which I mean people whose drinking doesn't create problems for them or people around them – you usually find that they drink to enhance good feelings.

For example, this type of drinker will usually drink when they are meeting friends for dinner, having family get-togethers, or to celebrate happy events. In other words, they drink in situations where they will be expecting to enjoy themselves. In these situations, alcohol may indeed work to enhance happy feelings, as this type of drinker doesn't normally drink enough for the bad side of alcohol to kick in.

By contrast, when it comes to problem drinkers – by which I mean people whose drinking creates chaos for them and people around them – you usually find that they drink to escape negative feelings.

For example, this type of drinker will usually drink when they feel offended, when they hear bad news, when someone says something they find objectionable, when they feel life is unfair, or when they feel overwhelmed. They will drink to excess, which brings on the bad side of alcohol and things just spiral down.

An experiment I have often carried out when I have been running meetings for drinkers is to pose this simple question: Why do you drink alcohol?

Having done this several times with dozens of drinkers, I can reveal that nearly everyone gives roughly the same reason: escape.

They might phrase it differently, they might say they want relief from pressure, or they want to get away from the grind of daily life, or they want to get away from a difficult situation, and so on. But it almost always boils down to the need for escape. Surprisingly few people say that they drink just because they like the feeling of getting drunk.

Naturally, heavy drinkers will also want to escape feelings of withdrawal, as we discussed in the chapter on withdrawal cycles. But if it was just a question of dealing with physical withdrawal, then alcohol problems would be very easy to deal with. You would just need to detox for a week, the alcohol would have left your system so the withdrawal would be over, and your problem would be solved.

But of course, it isn't that simple. If it was, then detoxes would always be successful. However, the majority of detoxes are not successful over time. The detoxed person will probably relapse, if not right away, then at a future date. I have met people who have had as many as 10 detoxes in the past, and are looking for another. Endless cycles of detox and relapse are achingly painful to go through, and desperately sad to see.

You can take the alcohol out of the body, but if the head is left untreated, relapse is inevitable. This brings me to my Second Law of Recovery from Alcohol Addiction, which states that:

"Control over alcohol is always dependant on control over emotional responses."

This is a massive concept. If you have a problem with alcohol and you cannot take this concept on board, you are doomed to a life where alcohol has the upper hand. This is why detoxes often don't work, because if you cannot control your emotional responses then relapse at some point is inevitable.

I have heard a thousand stories from drinkers who have relapsed, and 95% of them have been because an emotionally upsetting event had occurred and they have reached for a drink to cope. Therefore, I believe that the most important skill that a heavy drinker who wants to change can learn is a strategy for dealing with emotionally upsetting events.

How many times have your attempts to control your drinking come crashing down because someone upset you, or something happened to you that you thought was unfair? Perhaps it was unfair, but if you have alcohol problems, whether it was fair or not isn't the issue. What is important is how you respond.

I see so many drinkers going through life being bounced around like the silver ball in a Pinball game by their emotional reactions to whatever life throws at them. But it doesn't have to be like that. The key is to get into the habit of responding to events, rather than just reacting in the usual way – by reaching for a drink.

Whenever I hear a story about a relapse, or someone who has been controlling their drinking but it has suddenly shot back up to previous levels, there is always a reason that comes down to reacting rather than responding.

What I mean by responding is taking an action that is in accordance with your goal of moderation or sobriety, rather than simply falling back on the old habits that got you into the problems you face. Let's take a look at the sort of situations that cause problems.

Unpleasant feelings

Nobody likes to experience anxiety, sadness, loneliness, frustration or anger. But in life these feelings are bound to crop up, and with great regularity. We wouldn't be human if we didn't experience all of these at some time or other. So, given that these feelings are inevitable and unavoidable, if you reach for a drink every time one of these comes along, your recovery from alcohol addiction is never going to get off the ground.

Rather than trying to numb out the feeling with alcohol, think about making a response that will help to address the reason for the feeling. If you are feeling lonely, what can you do to speak to someone who will help you break out of that situation? If you are feeling frustrated, is there something else you can turn your attention to? If you are feeling in a low mood, rather than sit in self-pity, what can you do to put a smile on your face?

You notice I am saying: what can *you* do? Don't sit around waiting for someone else to bring you out of it. You are in the position of power - it's in your hands. You have the control if you can see that you have it.

The solutions to these problems of unpleasant feelings are often very simple. Getting out of your immediate environment is usually a good move. If you are at home, something as simple as going for a walk can change your perspective and break you out of your negative feelings. If you are lonely, you could simply pick up the phone rather than a drink. If you are feeling despondent, you could watch your favourite comedian on You Tube. Don't over-complicate it.

Alternatively, you could watch your mood and let it pass, because it will. This is getting into Mindfulness, and we'll be looking at that more in the Chapter 15.

Pleasant feelings

Feeling good can be a trigger to drink, you want to enhance the experience. As we discussed at the start of this chapter, in the case of "normal" drinkers, this is most often the reason why they drink. But normal drinkers don't overdo it. If you were in that category, you wouldn't be reading this book. Try experiencing and enjoying the good feeling for what it is, and before you reach for that drink, try using the "Play the movie through to the end" technique you learned in Chapter 12.

Social pressure

You may be in a situation where you feel you are the only one who isn't drinking; you feel the odd one out. But ask yourself, do other people really care? Do they notice? And even if they do, why should you put at risk your recovery, wellbeing and health just to please someone else?

One of my clients, Janine, was planning to go to a wedding. She was going through a period of sobriety, but she said:

"I will have to have an alcoholic drink to toast the bride and groom."

Me: "Why is that?"

Janine: "Because everyone else will be drinking Champagne. It will seem odd if I'm just drinking water. I don't want to upset anyone."

Me: "Who will be checking what you have in your glass? Who will be offended? Who will even notice when all eyes are on the bride and groom?"

The fact is that other drinkers are really only interested in what they are drinking, they really don't care what you're drinking. Ask yourself, when you have been on a session, has it really bothered you what other people were drinking?

Giving into social pressure to drink is just people pleasing. Put yourself first.

Expectations

To explain what I mean by expectations, let's look at a case study. Simon came to me for one-to-one counselling for his drinking. He was a middle-aged man who was living off savings, which were diminishing rapidly as his monthly bar bill was in excess of $1,000. Financial ruin was looming, but despite this, he couldn't get a grip on his habit, so wanted my help.

Simon was also very anxious, which is very common among heavy drinkers. The first time we met, he was sweating heavily (again, very common among heavy drinkers), his eyes were bulging, his hands were shaking, and he talked very rapidly in a desire to tell his story and all his problems.

Simon's story was full of examples of how he was the victim of other people's unkindness - at least, that was how he saw it – which gave him a long list of justifications to drink. Clearly, Simon was drinking to escape negative feelings rather than to enhance positive ones. His list of injustices which he claimed to have endured was exhausting, and I noted that most of them seemed to involve women.

We constructed a plan for him to reduce his drinking and start rebuilding his finances and his life. He was enthusiastic about this, and when we next met he was really fired up about how things were going, he had exceeded the targets we had set for week one, his demeanour was that of a man transformed, and everything looked rosy.

Then the following week, Simon almost fell through the door of the consulting room in a state of meltdown. The shakes and sweating were back and the demeanour had changed to a look of panic. I thought something truly awful must have happened. The conversation went like this:

Simon: "It's all terrible. I've had a terrible week. It's been awful. I haven't slept. And forget about the drinking plan, I've been bang at it. I had to have a drink this morning on the way here. It's all gone wrong."

Me: "Simon, what on earth's happened?"

Simon: "It wasn't my fault. I left my ex-wife a message. It was about me going round the house to get a few things I left in the loft when I moved out. It was nothing of hers, just some of my old bits and pieces that I wanted to collect."

Me: "So what happened?"

Simon: "She rang me back and.....you should have heard her. Swearing at me, screaming, like some animal. She was probably drunk herself; it wasn't just me who was the drinker. She was horrible. Anyway, I had to have a drink and I haven't been able to stop since."

Me: "So this was because your ex-wife rang you?"

Simon: "Yes, I know it sounds a bit weak when you put it like that. But you should have heard her. It was outrageous. She shouldn't be allowed to talk to me like that."

Me: "When you were together, did she talk to you like that?"

Simon: "All the time. I told her to go to the doctor. There's something wrong in her head."

Me: "So that's how she used to behave all the time?"

Simon: "Yes. You can hardly blame me for getting out of the marriage, can you? I mean, it's just not right."

Me: "So, in fact your ex-wife was behaving as she always does. This is why she is your ex-wife."

The whole reason for Simon's relapse was not his wife's behaviour. She was behaving normally for her. The problem was Simon's expectation that it would be different. He had no reason for this. If his expectation had been that his wife would be unreasonable, which would have been perfectly logical and in keeping with her normal behaviour, he would not have been upset, because his expectation and her behaviour would have been the same.

Having unrealistic or over-optimistic expectations are just setting yourself up for disappointment.

Outrage

You don't have to be a problematic drinker to suffer with outrage. It happens to us all, and it can come on quickly and unexpectedly.

Let's take a common enough situation. You are driving along and someone cuts you up. Suddenly, from being a rational human being, the red mist starts rising and out of nowhere wild thoughts of revenge start flying around your head, the person in the other car becomes the epicentre for all that is evil in your world, you want that driver to rot in the most foul and disgusting corner of hell.

If you acted on your urges - which probably involve running the other car off the road and thrashing the other driver until they beg forgiveness - who knows where it could lead and what trouble you might bring on yourself. So your rational mind starts to take charge, it tells you to calm down, that the important thing is to get to your destination safely, the other driver was just being stupid and probably didn't mean it - try to forget it. This is what you do. But that feeling of outrage simmers for the rest of the day.

There is nothing like a perceived injustice to bring on outrage and the urge to drink. Everyday life brings many opportunities for that feeling of injustice and outrage to crop up: dealing with bureaucracy, having to hold on for hours waiting for a call centre to answer you, the person in front of you at the checkout dithering around. And those are just the small things. When life throws a big, real injustice at you, the potential for outrage and alcohol relapse are very real.

This is another case where choosing how to respond, rather than just flying off the handle, will not only keep you away from booze, but can potentially save you from an escalating situation that you might live to regret. Try to get yourself away from the situation to give yourself time to calm down enough to think straight. Give yourself time to plan your response, rather than just reacting.

Blaming others

It's easy to blame other people for things that go wrong in your life, and therefore your need to drink. It makes you feel better if it was someone else's fault, not your own.

It was the barman's fault you got drunk for letting you have a drink on the house.

It was your boss's fault you got drunk, if she hadn't been so hard on you for coming into work late, you wouldn't have got angry and had a drink.

It was your wife's fault you got drunk, because she shouted at you when you crashed the car.

It's the economy's fault. If it was better you could afford to have what you want in life and wouldn't drink to drown your sorrows.

It was God's fault you didn't win the lottery, so you had to have a few whiskies to get over the disappointment.

It's life's fault you're a drunk. If life wasn't so unfair, you wouldn't need a drink.

It's very easy to pass the blame for your drinking onto other people, or even life or God. To be able to control your drinking, you need to start by taking responsibility for it. Drinkers don't generally like to take responsibility. In fact much of their drinking is to avoid responsibility. But if you take responsibility for your own actions, you then put yourself in a position of power over your life and your drinking.

Solution Focused Thinking

When a new client first arrives to see me, they usually float in on a raft of troubles. Although drinking is at the heart of their problems, it's not usually the alcohol itself that has brought them to see me, but issues it has created.

High on most people's list are relationships. Many clients have broken relationships in the past, frequently as a result of drinking. They are often separated from their children. Current relationships are suffering, too, and the fear of a current relationship breaking down is frequently the motivation for someone coming into treatment.

Mental health, and especially anxiety and depression, are often high on the list of problems. The majority of people I see are on anti-depressants. Anxiety and depression are alcohol's best friends. Wherever alcohol goes, anxiety and depression are usually not far behind. It is one of the great ironies of drinking that most drinkers believe that alcohol cheers them up, when it is in fact making matters worse.

Continued use of alcohol at high levels virtually guarantees that anxiety and depression will get worse.

Physical health features high in people's concerns, especially as the drinker gets older. They dread going to see the doctor, in case they are told they have some horrible alcohol-related condition. I would recommend that any heavy drinker goes and gets honest with their GP and at the very least has a liver function test and general check-up. The physician may then refer you to see a therapist like myself for focused treatment.

Money is often a worry, as heavy drinking is not a cheap hobby. It wrecks careers, making money worries worse. And then there are criminal justice worries. Many have had driving bans. Some have long criminal records for alcohol-related offences.

With all this going on in people's minds, it is not surprising that when they arrive to see me, they are very problem-focused. Their worries are swirling around in their minds all the time like some merry-go-round from hell. So they drink even more to numb it out, and the merry-go-round spins even faster.

While being problem-focused is understandable, it has to be changed. Problem-focused thinking is self-defeating. It is often said that you get in life what you think about. This is undoubtedly true when it comes to problems. If you think all the time about problems, you can be sure of what you will get – more problems!

Solution-Focused Thinking (SFT) offers the antidote to all this. It's a common sense way of addressing what is going on in your life, with its roots in proven therapeutic practice. But there is nothing complicated about it. You can easily learn how to do it yourself, and apply it not only to sorting out your drinking, but also to any issue in your life.

The origins of SFT are in the work of two American social workers, Steve de Shazer and Insoo Kim Berg and their team at the Milwaukee Brief Family Therapy Center in Wisconsin. Over thousands of hours of analysing therapy sessions, they developed Solution Focused Brief Therapy. This differs fundamentally from traditional, Freudian therapy, which works on the assumption that it is necessary to analyse the cause of a person's problem before it can be remedied.

I often meet drinkers who are obsessed with finding the root cause of their drinking, and feel that they need to do that before they can make any progress with sorting out their drinking. Where this type of approach fails the drinker, however, is that:

a) The drinker might die from alcohol abuse before finding the root cause.

b) If they find the root cause, it might not help them to find a solution.

c) They discover the root cause, only to realise that the reason they drink now has changed.

Solution Focused Thinking does away with all this. As Steve de Shazer said "causes of problems may be extremely complex, their solutions do not necessarily need to be."

Let's take an analogy. Imagine you are driving down the road, when you drive over a sharp object and get a puncture. If we take the thinking of traditional therapy, we would then have to walk back up the road, find the object and then examine the object to ascertain the root cause of the puncture. But by doing this we are focusing on the problem, not the solution, and we still have done nothing to fix the problem (the flat tyre). If we take the solution focused approach, we simply get out the spare tyre (the solution), put it on the car and drive on.

To put SFT to work for you, you need to grasp two key concepts, the first of these is:

If it works, do more

In SFT, we assume that you, the drinker, might already know the solution to your difficulty, without realizing it. It's just a question of uncovering that piece of information. To do this, take a look at what you do now. Are there times when your drinking isn't a problem, even for just a short time? What is going on then? Is what you are doing at that time something you can do more of?

Here's an example from one of my clients. Gloria was a lively 60-year-old in a happy marriage and having a good life. But she had one problem. She told me that for years she had been drinking a bottle of wine every night, often more. She was worried that at her age, this behaviour was catching up with her and that her health was suffering. She was concerned that her friends thought she was an alcoholic and talked about her behind her back. Also, it was causing arguments with her husband. He was an occasional drinker, and was worried about Gloria's persistent drinking and her increasingly more outrageous behaviour when she was drunk.

The breakthrough with Gloria came in this conversation:

Gloria: "I don't know why I do it, really. It's just a compulsion. It gets towards early evening and I just can't think about anything except having a drink."

Me: "The thought of drinking obsesses you."

Gloria: "Exactly. I just need that drink and then, well, I just can't leave the bottle alone once it's open."

Me: "And you say this is what happens every day."

Gloria: "Yes, every day. Well, almost."

Me: "Almost? Tell me what you mean by 'almost'."

Gloria: "Well, sometimes my friend Moira comes round on a Sunday, and then I don't drink."

Me: "Why is that? What happens when Moira comes round?"

Gloria: "Oh, we play Scrabble. I don't even think about drinking while I'm playing Scrabble!"

Me: "In that case, I suggest you play more Scrabble!"

Gloria: "Oh, I couldn't play Scrabble every day....But maybe a couple of times a week. Moira wouldn't mind."

Me: "Great. Now let's talk about what you could do on the other days."

What Gloria had done was to identify not what the problem was (we already knew that was drinking) instead she had identified a time when the problem went away for a while. She had found an exception. From that, we could start constructing a solution. We looked at her playing more Scrabble or taking part in other activities that would engage her brain as Scrabble did. We used the first concept of SFT. We found what worked for her, and then found ways she could do more.

Now let's look at a very different case. Gary was a classic black-and-white drinker. He was 55 and his life had been a painful series of periods of abstinence followed by horrible relapses when he would get arrested for fighting. Because of this he had rarely held down a job for long, and was unemployed. This made things worse, as alcohol was all he had to think about all day long. When we met, he had just detoxed yet again, and was looking for ways to stay sober.

Gary: "My problem is that I can get sober, but then all I think about is drinking. I can go for months without drinking, but then I just find that I have a drink in my hand. I don't know how it happens."

Me: "It sounds like being sober for you is mental torture."

Gary: "That's right, it drives me nuts."

Me: "But drinking brings you big problems also."

Gary; "I know, I hate drinking as much as I hate being sober. I can't win."

151

Me: "Gary. Indulge me for a moment. Cast your mind back. Tell me about a time when you felt content, even if it was just for a short time."

Gary: (after a long pause) "Well, there was a time about twenty years ago. For about two years, I was all right, really. Life was all right."

Me: "Tell me more about those two years. Why were they different from now? What was happening in your life?"

Gary: "It was all because of the pigs!"

Me: "Pigs! What pigs?"

Gary: "I was working on a farm looking after the pigs. It was great. I like pigs. I like animals"

Me: "Were you drinking then?"

Gary: "No, that was one of my sober periods."

Me: "And you were happy?"

Gary: "Yes, now you mention it, I think I was."

Me: "There's a farm near here where ex-drinkers like you sometimes go for a while as part of their therapy. They do some voluntary work with the animals, get closer to nature. How would you feel about getting involved in that?"

Gary liked the idea, so we had the start of a plan for him. Once again, it was the client who had found the solution by looking into the past and finding something that had worked before that could be done again. I had simply assisted in the process.

You can try this yourself. Look back at times when drinking was not a problem. It might be in the distant past. Or it might be that you had a short time recently when you didn't feel the urge to drink. Even if it was only for a couple of hours, it's a start.

Whenever it was, ask yourself:

What was different?

Where were you?

Who were you with?

What were you doing?

Does this show you something you could do now to overcome your excess drinking?

Now we come to the second concept of SFT:

If it doesn't work, do something different

When you look at that statement, it seems obvious, doesn't it? If something in your life doesn't work, then you would think it's common sense to do something different. Yet we human beings are constantly repeating actions that that don't work for us.

Drinking itself is a prime example. So why exactly is it that so many of us not only drink, but drink extraordinary amounts? I think part of the answer lies in the fact that we are talking about an addictive substance and addictions play mind games with you. They make you believe things that only someone with the addiction would believe, things that other people see is nonsense. Like a client who told me, in all sincerity, that drinking 20 pints of cider every day was normal. Even most drinkers wouldn't think that's normal, but he was totally convinced of it.

When we talked further, it emerged that he had been brought up in a pub, where he had seen heavy drinking from a young age, and had regarded it as being something good - after all, his father, the pub landlord, made his living from it. But by the time he met me, he had started to get a glimmer of insight that maybe alcohol wasn't working for him anymore, as his health was falling apart. It was time to do something different.

When I meet new clients, they often think there is something wrong with them, because they have followed a particular plan and failed. They beat themselves up about it. But as I point out, perhaps it's not you that's failed - it's just that the plan wasn't right for you. It's time to do something different.

For example, I met a woman who had been desperately struggling with her drinking for years. She was at her wits end with it. We had this conversation.

Eve: "I'm just a failure. I just can't stop."

Me: "Tell me, what have you tried?"

Eve: "I go to AA. I've done everything they say. I have a sponsor. I read the book. I go to lots of meetings. I have a morning routine. But I just can't seem to stay sober for more than a few weeks at a time. I see other women doing well in AA. But I just can't seem to get the hang of it. It must be me. There's something wrong with me."

Me: "How long has this been going on?"

Eve: "Two years. I've been going to AA for two years."

Me: "What else have you tried?"

Eve: "Well, nothing."

Me: "I know many people who have done really well in AA. But there is no one method that works for everyone. Even AA doesn't claim that their way works for everyone. After two years, no one could accuse you of not giving it a good try."

Eve: "Do you think I should stop going? I have friends there."

Me: "I'm not saying stop going. Having your sober friends in AA is really helpful. But maybe it would also be helpful to try something different. You could try a course in CBT running alongside your AA meetings. And there is a Mindfulness course starting soon that I could refer you on to. Would you like some information on those things?"

Eve was totally problem-focused: she thought she was the problem and was beating herself up about it, which was very unhelpful and just made her feel bad. In the course of this short conversation she started to focus on solutions, which was far more helpful.

Eve's experience also illustrates that sometimes you benefit from blending more than one approach. In Eve's case, AA was helping in that she had friends who could support her and she reported that she had had periods of several weeks sober in AA, so she had some success to draw on. By offering additional help and freshening up her approach to staying sober, I hoped to help her get over whatever roadblock she was facing. In fact, she found Mindfulness helped and it was complimentary to her AA attendance. (We will be discussing AA more in Chapter 17.)

In your efforts to control or stop your drinking, you have probably tried certain strategies already. Nothing has proved to be totally effective so far, which is why you bought this book. So take a look at what you are doing to deal with your drinking now. Are there self-defeating behaviours that you are repeating? For example:

Is there one friend you have that always talks you into having a drink when you are don't want to drink? Get a new friend!

Is there a place you visit where you are tempted to drink, like a particular restaurant that has an especially attractive bar? Eat somewhere else!

Is there a particular store you pass on the way home where you always stop off at to buy a bottle of wine? Take a different route home!

Can't resist the booze promotions in the supermarket when they are in your face? Shop online!

Now take a look at your regular behaviours. Is there something you are doing that you should just stop right now and do something different? A saying you will often hear in recovery circles is: the definition of insanity is repeating the same thing and expecting a different result. It might be a bit of a cliché, but it's true.

Stopping those Spinning Wheels

We saw in the last chapter Eve was beating herself up about what she saw as her failure to deal with her drinking. This is not unusual. Repeated battles to tame alcohol lead to drinkers having poor self-esteem. Then, when you finally get to grips with it and achieve a period of sobriety, things can get worse because, as the fog of alcohol lifts, you can see in sharper focus all the damage that your career of boozing has done.

As memories of arguments, damage and loss caused by drink come home to haunt you and self-esteem takes another tumble, then remorse and regret set in. If that wasn't bad enough, memory returns and you start getting flashbacks to events that had been totally forgotten. It seems like the reasons for putting yourself down just keep piling up higher and higher.

Thoughts of "what if" and "if only" set in.

What if I had done this......

If only I had done that.....

The thoughts go round and round like a wheel spinning in your head as you go over past events time and time again. The wheel won't stop spinning, because you can never resolve the issues. How can you, when they are in the past? You cannot go back in time. You cannot solve what has happened, but your brain keeps trying and that keeps the wheel spinning.

Going over past events you cannot change leads to depression, and depression can lead you back to a drink, putting you in a really vicious cycle.

But it's not just past events that can plague you. It's the future, too. You have damaged your prospects. You might find yourself unemployed because of your drinking, or divorced, or in prison. Your mind starts worrying that you have screwed up your future.

Once again "what if" and "if only" come to plague you, but this time it's slightly different:

What if the worst case scenario happens?

If only a miracle could happen!

You find yourself with another spinning wheel in your head. But this one's focused on the future, on events that may not even happen. Your brain tries hard to solve these puzzles, but as they are in the future, or just in your imagination, your brain can't do it, so this future wheel keeps spinning as well.

Going over imagined future events is where anxiety comes from, and anxiety can of course also lead to a drink.

So there you are with anxiety and depression like two wheels spinning in your head. Your normal way of dealing with those issues has always been alcohol, but you have now learnt that while a drink will help tonight, it will only make matters worse in the morning, it is self-defeating. You are caught in a painful place. What can you do?

The answer lies not in the future or the past. It lies in the present.

When we discuss the spinning wheels in my workshops, I draw a couple of big wheels on a flip chart, in the middle of one I write the word "past" and in the other I write "future". Then in between I write in large letters "NOW" with an arrow pointing to it to indicate that's where we need to focus.

We talk about how - despite all the worries people in the room might have - that right now, at this very moment, we are all okay. We have a nice room, coffee and biscuits, each other's company and something interesting to discuss. We talk about how we can create that feeling of wellbeing in the present when we leave the room.

We brainstorm what actions we can take today that will keep us in the present and stop those wheels from spinning. And you, the person reading this book, can do the same thing for yourself. What can you do today to keep yourself in the present?

A good start is simply paying attention to what you are doing and where you are. For instance, when you are walking through your local town along a familiar street, try actively looking around. It's amazing how much detail you see that you've never noticed before, even on a street you've been down a hundred times before. It makes you realize how usually you are so preoccupied and self-absorbed that you miss what's going on around you.

As you walk with a heightened sense of your surroundings, you will notice other people, hands in pockets, serious faces, looking down at their shoes as they walk – you can bet those people have the wheels spinning in their heads as they walk and are totally oblivious to what's going on in their present.

A favourite exercise of mine when I am walking through the town is to actively open up my attention to the sounds around me. I am not trying to think about the sounds, I am just trying to be aware of sounds. You realize just how much is going on, sounds of birds, people talking, traffic, wind in the trees, it really gets your mind away from those spinning wheels.

Think about your activities. What can you be doing that will keep your attention on the present? In the last chapter we talked about how Gloria found that she didn't even think about drinking when she was playing Scrabble, and how Gary was happy working with his pigs. They were doing things that kept them happily centred in the here-and-now.

I had one client, one of the heaviest drinkers I have ever worked with, get over his problems by focusing on learning to play golf. Another found that doing huge jigsaw puzzles worked for him. I knew one woman - who was cross-addicted to alcohol and heroin - who got clean and sober by learning knitting! The one thing these activities had in common was that it kept people in the present.

Working with other people is a great way of keeping your mind in the present. If you turn your focus to other people, those wheels in your head stop spinning. In drug and alcohol services, we encourage people who have become sober to do a little voluntary mentoring with people new into treatment, because it's good for them as well as the people they mentor. Or you can get involved in voluntary work, as well as helping a good cause, you can help yourself by focusing on other people and giving you mind a rest from your own issues.

I know that if I have concerns myself about things that are happening in my own life, one of the best things I can do is go and work with my clients. If my mind is focused on someone I am helping, I cannot think about my own troubles at the same time, it's impossible.

Mindfulness-Based Relapse Prevention

A great way to bring your attention to the here-and-now and stop those wheels spinning is Mindfulness. If you've ever thought that Mindfulness sounds a bit hippy-ish, consider that Mindfulness is clinically proven to work. In the UK, for example, it has been recommended by the Health Service since 2005 as a treatment for anxiety that is at least as effective as medication – and you don't get the downside of taking pharmaceuticals.

Mindfulness is a form of meditation that is quite accessible to anyone. It usually begins with turning your attention to your breathing, or sensations in your body, or sounds. It helps you begin observing your thoughts, rather than being wrapped up in them. Being detached from your thoughts and looking at them as they come and go through your mind is an experience new to most of us. It gives a detachment and a new level of self-awareness that is really useful to someone struggling with an addiction. Regular practice of Mindfulness can lead to a generally improved sense of contentment and wellbeing.

It's really easy to get into Mindfulness. Pre-recorded guided meditations make it very accessible to anyone. Simply download a meditation, get comfortable and follow the instructions. There are masses of free downloads you can find on Google or You Tube. But a couple of web sites I can recommend to find good quality downloads are franticworld.com and freemindfulness.org.

Although Mindfulness has been around in the East for thousands of years, the origins of its current popularity in the West owes a lot to the work of Jon Kabat-Zinn, a professor at the University of Massachusetts Medical School, who in the 1980s pioneered Mindfulness Based Stress Reduction (MBSR) for the treatment of stress, chronic pain and illness.

One version of Mindfulness that may be of particular interest to readers of this book is Mindfulness Based Relapse Prevention (MBRP). This was developed at the Addictive Behaviours Research Center of the University of Washington for the use of people in recovery from addictive behaviours. MBRP helps to create greater awareness of the triggers and habitual behaviours that cause relapsing.

MBRP is a course of about two hours per week over eight weeks. I have attended one of these courses myself as a co-facilitator with a group of mixed former drug or alcohol users. The difference I could see that MBRP made to some of the course members was impressive. Sadly MBRP isn't available everywhere, but a particularly useful web page is www.mindfulrp.com/For-Clients.html.

This page gives you

a) A list of MBRP therapists around the world who you can contact for local courses if there is one in your area.

b) Free MBRP downloads you can use right now. Clearly this isn't as good as physically attending a course, but it will still be helpful. Simply download, get comfortable and listen.

Recruiting your Cheerleaders

Research shows that the majority of people who drink seriously enough to have diagnosable Alcohol Use Disorder at some point in their life will be able to resolve their problem with little formal help.

Earlier in the book we looked at how young people often drink heavily for a few years, but then cut back or stop when major life events happen: they fall in love, become parents, or start careers. This process is known as maturing out. It is simply part of the process of growing up for many people.

Other people, particularly those at the mild end of the AUD spectrum, will sort out their issues on their own. The motivation may come from a wake-up call such as a doctor's intervention or a driving ban. If you are one of those people, you might find that learning a few of the techniques in this book is all the help you need.

Social support

Nevertheless, it has been shown in many studies that people who reach out for support are far more likely to succeed in overcoming alcohol issues than people who try to go it alone. At the very least, you need a few cheerleaders, people who will encourage you on the days when it all seems just a bit too difficult. This is why early on in this book I asked you to make public your intention to moderate or stop your alcohol use. This helps you find the cheerleaders in your life.

If you go on to social media and say that, for example, you have decided to stop drinking for three months, this could draw a couple of responses. Some people might say "Rather you than me", "You'll be lucky to last three days" and so on. These people are the doom merchants who have their own alcohol issues. They don't want you to succeed because it makes them feel uncomfortable about their own levels of alcohol use. These people are to be avoided. They will try to poison your mind with negativity. They want to see you fail.

On the other hand, some people will say "Well done", "Good luck" and "What a great idea". These people are golden. You have found your cheerleaders. These are the people you need to be spending your time with. Be honest with these people. Share your ups and downs with them. Give them the opportunity to cheer you on more.

Social media is an increasingly important source of support. On Facebook there are a huge number of groups of people who use the platform to cheer each other on. Some are local groups, but most have members from around the globe. You have to be a little careful as these are often not moderated and there are people out there who are looking to promote their own agendas, which might not be helpful to you. I would suggest getting involved with a more formal and established kind of support, known as mutual aid.

Mutual Aid Groups

These are voluntary groups where members can share their experiences and draw support from each other. The colossus of the mutual aid world is Alcoholics Anonymous (AA) which started in the 1930s and has face-to-face meetings over much of the world. AA's philosophy is based on what it calls the 12-steps. AA has spawned many other 12-Step groups for other issues, the best known of which are Narcotics Anonymous (NA) which covers all drugs not just alcohol, Cocaine Anonymous (CA), Gamblers Anonymous (GA), Overeaters Anonymous (OA) and Co-dependents Anonymous (Coda). We will be discussing AA and the 12-Steps in detail in the next chapter of this book.

For many years, AA had the field of mutual aid for drinkers to itself. In the 1970s onwards, however, other rival organisations started to spring up. Organisations like Rational Recovery and Life Ring offer an alternative to AA's 12-Steps.

Unfortunately, many people in these organisations are so vociferously opposed to AA that a huge bun fight has broken out over the last few decades which I don't think is particularly helpful to people trying to get sober. You don't need to do much research on these organisations on the internet to encounter people with deeply entrenched positions on either side, which is a shame as this draws attention away from the good advice and genuine willingness to help that can be found in all these organisations.

An organisation that has emerged from all these AA alternatives that has also managed to keep itself aloof from the bickering is Smart Recovery. Smart is based around something called REBT, a kind of cognitive therapy. Smart is well-run and has managed to establish itself outside of its native United States. For example, in the United Kingdom Smart has become well-established in mainstream treatment and I have facilitated many Smart meetings while working for services commissioned by Public Health England. We will be discussing Smart in detail in Chapter 18.

All these organisations were based on face-to-face group meetings, a model with its roots firmly in the 20th century. The omnipresence of the internet since the development of broadband this century, however, offers us a new layer of support. Smart Recovery and AA both have a big online presence, but now we are starting to see the emergence of mutual aid that is solely online.

A new player in mutual aid is the Australia-based Hello Sunday Morning (HSM) which provides support through introducing people with similar goals. This site was started by Chris Raine as a result of the support he got from people when he decided to take a public decision to go sober for a year. On HSM you sign up with an aim, which could be either sobriety or moderation, and a time frame you want (so for example I want to be sober for 6 months) and you will be invited to approach others with the same aim. You can find HSM at hellosundaymorning.org.

On the subject of internet support, I have set up a Facebook page to accompany this book. I put out occasional posts, if I see something that might be of interest to my readers. So, if you are a Facebook user, please go along and "like" the page. The address is:

facebook.com/alcoholandyou.info/

I also occasionally post on the page: Wins Health & Wellbeing Publishing. This is for anyone who would like to improve their life. You can find that page at:

facebook.com/winspub/

Formal Support

Your GP or local drug and alcohol agency are good places to start if you are looking for more formal help. They will be able to assess your needs and refer you to the treatment you require. Usually, what is required is information and alcohol-specific counselling; but if you are physically dependent, they can refer you for medically assisted help.

Depending on where you are geographically, help might be state-funded or private sector. If you are using private sector help, ensure that you are dealing with someone registered with the governing body for your country. In the United States, you would look for a substance abuse counsellor who is registered by your state. Where I work in the UK, you would look for a member of the Federation of Drug and Alcohol Practitioners, of which I am a member.

Much of the support available is based around group meetings. A lot of people are really reluctant to attend meetings, which is a shame as the research shows that people who isolate and rely just on one-to-one help are less likely to get over their difficulties, so I would urge you to give meetings a go.

How you react to a meeting is going to depend partly on the skill of the meeting leader, and whether you get on with the other people who attend. But the most important thing is your own open-mindedness and willingness to take part.

I get a lot of people who see me for assessment who panic at the suggestion of attending a meeting. The phrase I hear trotted out is "It's not for me." Often, the person has never even been to the meeting they say is not for them, so it's impossible for them to know. Or maybe they have been to just one or two meetings and been put off by something relatively minor.

This is not just a pity - it's potentially life-threatening. I was talking recently to a member of a mutual aid fellowship who joined years ago with a work colleague, as they were both heavy drinkers. He told me that he had stuck with the group, had been attending meetings for many years, and was now comfortably off and happily retired having enjoyed all the benefits of sobriety. And the colleague? He had decided the meetings were not for him and shortly afterwards had checked into a hotel and killed himself. I can't help wondering if he had persevered with the meetings, there could have been a much happier outcome.

So why do a lot of people struggle with the idea of attending meetings that are designed to help people exactly like them? The most often quoted reason is anxiety. I understand this. Alcohol causes anxiety, so this is not surprising. But it is only by confronting situations that make you anxious that you can overcome anxiety. Ironically, I have often found that it is some of the most anxious people who, when they finally try one of my meetings, enjoy them the most. Also, it's quite funny that it is the people who say "I'll try going to a meeting but I don't want to say anything" who are often the same people who never stop talking once they arrive – you can't shut them up!

I believe, however, that the most common reason for people not wanting to go to meetings is judgmental thinking. People come to a judgment about what the meeting will be like before they even attend. Or they attend but spend the whole time judging the other people at the meeting. We can't help being judgmental. It is a natural human characteristic. Our ancestors lived in a dangerous world, so evolution has given us the ability to make snap judgments all the time to protect us from harm. But the judge in your head isn't usually very useful at a recovery meeting.

I would like to suggest that if you attend a meeting, you go with the attitude that you are going to try to contribute to the meeting, rather than sit in judgment of what you think the meeting can give you. At the very least, you can contribute a spirit of compassion to the meeting, even if you say nothing. You might find it much more rewarding as a result. It is a simple shift in perspective that can make a huge difference.

I like the meetings I run to be full of great advice, lively discussion and laughter. I don't want people leaving looking glum. Getting over addiction doesn't have to be all hard work. If you find a local meeting that just leaves you feeling down, try another meeting, you might find one more to your tastes.

Comparing different approaches

The common therapies that are used in outpatient facilities like the hospital where I work are called Motivational Enhancement Therapy (MET) and Cognitive Behavioural Therapy (CBT). These are also used in residential treatment, but in rehabs Twelve Step Facilitation (TSF) is also very common.

So, which should you sign up for?

A good question – and in fact it was a question that the United States government spent $27 million on trying to answer. It was a study called Project Match, and it was the King Kong of alcohol research studies. There had never been a study of its size before and may never be one again.

How the study worked was that there were three study groups. In each group were drinkers diagnosed with Alcohol Use Disorder. MET was used with one group, CBT with another, and TSF with the third. The reason it was called Project Match was because it wanted to establish if different drinkers should be matched to different programs to improve results. Top notch therapists were used who were expert in the type of treatment they were delivering. The study started in 1989 and was eventually reported on in 1997.

So which came out on top? Which was the best type of therapy? Well, the answer that came out was:

All of them!

They were all found to be more or less as effective as each other. Interestingly, though, it seems that the most important aspect of the therapy for a lot of the drinkers was not so much the therapy itself, as their relationship with the therapist. A logical conclusion of this is that it's really about finding people you are comfortable with, and why a theme of this book is trying to find what is right for you, rather than me saying you should do this or that.

Now in the following chapters, let's look at some of these different approaches in more detail.

AA and the 12-Steps

I meet many people in my work who say AA is wonderful, that it has saved their lives. Equally I meet many people who just cannot get on with it. AA divides opinion.

One thing that is not in dispute, however, is its size. It is the colossus of alcohol recovery. AA states that it in 2015 it had 117,000 groups with an active membership of more than two million people and a global reach of 181 countries.

This is fantastic news for AA members, as it means that there is always an AA meeting somewhere near in most parts of the world. Indeed in large cities, meetings start at breakfast time and can be found all day long. The only other mutual aid organisation that comes anywhere near AA in its amazing coverage of face-to-face meetings is AA's sister organisation Narcotics Anonymous (NA), which deals with addiction to any drug, not just alcohol.

The history of AA starts in 1934 with a man getting sober in Manhattan. That man was Bill Wilson. Wilson had spent years drying out and then relapsing. Drinking had wrecked his career on Wall Street and his health. He was in Towns Hospital for the fourth time. He was under the care of Dr William Silkworth, a man who has a place in AA history for this theory that alcoholism was a combination of mental obsession and physical allergy to alcohol. It was an illness, rather than a personal failing. It was while under Dr Silkworth's care that Wilson received a treatment called the Belladonna cure, a concoction of plants including Belladonna that causes hallucinations.

It was at this time that Wilson had what he called a spiritual awakening. It was a dramatic, white light event. He says in AA's main text (known to all AA members as the Big Book) that he experienced "such a peace and serenity as I had ever known."

It would be easy to be cynical about of the idea of Wilson having some sort of psychological upheaval under the influence of a hallucinogenic drug. But whatever happened, there is no doubt that Wilson had a dramatic shift in his personal perspective and didn't drink again until his death in 1971, and what followed from that day in 1934 was going to help millions of people. Time Magazine posthumously named Wilson as one of the 100 most influential people of the 20th Century.

In 1935 Wilson turned his attention to helping other hospitalised drinkers. History tells us that he didn't succeed in getting anyone sober, but he discovered was that this was a great way of keeping himself sober. This makes a huge amount of sense. I have recommended in this book working with other people as a way of helping yourself. If you are thinking about other people, it is impossible to be thinking about yourself at the same time, which can be very helpful in recovering from alcohol addiction. The concept of "doing service" has become enshrined in AA, with members given jobs to help their group to function: it could be making the coffee, or maybe looking after the group's accounts. The important thing is that it gives the individual a sense of purpose and turns their attention to helping others.

A few months into his sobriety, Wilson found himself away from home on a business trip and was tempted to drink. He set out to find another alcoholic he could work with, in order to help take away his own urge to drink. This led him to meet Dr Robert Smith, an extreme drinker, just as Wilson had once been. Their relationship blossomed, Smith got sober, and Bill and Bob became the founding fathers of a fellowship that at that time had no name.

Their fellowship started to grow as new members joined, originally meeting at Wilson's house. Eventually the membership reached about 100. Wilson and the others set about writing a book about their experiences which was published in 1939. This book, which AA members usually call the Big Book, was officially called "Alcoholics Anonymous" and the fellowship found its name. It also found a lot of publicity when in 1941 the Saturday Evening Post ran an article about Alcoholics Anonymous, and AA took off.

AA meetings vary in terms of their format, but one thing common to all meetings is the concept of "sharing", which simply means having your say. Debating isn't allowed, you can have your turn to speak, but then are expected to be quiet to give someone else a chance. AA is kind of therapy with a story-telling tradition. Members share what is often called their "experience, strength and hope". This frequently involves going into quite graphic detail about their drinking past, what are often called war stories. Some people find it helpful to hear other people's war stories, while others say that they make AA meetings seem negative. You need to make your own decision on this.

Anyone can join AA, as they say in AA "the only requirement for membership is a desire to stop drinking". And they do mean stop. AA is an abstinence program. If you went there talking about moderation, you could expect a frosty reception. It doesn't cost you anything to join. They usual take a collection to cover the cost of running the meeting, like hiring the room and providing coffee and biscuits.

Central to AA's way of working is that all meetings are self-funding and autonomous. Any two members getting together can start an AA meeting. As long as they adhere to AA traditions, they don't need to make any formal application to AA.

Although you don't make any sort of financial commitment when you join AA, if you become a regular, you are expected to help run your local group, which is fair enough. This could be as simple as helping put the chairs out at the start of the meeting or helping with the tea and coffee. For long-standing members with stable sobriety, it could mean running the meeting, or even organising for AA on a regional or national level.

I find AA's way of self-funding and autonomy on a local basis refreshing in its independence. One of AA's traditions is "declining outside contributions". You won't see a "donate" button on the AA web site.

AA is very much an organisation run by its members for its members. The officers of AA are all elected by their peers and, with the exception of a few administration posts, are unpaid. Anonymity, as the name Alcoholics Anonymous suggests, is a core tradition. Your attendance at meetings is not recorded and nobody asks for your second name. Even Bill Wilson was known as Bill W within the fellowship during his lifetime.

Whilst this helps to ensure your privacy, it means that there is no vetting of people in AA, which is worth considering at meetings if you divulge personal information. AA literature talks about disclosing your story in a "general" way, which would seem good advice if you don't know everyone in the meeting. And it's worth bearing in mind when you are looking for help from members of the group that AA is a fellowship of peers, people who are there because they have a similar problem to you, which doesn't qualify them as therapists. Advice from other members may be well-intentioned, but there is no quality control on people's opinions. Fortunately, AA is backed by much literature and advice that members can refer to.

When you go to AA, you will hear standard advice like "don't pick up the first drink", "one day at a time" and "keep coming back to meetings". It's a simple message that has kept many people sober for years. But AA goes much deeper than that. Central to AA's philosophy are the 12 Steps. This is a program of recovery that has its roots in an evangelical organisation which pre-dates AA called the Oxford Group, of which Wilson had been a member.

This is where a lot of resistance to AA comes in, because there is no getting away from the fact that in the Big Book and the 12 Steps there is a lot of talk about God, which puts many people off. But I should say that in AA the concept of God is not a religious one. AA says that it is "a God of your understanding", so it is something that makes sense to you. It is what AA calls a power greater than you or a higher power. It can be what you want. It can be nature or the universe. It can be a higher form of you. AA likes to say that it is spiritual program, not a religious one.

To many people, the concept of having a higher power and a spiritual program sounds like so much hocus pocus and they reject AA outright because of that, cutting themselves off from the biggest support group on the planet for problematic drinkers. I think there is a lot of misunderstanding because of the terminology used and that the language of AA goes back to the 1930s.

How I try to explain AA to drinkers who have never been is that AA encourages you to put your faith in a higher power and live one day at a time. This higher power can be anything. For example, it could be your plan for recovery from your addiction. If I suggested to you putting your faith in your plan and living one day at a time, you would probably think that sounds sensible and not like hocus pocus at all.

Looking at this from a scientific point of view, this is likely to result in less stress and anxiety and better outcomes. If you are focusing your attention on the day in hand rather than projecting ahead, you are likely to make a better job of whatever you are doing, hence the likelihood of a better result.

This is something that people pay money to achieve through CBT, Mindfulness, or Life Coaching, but is available from AA for free. And having a healthy spiritual attitude to life is an indicator of good mental health.

Here are AA's famous 12 Steps:

"1. We admitted we were powerless over alcohol - that our lives had become unmanageable.

2. Came to believe that a Power greater than ourselves could restore us to sanity.

3. Made a decision to turn our will and our lives over to the care of God as we understood Him.

4. Made a searching and fearless moral inventory of ourselves.

5. Admitted to God, to ourselves and to another human being the exact nature of our wrongs.

6. Were entirely ready to have God remove all these defects of character.

7. Humbly asked Him to remove our shortcomings.

8. Made a list of all persons we had harmed, and became willing to make amends to them all.

9. Made direct amends to such people wherever possible, except when to do so would injure them or others.

10. Continued to take personal inventory and when we were wrong promptly admitted it.

11. Sought through prayer and meditation to improve our conscious contact with God as we understood Him, praying only for knowledge of His will for us and the power to carry that out.

12. Having had a spiritual awakening as the result of these steps, we tried to carry this message to alcoholics and to practice these principles in all our affairs."

The wording of the twelfth step indicates that the steps are a way of achieving that spiritual awakening, a great perspective shift, which Wilson believed alcoholics needed to recover. Working on a one-to-one basis with a sponsor -

an experienced member of the group with a good period of sobriety - is the usual way of learning the 12-Steps. The choice of a sponsor is down to you.

It is not obligatory for members to follow the 12-Steps, however, so if you are unsure, I would not let it put you off trying AA. There are a lot of people out there living their lives by the 12-Steps and are very grateful for it. There are many other members who don't follow it. As they say in AA, you can take what you need and leave the rest.

I think the antiquated language of the Big Book is a big problem for AA in this century. But the members seem to like its old-fashioned language. Change happens very slowly in AA. Even in the very early days when AA was so small that the members could all meet at Wilson's house, Wilson found the members very reluctant to change. Wilson himself was a radical and he seems to have found conservatism in the organisation frustrating.

The upshot of this is that the language of AA's core text written in the 1930s becomes more difficult to understand for new members with every year that passes. The Big Book also gets quite a lot of criticism – including from AA members – for being sexist. I doubt it would have been seen that way when it was written, but it is now. However, as so many members treat the Big Book more like a sacred text than a self-help book, it is unlikely to change any time soon. The writing in the Big Book varies from the prosaic to the truly inspiring, as in this famous extract, known as the Step Nine Promises:

"If we are painstaking about this phase of our development, we will be amazed before we are half way through. We are going to know a new freedom and a new happiness. We will not regret the past nor wish to shut the door on it. We will comprehend the word serenity and we will know peace. No matter how far down the scale we have gone, we will see how our experience can benefit others. That feeling of uselessness and self-pity will disappear. We will lose interest in selfish things and gain interest in our fellows. Self-seeking will slip away. Our whole attitude and outlook upon life will change. Fear of people and of economic insecurity will leave us. We will intuitively know how to handle situations which used to baffle us. We will suddenly realize that God is doing for us what we could not do for ourselves."

If you have never been to AA and want to stop drinking, it is worth your time going to see what it's all about. All you need to do is Google AA meetings in your area and turn up with an open mind, as simple as that. You will also find telephone helplines you can call on AA's regional web sites.

If you are one of the people who can get on with AA, you will have found yourself a huge resource, somewhere you can make like-minded sober friends, and find unparalleled worldwide support.

Smart Recovery and the 4-Point Program

Smart Recovery has its roots in the AA alternatives that started towards the end of the last century and seems to be the most successful of the bunch. Smart stands for Self-Management and Recovery Training. The Smart Program was put together by a collaboration of professionals and people in recovery and launched in 1994. It is very practical.

Smart is not so much one original philosophy as a collection of techniques that have been assembled to make one program. At its heart is something called Rational Emotive Behaviour Therapy (REBT) which was created in the 1950s by a psychiatrist called Albert Ellis. REBT focuses on our thinking habits and rooting out the kind of faulty thinking that often leads to drinking.

Smart has built around REBT many recovery support and relapse prevention strategies which it calls the Smart tools. The whole program, which Smart likes to call science-based, is flexible in that as new breakthroughs in recovery are made, they can be added to Smart. For example, Mindfulness has started to make an appearance in Smart. The whole program can be found in the Smart Recovery Handbook, which is updated on a regular basis, as is the website smartrecovery.org which is packed with resources.

Smart's strap-line is "The Power of Choice". In Smart's philosophy, if you have chosen to maintain an addictive life, you can choose to stop it. There is much talk of self-empowerment. The Smart program has a 4-point structure.

1. Building and Maintaining Motivation.

2. Coping with Urges.

3. Managing Thoughts, Feelings and Behaviours.

4. Living a Balanced Life.

Smart is not specific to alcohol, it covers any drug and also any addictive behaviour, so it could be applied to anything from heroin to gambling to smartphone addiction. But as alcohol is the giant of the addiction world, there is plenty in Smart for the drinker. It is abstinence-based, but it does leave the door open for people who are not committed to abstinence to come in and take a look.

A Smart meeting is led by a facilitator, whose job it is to ensure the smooth running of the meeting and keep it relevant to Smart's principals. The facilitator is Smart-trained. Smart runs a thirty hour online training course from Ohio to skill up facilitators. As I have done this course myself, I can confirm that it's a thorough, well-constructed course, and this means that there is consistency and quality-control between Smart meetings wherever you attend one.

If the Smart meeting is based in a treatment facility, such as the out-patient location I work in, the facilitator may be a recovery professional like myself. However, ideally Smart meetings will be peer-led, meaning that the facilitator will probably be someone who entered Smart initially as a service-user. In this way Smart can grow organically.

Smart meetings follow a standard format. This begins with a check-in, at which participants can share their ups and downs, usually focusing on recent events. Unlike the 12-Step tradition, in Smart the telling of war stories is discouraged. Smart also discourages the use of labels like alcoholic or addict. At the end of the check-in, the facilitator will draw up an agenda for discussion, based on key points that participants have talked about in the check in, and the meeting will be open for discussion.

So for example, let's say that boredom as a trigger to drink had come up as an issue for people in the check-in, the facilitator might lead a group brainstorm (a common Smart technique) to come up with solutions to this, perhaps ending up with a flip chart full of helpful ideas. The meeting would then move on to the next agenda item. It is part of the facilitator's role to keep the discussion flowing and to relate issues raised by the participants to tools in the Smart program. The meeting finishes with a check out, at which participants can reflect, for example, on what they have learned from the meeting, or plans for the week ahead. A hat might be passed for donations to help finance the meeting.

As part of my work for government-commissioned services in England, I have been facilitating Smart Recovery meetings for four years. During this time I have seen a lot of drinkers and users of other drugs pass through the meetings. I have found that Smart has been well-received. The one area that people sometimes struggle with is that Smart can use a lot of rather academic language and it loves its acronyms (Smart itself being an acronym) which people can find confusing. But that aside, people generally seem to take well to Smart.

I was once asked to facilitate a Smart meeting I had never previously attended. As I didn't know the people in the room, I wanted to get an idea for how much they knew about the Smart Program, so I asked what they understood about the Smart program.

I got an immediate response from one person: "Learning how to handle PIGs and DIBs." I thought this was great, as it does sum up a lot about what Smart teaches.

A PIG is a "Problem of Immediate Gratification". A person with an addiction is someone who is used to immediate gratification: when the urge to drink comes on, you want to get that drink right away. If you can't get that drink, it starts to be difficult to think of anything else, it becomes a craving. But every time you give in to that craving, the problem gets worse, your PIG gets bigger, then before you know it, your life is all about feeding your huge PIG. In Smart, you work on how to put control back in your own hands and take it away from the PIG.

DIB is short for Disputing Irrational Beliefs. An Irrational Belief is one of those it-was-a-good-idea-at-the-time thoughts that can get you into trouble if you act on them. When the idea pops into your head, it might sound reasonable. But if the thought came from your addiction, watch out! So how do you spot an Irrational Belief and what do you do about it?

An Irrational Belief is:

Unrealistic, there is no evidence to support it

When you look at it carefully, it doesn't make sense

It's harmful to you and will sabotage your goals

The way to deal with an Irrational Belief is to turn it into a question, then give an answer, like this:

Irrational Belief: "I'll die if I don't get a drink."

Question: "Will I really die if I don't have a drink?"

Answer: "No, I won't die - I'll just feel uncomfortable for a while. In fact, I'm more likely to die if I do have a drink."

Here's another example:

Irrational Belief: "I haven't had a drink for a week, so I'll be okay to go and see the guys at the bar. I'll just have an orange juice."

Question: "Will I really just have an orange juice?"

Answer: "Who am I trying to kid? I've never drunk orange juice with those guys ever! This is just my addiction trying to fool me into picking up a drink."

Another example:

Irrational Belief: "I drive better if I've had a drink, because I feel more relaxed."

Question: "Do I really drive better if I've had a drink?"

Answer: "No, I just feel like I do. The reality is that my reactions are poorer like everyone else. I could lose my licence or worse, I could kill someone."

Another one

Irrational Belief: "My life is such a mess, I deserve a drink."

Question: "Do I really deserve a drink because my life is a mess?"

Answer: "No, my life is a mess because of my drinking. Having more to drink is likely to make it worse."

And another

Irrational Belief: "I need a drink because I'm bored."

Question: "Will a drink really help with boredom?"

Answer: "No, I'll just end up bored and drunk. The cure for boredom is finding something to do."

I hope you get the idea now of how to dispute irrational beliefs. If you like, you could have some fun with DIBs and think up some of your own. Think back to the last time you had an unplanned drink that you regretted. Was there an irrational belief to blame? Can you remember what it was? If it happened again, how would you dispute it?

The examples I have given only relate to drinking, since that is what this book is about. But if you practice disputing irrational beliefs, you can turn it into a skill that can benefit every part of your life.

The problem you might have with Smart is in getting to a face-to-face meeting. It simply doesn't have the global reach in that respect of AA and the other larger 12-Step organisations, especially outside the USA. If you can't get to a physical meeting, try an online meeting. Smart is well geared up for this, and as with the physical meetings, the facilitators of the online versions are Smart-trained. The web site can be found at smartrecovery.org.

As mentioned earlier, Smart owes a lot to the work of the psychiatrist Albert Ellis, and his ideas are also fundamental to CBT. So let's take a look at that next.

Cognitive Behavioural Therapy (CBT)

Cognitive Behavioural Therapy (CBT) is a treatment method, a talking therapy that is frequently used to treat addictions as well as conditions like anxiety, phobias, depression, and PTSD. I am including it in this book because its use in addiction therapy is so widespread and, although you are better seeing a professional CBT counsellor to get best results, you can gain a lot from grasping a few basic CBT concepts right now.

CBT treats emotional disturbances. This is important from the point of view of the drinker as research shows that problematic drinkers overuse alcohol as a way of dealing with emotional upsets. True, you can drink because of good news, but mostly it is to shut out the bad. This is a hypothesis that I know few of the drinkers I have worked with would disagree.

A basic belief in CBT is that you feel how you think. Those emotional disturbances come from your thoughts and opinions. To illustrate this, let's take the example of a big sporting event like a football final. At the end of the game, the followers of the winning side will be in a euphoric emotional state, cheering and clapping, whereas the followers of the losing side will be in a negative emotional state, frowning and slump-shouldered.

But why should this be? After all they have both seen exactly the same game. It is simply because the fans of the winners will have the thought that the result was good and will feel good, whereas the fans of the losers will believe the result to be bad and will feel that way. Therefore, what you believe about something does indeed dramatically affect your emotional state.

CBT is very practical and indeed a lot of CBT seems like common sense when it is pointed out to you. With a little knowledge, you can start to become your own therapist, simply by being able to spot common traps that our thinking often falls into, causing us emotional distress. To start with, let's look at some common forms of unhelpful thinking. These are situations that can affect anyone, not just drinkers. But if drinking is a problem for you, these mind traps can easily bring on a relapse or a bout of heavy drinking that makes matters much worse. Take a look through this list and try to identify instances where you might have been caught out in the past.

Mind Traps – types of unhelpful thinking

Black and White Thinking: You believe that everything depends on one thing. "I'll never be happy until I get a new house." Or "I can't relax until all my debts are paid." This kind of thinking puts all your eggs in one basket and makes you vulnerable to serious disappointment that can lead to heavy drinking. It is never the case that everything depends on one thing.

Ignoring the Positives: You focus on negative things that happen to you and filter out the positives. "Nothing ever goes my way." In this way you build up in your mind the idea that you are a victim. But positive things happen to everyone, so this is untrue.

Negative Self-Labelling: Putting a label on yourself is unhelpful, as is labelling other people. You believe the label. "I'm an alcoholic and there's nothing I can do about it." "She's just a lucky person." But a label isn't really you.

Catastrophizing: Imagining the worst-case scenario all the time. "If I don't get that new job, my life will fall apart." True, the worst can sometimes happen, but usually it doesn't.

Mind Reading: Thinking that you can tell what other people are thinking. "I know they all hate me at that meeting, you can see it by the looks on their faces." Sometimes you might guess right, but mostly you will be way off mark. You can cause yourself a lot of emotional distress because you believe someone is thinking something that they are not.

Self-Pity: Sitting at home lamenting how cruel the world is to you. "It really isn't fair the way they treat me." Or "It shouldn't be like that." This thinking is always self-defeating and almost guaranteed to cause a relapse.

Approval-seeking: Basing your value on what other people think. "If people don't like me, it's my fault." Of course it's pleasant if other people think well of you, but placing your value on what other people think is setting yourself up for disappointment.

Ignoring the Present: Constantly prioritizing the future over the here-and-now. "I can't think about doing this now. There are things I need to get done for next week." You end up feeling overwhelmed, which is a major trigger for drinking.

Focusing on Past Pain: Staying in a painful place rather than looking at what can be done now. "I'll never be able to be happy until I work out where I went wrong." This really opens the door to the downward spiral of depression and drinking.

Fortune Telling: Believing that you can see into the future. "There's no point in trying to stop drinking. I know I'll fail." Unless you are genuinely clairvoyant, I suggest putting away the crystal ball. Fortune telling just leads to self-defeating thinking.

Blame Shifting: Not taking responsibility for your own actions. It's always someone else's fault "If she hadn't upset me, I wouldn't have relapsed." If you avoid taking responsibility for how you respond to events, you will always be vulnerable to relapse.

Over-optimism: Assuming that something will be okay, even though the evidence is to the contrary. A common example with alcohol is thinking "I'll just have one drink" when that has never happened before.

The ABCs

A method that is used in CBT to help combat thinking errors is called the ABCs, which Albert Ellis developed in the 1950s. His idea was that he was looking for a way of working with his clients that would produce much quicker results than traditional therapy. This technique is a core skill in both CBT and Smart Recovery. It works like this:

A stands for Activating Event: This is an actual external event which happens in real life that sets off an emotional

202

response. It could also be a thought (usually a fear) about an imagined future event that sets off a reaction. Thirdly, it could be an internal event in your head, like a memory or idea.

B stands for your Belief about A: So for example, if A was a strong craving for alcohol, your B might be the belief that you must have a drink to get rid of the craving.

C stands for the Consequences of A and B: So following on from the above, if you have as A a strong craving for alcohol and B is the belief that you must have a drink to get rid of the craving then C will be having a drink.

So how does this help?

If you can recognise the A and the B, you can question the B. You go in search of the evidence that it is true. In the above example, if you looked for evidence to support the belief that you must have a drink to get rid of the craving, you might then conclude that, in fact, it isn't true. If you just did something to distract yourself for a few minutes, then the craving would fade away. You would then end up with a different C, which would be that you didn't have a drink.

Let's take another example.

A: You are having a period of sobriety, when a drinking buddy rings you up and invites you for a game of pool at your local bar.

B: You think, oh well, it would be good to get out, I will drink Pepsi.

C: You go to the bar, your friend buys you a beer without asking and you relapse.

If you had challenged your B looking for evidence that you will drink Pepsi, you might have realized that in the hundred times that you have been to that bar, you have never drunk Pepsi, always beer, therefore the evidence points strongly to a relapse being inevitable. So you decline your friend's offer, and instead your C is that you stay on track with your plan.

Cascading ABCs

When I am doing the ABCs with a group, I like to develop what I call cascading ABCs. This is where one ABC leads on to another. It can take you a long way in terms of consequences. Here is an example.

A: You are minding your own business at home when the phone rings. It's your ex who wants to change the access arrangements to see the kids at the weekend.

B: You think this is out of line. You have something arranged for the weekend.

C: You have a fight on the phone.

You could have looked for the evidence in the B. Was your ex being out of line, or was there a good reason? Could there have been a compromise that could have suited you both and the kids? However, you flew off the handle and next, the C above becomes our next A.

A: You have a fight on the phone with your ex.

B: You think it's outrageous that your ex speaks to you like that. You need a drink.

C: You go to the store, buy a bottle of wine which you bring home and drink.

You could have looked for the evidence in B, do you really need a drink because of the argument, or was it just an excuse to drink? The C now becomes an A in the next ABC.

A: You've drunk the wine. It's still early. You want another bottle.

B: You think you could just drive back down to the store. It's not far. You'll be safe to drive.

C: You crash your car and end up in a cell.

You could have looked for the evidence in the B, which was that you are not safe to drive when you have drunk a bottle of wine; it's just the booze talking.

You can see how the ABCs cascade one into another. In the above scenario, this could continue to cascade until you lose your job or end up with a prison sentence, and this could all have been avoided if you had looked for the evidence that your ex was being unreasonable on the phone.

This gives you an overview of some of the basics of CBT. There is much more to CBT that is beyond the scope of this book which you can explore with a CBT counsellor. But even if you can just master what you have read in this chapter, you can make big strides in controlling your drinking and in your life generally.

Relapse Prevention

We have covered a lot of ground in this book, you and I. We have looked at how society and advertising condition our thinking about alcohol; we have exploded common alcohol myths; we have discussed AUD, and investigated different treatment methods and useful drugs; we have explored the pros and cons of moderation and sobriety, detox and reduction, withdrawal cycles and how time can perform wonders with your body and mind if you give it a chance; we have gone into the head game of overcoming alcohol, using many techniques like Solution Focused Thinking and Mindfulness; we have compared AA, Smart Recovery and CBT-based treatment.

In the introduction to this book, we talked about how alcohol can seem like a huge overpowering dark force that always gets the upper hand, but how demystifying alcohol takes away its power. I hope that having read this book, you find that alcohol is demystified for you now and you feel equipped to take the power back into your own hands. I hope that you have a plan and are starting to make progress.

But what's next?

Alcohol Use Disorder is by its very nature a relapsing condition and inevitably most people don't beat it at the first attempt. There can be many slips along the way. This is normal. If you have a slip, this is not something to beat yourself up about. Apply Solution Focused Thinking. Look at what happened. What worked, if only for a while, that you can do more of? What didn't work and what can you do differently?

But how can you avoid the pain of a full-blown relapse? Opinions differ on what exactly constitutes a relapse, but I would define it as follows: A relapse is where you return to your original behaviour for several days. What exactly that original behaviour was, only you know.

If you have become abstinent of alcohol, then a relapse is obvious – you are drinking alcohol again. The remedy is to put the alcohol down right away. Don't start thinking "Oh, I'll just have a few today and start again tomorrow" or "It'll be okay just for the weekend". The more you drink the harder it will be to stop again. The voice in your head that is telling you that it's okay to have a few is the voice of your addiction, and your addiction wants to destroy you.

If you have gone down the route of moderation, a relapse can be trickier to see starting. It might just be one extra drink above your self-imposed drinking limit. In this case the voice of your addiction can sound very soothing and beguiling "Oh, it was only an extra one, you're doing well, and it won't hurt". But it will hurt. Before you know it, you will be back to drinking at your problematic level, while your addiction is saying "It's okay, you can cut back again tomorrow".

In the early days of your plan for recovery, a relapse can happen very quickly. It might take a few attempts to get your plan off the ground. But as your plan starts to get going and you get days and then weeks of achievement under your belt, it's easy to become a little over-confident.

Relapse can be a subtle foe. It doesn't always happen suddenly. Indeed, the longer you get into your plan, the more likely it is that relapse takes its time. If you can spot the early signs, you can nip it in the bud before it takes hold. Here are warning signs to look out for:

1. You start finding reasons not to do the things that have been working for you. For instance, if you have been going to lots of recovery meetings and you suddenly start to cut back. Or maybe you have been seeing a counsellor and you start to think you are too busy to see her anymore. Or you have been going to yoga or meditation groups, and you stop. Whatever it is, have a serious talk with yourself, ask

yourself if there is really a good reason for this change in behaviour, or are you starting to backslide?

2. You start to see old drinking friends or visit places where you used to drink. You might tell yourself that you can do this now, you have done well and you are strong. But is this really you that's talking, or is it the voice of your addiction? You might be able to see those people or go to those places at some date in the distant future, but if you are just weeks into your plan, it is much too dangerous. Ask yourself if it is really a desire to drink that is drawing you closer. Are you courting relapse because deep inside you want to find an excuse to drink?

3. You start to think about the good times you had drinking and romanticising your past. You start to forget all the terrible things that alcohol brought into your life. This leads you to feeling hard done by. It makes you think that life is unfair. You should be able to enjoy yourself. Self-pity starts to take hold, and before you know it, the voice of your addiction is putting up powerful arguments for drinking. It starts telling you that you are better with a drink, you are wittier, you have more fun, and so on. If this happens, take a piece of paper, write down all the horrors that alcohol caused you on one side. On the other side, write down all the benefits that your new life is bringing you. Then compare the two.

4. You start thinking that perhaps things weren't as bad as they seemed. You think you can cut corners. You begin wondering if the reasons why you took action on your drinking were exaggerated. You wonder if all those dire health warnings you read about alcohol are all so much hot air. You begin to think that you don't need to keep following your plan. You're okay now. You deserve a break. One day off the plan won't hurt. In short, you start to think that all you have learnt doesn't apply to you.

This leads us to my Third Law of Recovery from Alcohol Addiction:

"You are not an exception."

The idea that everything you have heard doesn't apply to you has launched a billion relapses. Ask yourself, what evidence is there that I am different? Why should I be able to get away with drinking now in a way I couldn't in the past? Where's the proof?

Post-Acute Withdrawal Syndrome

It is my belief that a major reason for relapse is Post-Acute Withdrawal Syndrome (PAWS), and yet very few of the clients I talk to have ever heard of it. In fact, a lot of my fellow recovery professionals know little about it. But if you understand what it is, you can save yourself a relapse and much pain.

In the early stages of giving up any addictive substance, you expect to suffer with withdrawal. It's no surprise. This is called the acute stage, when the substance is still in your body but the levels are dropping. In the case of alcohol, it takes about 10 days for the body to be completely rid of the drug.

However, you will find that you still feel like you are in withdrawal from time to time afterwards. These feelings can come in waves. This can be confusing, because you know that alcohol can't be in your body any longer. As this comes on top of the mental games that coming off alcohol produces, it is not surprising that people need a lot of support in these early days.

What is happening is that your brain chemistry is readjusting after a long period of alcohol abuse. It is normal, but it feels like something is going wrong. What's more, Post-Acute Withdrawal Syndrome can occur for anything up to two years after you stop drinking. Most people don't know that. This is the story of Pamela and her experience with Post-Acute Withdrawal Syndrome:

"Getting into recovery from alcohol was much easier than I had expected. True, the first couple of weeks were difficult

- I often felt as though I didn't know what to do with myself. But that soon passed. I had heard ex-drinkers say that when you stop drinking a lot of people get what is called a 'pink cloud' period, when everything seems lovely, and that is what happened to me.

The world without alcohol just seemed marvellous. I absolutely loved the feeling of being clean and clear-headed. Everything seemed so colourful. My senses seemed to have been heightened. Even my eyesight started to improve, and after a couple of months I didn't need to wear glasses for driving any more.

I went to recovery meetings all the time, five or six a week. It didn't matter which ones. I went to AA, NA, Smart, and meetings at the local drug project. I loved hearing other people's stories. Some were real eye-openers, especially people who had been cross-addicted. But it didn't matter how gritty the stories were, and even if they were very different from me, I got a lot from them. In fact, if I couldn't go to a meeting for a few days, I really missed them. They were a vital part of my recovery.

During all this time, I had days when I would feel the urge to drink, lots of them. But I just kept myself busy, which helped a lot. I didn't give myself time to think about it. Something that had been drummed into me at meetings was not to allow self-pity a chance to take over my head, and that was good advice. The urges would always pass pretty quickly.

It all went well and before I knew it, I was a year sober. I was still keeping busy. I was helping out at some of the groups I attended. I had made lots of sober friends. Life was good.

Then it happened. Completely out of the blue one morning I woke up with a raging craving to drink, as bad as anything I could remember in my first few days after quitting. But this was after about 16 months of sobriety.

I was devastated. I started to panic. My thoughts were that it had all been a waste of time. All the meetings I had been to, all the good stuff I had done was all for nothing. Here was alcohol back to claim me. And it didn't go away. I was in tears. I felt beaten, alcohol had got me. It all seemed so unfair.

It would have been easy to pick up a drink that day. I just felt like giving up the battle with alcohol. But I didn't. Instead I rang up a therapist who had given me some counselling in my early days. Luckily he was available. When he heard what was happening, he told me to come and see him that afternoon.

When I saw him, the cravings were still raging. I told him the full story. He told me not to panic. He said it sounded like Post-Acute Withdrawal Syndrome. I said I had never heard of it. He explained that it was just my mind settling. That it would pass. I was just to stick to my normal routine. He was right. It took a week, but it did pass. Thankfully, it never returned."

How to manage Post-Acute Withdrawal Syndrome

1. Expect that it could happen to you. That way you won't be in panic as Pamela was.

2. If it does happen, don't think that something has gone wrong. In fact, although it feels bad, it's a sign that something is going right. It is your brain recalibrating and returning to normal.

3. Stick to your routine and trust in the things that have kept you sober up until that point. It will pass.

Now the nightmare is over, what do you want the dream to be?

Being a heavy drinker takes a lot of time, money and effort. Leaving alcohol behind creates time and opportunity in your life. It's now up to you to decide how you want to enjoy that time.

On one level, it's important to keep up the practices that have helped you. Don't drop any practices that have worked for you unless you are sure they really have passed being useful. For example, if you went to lots of recovery meetings, cut back on them by all means if you think you don't need to attend so many, but don't just stop. That could trigger a relapse.

On another level, however, it's important to start getting on with your life. Recovery from alcohol is often described as being a bridge to normal living. It is not normal living in itself. I have met many people who seem to have got stuck in a recovery bubble and, while they might not be drinking any more, you wouldn't really describe them as being

216

sober. It's time to move your focus away from alcohol altogether. Try this exercise:

1. Take a notebook and find somewhere you won't be disturbed. Do a little brainstorming just with yourself. Ask yourself, now the nightmare is over, what do you want the dream to be?

2. Keep writing until you have a long list and have exhausted your mind of all the things you might want to do. Now go through your list. Put a circle round the ones that appeal to you the most.

3. Next, draw up a short list. Then number them in order of preference. Keep working on your list until one thing emerges as the number one thing you want to do with your sober life.

4. Now go and do that.

I wish you well on your journey.

My Default Program

The idea of this book was to present to you a variety of ways for you to choose from to construct a program that works for you.

Have you done that?

Or are you still confused?

This appendix is for the benefit of anyone who is still unsure. It is my default program - one that I believe is likely to work for the majority of drinkers.

1. Reduce down in 20% steps as described in chapter 6. If you find this is really difficult, you could talk to your physician about whether Nalmefene or Naltrexone could help, as described in chapter 7.

2. Get as much support as you can, as described in chapter 16. Consider getting CBT counselling or doing Mindfulness.

3. When you have reduced down to zero, begin a sober break as described in chapter 9. I would recommend at least six months. If this is really difficult, consider asking you physician if acamprosate could help you handle the cravings.

4. Don't let up on the support. Research shows that in the early days of sobriety, people who get help and make sober friends are most likely to succeed.

5. When you reach the end of your sober break, you can now take a decision. Do you want to extend your sober break? Do you want to try moderate drinking? Do you just want to stay stopped? This is your decision.

My Three Laws of Recovery from Alcohol Addiction.

1. Misery increases in direct proportion to the amount of alcohol taken.

2. Control over alcohol is always dependent on control over emotional responses.

3. You are not an exception.

Suggested Reading

William Miller and Ricardo Munoz - Controlling Your Drinking

Steve Chandler – Death Wish

Smart Recovery – The Smart Recovery Handbook

Alcoholics Anonymous World Service – Alcoholics Anonymous

Philip Tate – Alcohol: How to Give It Up and Be Glad You Did

Albert Ellis – How to Stubbornly Refuse to Make Yourself Miserable about Anything

Mark Williams and Danny Penman – Mindfulness

David D Burns – Feeling Good

Kelly Wilson - The Wisdom to Know the Difference

Book 2

Reversing Alcoholism:

Real Recovery from Alcohol Addiction

Preamble

This is a book of hope, written in a spirit of compassion both for alcoholics and their loved ones. I also expect this book to be read by my fellow addiction therapists and clinicians. It may even be read by sceptics – I realize the title of this book will raise many eyebrows, particularly among members of Alcoholics Anonymous and other 12-Step groups. Whichever category you fall into, I welcome you to this book, and I hope you find much that is helpful in your life. I will be using examples from my own work, case studies of clients I have worked with, and will be referencing some of the most highly credible scientific research available.

A few years ago, I was working in an outpatient facility at a hospital in England. The service was focused on addictions. I worked with a wide range of people who had problems with a wide range of substances. Keeping up with new substances was a challenge - it is quite amazing how humanity, and in particular chemists, can keep coming up with newer ways for us to find a mental outlet, or in common parlance, get high. But there was one substance that stood out from the rest, one which affected 80% of clients in addiction and which had been around for millennia – alcohol.

My job covered carrying out clinical assessments, care planning, one-to-one counselling, and running therapeutic groups. As you can imagine, the clients could be challenging, sometimes threatening, but always rewarding to work with. However, there was one group of clients I found particularly stimulating to work with – the drinkers.

I think this was because I could relate most strongly with them. I have never smoked crack, taken ecstasy, chased the dragon, or swallowed handfuls of Diazepam. But I do know what it's like to wake up with a hangover, to have forgotten what I did the previous night, to have regretted decisions made while drunk, to have been dying for a drink without knowing why. That doesn't mean I had a problem, in fact it probably indicates that I was pretty normal - since alcohol is condoned in our culture, I doubt many people grow up without having at least one experience of the negative side of drinking.

True, my negative experiences with alcohol might not have been as extreme as most of the clients I have worked with.

But those experiences gave me insight into the thinking of my alcohol clients. It gave me the gifts of empathy and compassion. I could understand their confusion, pain and frustration at finding themselves in the grip of a mysterious substance that was pulling their strings like an unseen puppeteer.

Something else that fascinated me about alcohol was the diversity of problem drinkers. I find it remarkable how this particular drug, alcohol, works in so many ways with different people. My clients ranged from highly successful and rich business people through to street drinkers whose lives were in total chaos.

At one end of the scale was Terry, who ran one of the largest privately-owned companies in the United Kingdom. He would arrive at work in his chauffeur-driven Bentley, passing his workers who were walking up the drive up to his grand Edwardian mansion from where he ran his business empire. When he arrived in work, his chef would make him his breakfast of eggs, bacon and mushrooms, accompanied by his first brandy of the day. Terry had just about everything a man could want, apart from happiness.

At the other end of the scale was Martin, who lived on a bench on the seafront. All his possessions were in his rucksack. I would often pass him while I was walking into work in the morning. Most days he would be clutching a large plastic bottle of cheap, rocket-fuel cider, unless he had got some money, in which case he would be drinking Jack Daniels straight from the bottle. Some days he would shout out when I passed by. Other days he would not seem to recognize me and his gaze remained fixed on the horizon. He passed his time looking out to sea, trying to keep warm, dodging the police and getting into fights with his peers.

Then there was Jenny, a well-dressed and well-spoken middle-aged mother who worked as an administrator of a college. She really wasn't the kind of person that you would suspect of having a problem, she seemed so proper. But she had half a bottle of vodka mixed in with the orange juice she kept in her bag at all times. She had also been embezzling money from the college and was full of fear that she would be found out. Her apparently comfortable, middle-class life was in danger of crashing in spectacular style.

There was Harry, who tried to keep how much he drank from his family. He was a recently-retired army officer, a big man with a big personality. He had a special long pocket inside his overcoat that was just right for him to hide a bottle of wine in. When he took the family dog out in the morning, he would insert a bottle of wine, and then drink it straight from the bottle as soon he was out of view of the house. He could drink the whole bottle in seconds. He told his family he liked exercising the dog as it kept him fit, which is why he walked it so often.

I have worked with drinkers who would only drink good wine. I have worked with drinkers who would drink mouthwash if it contained alcohol. I have worked with drinkers who were so sensitive to alcohol that a couple of glasses of wine would send them off into another world where they totally lost control. I have worked with drinkers who could consume amounts of alcohol that would kill another human being, yet could carry on as if they were sober. I have worked with clients who were so extremely physically addicted to alcohol that a mere mouthful of beer would spark off the most frightening and life-threatening bender. I have worked with others were totally obsessed with alcohol, but showed no signs of physical addiction. Many were pure drinkers, uninterested in other drugs. Others were cross-addicted, with alcohol being just one item on their daily drug menu.

This all goes to demonstrate that drinkers – the ones that we colloquially call alcoholics - vary enormously. Yet despite this, there is a perception that all problem drinkers are the same and there must be a similar way of treating them all.

I have to disagree. Alcoholics are people, not clones. There is no universal solution that works for everyone, and treating all alcoholic drinkers the same way doesn't make any sense.

Yet treatment services often try to treat them in the same way. There is a widely-held view that the way to treat alcoholics is to put them through a detox for a week, followed by some therapy groups in aftercare for a few more weeks, and expect them to live a happy live of total abstinence thereafter. Or if drinkers go to Alcoholics Anonymous, they are expected to follow the 12-Step program, never drink again, and attend AA meetings until they die.

I would like to clarify that I am not against being abstinent from alcohol – far from it. I believe that for a minority of alcoholics that abstinence is in fact the only hope for their survival. But as we will be seeing, that is not the case for everyone, and what is really going on out there is rather different to what most people believe to be true.

Also, I am not against Alcoholics Anonymous. Indeed, I have a great respect for what AA has achieved over many decades, even though I believe that their program has some fundamental flaws. But AA is nevertheless a valid form of treatment, and I am sure that it has saved the lives of thousands of people. I'm also sure it has saved innumerable marriages and careers along the way. But it is just one way of dealing with alcoholism. Many people I meet who are AA members believe that Alcoholics Anonymous is the only way, and often argue this with a great and genuine passion. But the world of treatment is much wider than AA, or indeed any single treatment method.

Alcoholics are a diverse group, and need to be treated as such. In fact, it sometimes seems to me that there are almost as many ways of treating alcoholism as there are alcoholics. But this brings up the practical question of how to accommodate all this diversity, and how to coherently explain the solutions. This is what eventually brought me to writing.

In my work, I have at any one time been working with 60 or more alcoholic drinkers on my caseload. This is far more than ideal, but given the funding constraints of working in government-backed services, it had to be done. Getting to see them all regularly was a real headache, and it was a concern that the lack of time I had for each individual meant that I wasn't able to give them the level of service they needed.

One way to see all these people on a regular basis was running weekly workshops. These were well-attended, with as many as 20 drinkers in the room at any one time. But there was still too much time between them attending sessions without contact with the service – too much time for them to be able to go off-track.

What I needed, I concluded, was some sort of guide book, specific to drinkers, that they could refer to when they were alone. In this way, they would have instant access to support at any time. I thought such a book must exist. But when I searched through what was available, I was surprised to see that most books on the subject were written by people calling themselves ex-alcoholics, who wanted the reader to follow the way they had got sober.

I realized that, while these books are probably written with the best of intentions, they were fundamentally flawed and did not meet the standards needed for clients in a clinical environment.

Firstly, by promoting one particular way, this falls into the trap of a one-size-fits-all solution. Just because they had found a way that worked for them, didn't mean it would work for others, and there was no supporting research to suggest otherwise. Secondly, the writers had no clinical training, which was deeply worrying, as wrong advice given to dependent drinkers could result in a medical emergency, even death.

I found some more reliable books, written by professionals. Some were great, but none of these was quite right. Some were too academic and lacked the reader-empathy I was looking for. Some had been written in the last century and seemed too dated. Others were general to addiction and not specific to alcohol.

I concluded that the book I was looking for simply wasn't out there, and the only logical thing for me to do was to write it myself. So was born my first book, Alcohol and You: How to Control and Stop Drinking. This book is a comprehensive guide for the problem drinker, based on reliable science, and written in a way that I hoped drinkers would find accessible and even enjoyable. I realized that I could pass on to drinkers around the world the great techniques that were working for my clients. This was exciting and inspiring.

The results have been encouraging. Alcohol and You sells around the world on Amazon, Apple Books, Kobo and other platforms. I have heard that the paperback version is now being used as a standard text in some treatment services in the USA. Most rewarding of all has been the feedback from readers who have found the book a revelation.

In writing that book, however, I had to be careful about what I used and left out. The reason was that that Alcohol and You is so information-packed that I didn't want it to become overwhelming, with too much information. Also, I realized that the topic of this book, Reversing Alcoholism, was too big and important to include as a chapter in Alcohol and You, where it might get lost among all the other chapters.

So, I present Reversing Alcoholism to you today as a stand-alone work. Although there is inevitably a certain amount of overlap with Alcohol and You, I have tried to keep this to a minimum. In writing this as a separate work, I have also been able to create a shorter book that some might read in a single sitting, and that is at a low price accessible to all.

I believe that what you are about to read in this book is important for anyone who is suffering with alcohol dependence, those already in recovery, the families and friends of problem drinkers, and workers in caring professions who want to better understand how to serve clients with such problems.

Free PDF Download:
How to Self-Diagnose Alcohol
Dependency in Minutes

If you downloaded this from the link in "Alcohol & You", you don't need to download it again.

If you are experiencing alcohol problems, before going any further in this book, you might find it useful to answer a questionnaire that will show you where you are on the scale of alcohol dependency. To get a copy, all you have to do is send a blank email (it doesn't need a subject or anything else) to alcoholfix@gmail.com, and an autoresponder will send you what you need immediately.

The questionnaire is of a type widely used by clinical staff in addiction services. I use it as part of the assessment process when I see a new client. The PDF explains how it works. I hope you find it useful.

If you are reading this book because you have someone in your life that has a drink problem, or if you are a health worker, you might also like to take a look at the PDF, as I will be referring to it during the book.

Your email goes to my private account, so you need have no worries about privacy. I will not share your address with anyone. I might send you an email very occasionally such as when I release a new book, but you won't get spammed.

Reversing Alcoholism

Can alcoholism really be reversed?

Yes, it can. In fact, I believe that reversing alcoholism is a very common phenomenon. But most people are simply unaware that it happens.

When I first started working as an addiction therapist, if anyone had suggested to me that alcoholism could be reversed, I would probably have accused them of wishful thinking. I had been exposed through my work to the full horror of alcoholism. Even at the milder end of the alcoholic spectrum, I saw people who had destroyed careers and homes in their single-minded pursuit of the next drink. At the severe end of the spectrum, I worked with drinkers who had the most horrific stories to tell of the harm they had done to themselves and to others. Most shocking of all were the drinkers who carried on drinking even though physicians had told them it would kill them in months – being without a drink was more frightening than death.

Conventional wisdom was that "once an alcoholic, always an alcoholic". I was told that alcoholism was a chronic brain disease for which there was no cure. The only way of dealing with it was for the alcoholic to abstain from alcohol and spend the rest of their life in recovery.

Essentially, recovery is a strategy of containment. The ex-drinker is constantly vigilant to the risk of picking up a drink, while following a plan to keep occupied by living life in a more meaningful way. For example, recovering alcoholics are encouraged to refocus on work, fitness or family. For some it means attending Alcoholics Anonymous meetings for life and following their program, the 12-Steps. For others, it could mean being in long term therapy.

For me, that isn't really recovery at all. If you have an illness and you recover, the illness is gone. When most people talk about recovery in relation to alcoholism, what they really mean is a life of constant maintenance, of learning how to manage the problem. But the value of recovery is not questioned as it is without doubt a happier outcome than being a slave to alcohol. My job was to help people get into the recovery system in the first place, and then keep them there.

Some people spend their lives in recovery and are happy that way, which is great when it can be achieved. However, the weakness of recovery as a strategy lies in the word I used earlier: containment. Recovery is about containing the problem, not about solving it, as we are told there is no cure for alcoholism. And with containment, there is always the risk of the problem breaking out, or as it is generally termed, relapse.

Sadly, relapse is only too common. A frequent scenario – all too familiar to people in my type of work - is that of a drinker who spends weeks in preparation, then is detoxed, and subsequently spends weeks, sometimes months, in rehab, only to come out and start drinking almost immediately. Many will have repeated detoxes, followed by the same result.

It seems that for the alcoholic drinker, there are three outcomes.

Drinking to destruction.

Living in a loop of getting sober and then relapsing.

A life of total abstinence, following a treatment plan.

But does it have to be that way? Are there other possibilities out there?

Yes, there are.

As you will see, there are huge numbers of former alcoholics out there who have seemingly reversed their alcoholism. They are not "in recovery".

In fact, as many as 75% of people who recover from alcoholism do so without ever being in treatment.

This goes a long way to explaining why the phenomenon of reversing alcoholism isn't more widely recognized. If it mostly happens outside of treatment, who knows about it? Treatment providers obviously don't know what happens with people they never meet.

If you have experienced reversing alcoholism, without being in treatment, who are you going to tell? Probably no one. More likely you will be busy getting on with your life. You may not even recognize that you were once an alcoholic, you just know you drank a lot, but now you have moved on.

But what about the drinkers who were in treatment? Well, if you have been in treatment and you realize you are okay and you no longer have a problem with alcohol, do you go back and report this to the staff at your drug and alcohol service, or do you just get on with your life? You probably didn't like being in treatment anyway. You will fob them off when they call you. The treatment centre can't compel you to come in, so they close your case, and you're gone.

If you have been a member of Alcoholics Anonymous and you realize you are okay now, do you go back to your AA meeting and say you are no longer an alcoholic? Pretty unlikely. You know that at AA they don't believe you can stop being an alcoholic, and you would expect a sceptical, even hostile reception from the group. So naturally, you don't go back, and no one knows. If you do meet someone from the group in the street and tell them you are okay now and don't need to go to meetings any more, they probably won't believe you.

******

So, what exactly do I mean by reversing alcoholism? Well, let's start by defining what we mean by alcoholism and an alcoholic, as we cannot define reversing if we are unclear about what it is that we are reversing.

The word alcoholic itself seems to have originated in the 19th century, when it became a popular term in the temperance movement to describe a drinker. There was an alternative word, "alcoholist", which sounds rather more elegant, but that didn't stick like "alcoholic".

Personally, I don't like the terms alcoholic or alcoholism. This is partly because they are often used as insults. In treatment circles, we rarely use the word alcoholism, we more normally nowadays talk about Alcohol Use Disorder. I had to think long and hard about whether to use the word alcoholism in the title of this book. In the end, I decided to use it for purely pragmatic reasons. I wanted to sell this book online, and that means search engines need to find your book, like the search boxes on Amazon. People search on the term alcoholism a lot. So, put simply, if I had called this book Reversing Alcohol Use Disorder, it might have sunk without trace in the digital warehouses of Amazon. Whereas using the word alcoholism, I know that it will come up in searches.

But the main reason why I don't like the terms alcoholism and alcoholic is that they are unspecific. How exactly do you define alcoholism? If you do a search of dictionary definitions, you will find a wide variety of definitions.

My favourite definition of alcoholism is this: alcohol dependence. There is a big reason why I like this definition - alcohol dependence can be measured. It takes away the guess-work. It takes away opinion. It is clear. What's more, it doesn't just tell you whether someone is dependent, it tells you where on the spectrum of dependence they are.

Many problem drinkers drive themselves crazy trying to decide if they are alcoholic or not. If you are reading this book because you have a problem with drink, then you probably know what I'm talking about. In particular, drinkers in the early days of membership of Alcoholics Anonymous can get into a stew about this, as they worry about whether to call themselves alcoholic. Although it's not compulsory to say you are an alcoholic at AA meetings (as in "Hello, my name is Joe and I'm an alcoholic.") it is the general custom. AA doesn't really help in this respect, as it says the only person who can say if you're an alcoholic is you.

But it's not a simple yes or no question. It's not black and white. Alcoholism, or alcohol dependence, is a sliding scale. It would be much more helpful if, instead of worrying whether they are alcoholic, drinkers should be asking themselves how dependent they have become. Crucially, they should also be asking whether they have become physically, as well as psychologically dependent.

In my work, when I first see someone about their drinking, I carry out a clinical assessment. This is a vital first step in treatment. Without getting the full picture of what's going on with a new client, I cannot be sure I am giving them correct advice, because – as we will be discussing later in the book – alcoholism doesn't just occur in isolation. It always appears as part of a wider mix of issues. So, it's important that to do my job well and serve the new client best, I find out about their medical history, prescribed medication, recreational drug use in addition to alcohol, their home life and relationships, work, hobbies, background, any history of trauma, criminal record, and so on.

But most important of all, I need to take them through a questionnaire to establish where they are on the alcohol dependence scale.

A new client might want to talk a lot, as I could be the first person they have ever honestly discussed their drinking with, and it can be a relief for some people to finally let it all out. Conversely, some people can be very guarded, especially new clients who have been coerced into seeing me in order to please their family.

Either way, it would be easy for me to be misled or come to false assumptions, but using the clinical questionnaire cuts through that and gets to the truth. From a medical perspective, the score that the client comes out with from the questionnaire helps nursing staff make a judgment on whether the client needs a medically supervised detox. It's important.

The questionnaire that you were given the chance to download at the end of the last chapter is exactly the sort that is used. So, if you believe you have a drink problem and haven't downloaded it, I suggest you take a look when you've finished this chapter.

If we were able to use one of these questionnaires over time with a drinker, we could use it to establish scientifically if alcoholism reversal had taken place. For example, if I assessed a new client today, and the score showed us the client was clearly dependent, then we repeated the assessment in, say, three years from now, and the score showed us the client was no longer dependent, we would have evidence that the alcoholism had been reversed.

But waiting three years for the results from one person would not be very efficient or conclusive. To establish that alcoholism reversal really exists we would need a study that:

used a massive random sample of the population, not just people in treatment.

was carried out by qualified professionals.

was commissioned by a world-class organisation.

It sounds like a big ask, because if such a study already existed, surely everyone would already know about it, wouldn't they?

Does it really exist?

Yes, it does!

The Research

In the United States, there is a government agency whose job it is to advise on alcohol misuse issues, the National Institute on Alcohol Abuse and Alcoholism (NIAAA).

Back in 1992, the NIAAA commissioned a piece of research of immense size and importance, the National Longitudinal Alcohol Epidemiologic Survey (NLAES). Staff from the United States Bureau of Census carried out the face-to-face research in the field. The randomly-chosen sample was a massive 42,862 respondents.

In order to carry out the clinical assessment for Alcohol Use Disorders, the researchers used the Diagnostic and Statistical Manual of Mental Disorders, fourth edition, of the American Psychiatric Association, known for short as DSM-IV. According to the NIAAA, DSM-IV "recognizes alcohol dependence by preoccupation with drinking, impaired control over drinking, compulsive drinking,

drinking despite physical or psychological problems caused or made worse by drinking, and tolerance and/or withdrawal symptoms."

The random sampling in this research gives us a great view of what is happening in the population generally. Most research on alcoholism is done with people in treatment, which gives a distorted view. I believe that drinkers in treatment tend to be at the more severe end of the alcoholic spectrum. Also, many drinkers in treatment are resistant to being helped, because they have been coerced into being there, perhaps because of family pressure, a court order, or social services intervention.

Using DSM-IV, the researchers found that around 11% of the sample were, or had been in the past, alcohol dependent, or alcoholic in common parlance. The amazing take-away from this research is that half of all these alcoholics were still drinking, but were no longer abusing alcohol.

According to what most people believe, including people working in treatment like myself, this should not be possible: alcoholics cannot become regular drinkers. Yet, this research shows that in fact not only can some alcoholics get over alcoholism, but also it is really quite common. Alcoholism can be reversed, and often is.

Going forward ten years to 2001-2, the NIAAA followed up with the National Epidemiologic Survey on Alcohol and Related Conditions (NESARC). NESARC again sampled 43000 adults in the United States using DSM-IV. The key highlights of this amazing body of research are:

Most dependent drinkers fall in the mild or moderate categories. They have difficulties controlling their alcohol use, but still function in society - they have jobs and families.

Alcohol dependence can begin any time from mid-teens till middle age, with 22 being the average age of onset.

72% of dependent drinkers have an episode of alcoholic drinking lasting up to four years, while the remainder can have up to five episodes of recovery and relapse back into alcoholic drinking. The NIAAA concludes that there appear to be two forms of alcohol dependence: time-limited, and recurrent or chronic.

Twenty years after the onset of alcohol dependence, 75% of people are in full recovery.

More than half of those that have achieved full recovery continue to drink, but at non-problematic levels.

This blows a big hole through what most people believe about alcoholism. Let's just look at that again: 75% are in full recovery, and over half of them are still drinking without it being a problematic. Their alcoholism must have been reversed.

As Mark Willenbring, director of NIAAA's Division of Treatment and Recovery Research, said, "These and other recent findings turn on its head much of what we thought we knew about alcoholism."

The stereotypical view of the alcoholic as being a vagrant living on a park bench does have some truth in it. I have worked with people like that. But they are just a tiny minority. As Doctor Willenbring stated, "The fact is that most people who develop heavy drinking or alcohol dependence do not fit that stereotype. There are many who are not falling apart — their marriage is intact, they parent, they go to work, and in many cases, nobody even knows they are coming home and drinking a pint or more of whisky, and these people are not getting any attention at all."

But given that this vastly-important research has been around for a few years already, why is it that it isn't generally more widely known? In my experience, it isn't even that widely known among people who work in recovery.

I think the answer lies in something else that NESARC revealed: 75% of people who recover from alcohol dependence do so without ever getting any kind of help from drug and alcohol services and they never attend Alcoholics Anonymous.

The simple fact is that people working in recovery or attending AA never get to see these people. They are unaware that those people are out there.

In fact, the NIAAA found that only 13% of alcoholics get specialist treatment like detox. So, the drinkers I see in my work are, as I have long suspected, at the extreme end of the alcoholic spectrum.

Also, the fact that 75% of alcoholics get well without help is an inconvenient truth for the $35-billion rehab industry. If I was running a commercial rehab, I would be keeping quiet about that.

But Isn't It A Disease?

It has been widely accepted for decades that alcoholism is a disease, a chronic relapsing condition. What's more, it is progressive, meaning that it gets worse with time. There is no cure.

The only way to control it is to stop drinking entirely, which effectively puts you in remission. But if you subsequently drink again, you will relapse and be worse than when you stopped: because of the progressive nature of the disease, you will have got worse. Consequently, the usual advice is to become totally abstinent.

This theory, often referred to as the Disease Model, is not questioned within Alcoholics Anonymous. If you go to an AA meeting, you may well hear stories from members who have "gone back out there" (AA slang for relapse), and how it was indeed terrible, which is why they are back at an AA meeting. I am sure these people are genuine. But as we have already seen, if they are in Alcoholics Anonymous in the first place, they are more likely to be at the extreme end of the alcohol dependency spectrum, so are more likely to have a bad relapse if they touch alcohol.

The disease model is also the cornerstone of the rehab industry, most of which, in the United States especially, uses AA's 12-Steps as part of the treatment. But again, we now see that if the people who get into rehab are likely to be at the extreme end of the alcoholic range, they are not typical of the average dependent drinker at all.

The disease model was even the received wisdom of the NIAAA, until the penny dropped that their own research was telling them something very different.

According to Marc Willenbring, director of the NIAAA, "It can be a chronic, relapsing disease. But it isn't usually that."

Having worked with thousands of alcoholics, I agree with that. There is a minority of alcoholics for whom alcoholism is a terrifying, chronic condition. They face a stark choice between forced abstinence and early death. But for most alcoholic drinkers, it isn't like that.

In a way, it would be simpler if it was a disease. If every alcoholic suffered from the same disease, they could be treated in the same way. But they cannot. So why is alcoholism so different in different drinkers?

I believe that much of the explanation lies in that alcoholism rarely exists as a free-standing issue. It comes as part of a complex mix. Thinking about all the dependent drinkers I have worked with, I cannot remember one where alcoholism has been the only issue, where everything in their life was okay except the drinking. These people were drinking because of something else.

This is where the alcoholic drinker differs from the normal drinker. The non-problematic drinker usually drinks to enhance good feelings, like having dinner with friends or to celebrate their team winning, or simply to amplify the feeling of relaxation at the end of a busy day. The alcoholic drinker, by contrast, usually drinks to lessen the pain of something else that is going on, to self-medicate.

In most cases, alcohol misuse wasn't the main problem; it was a symptom of the problem. And this is why I believe that treatment of alcoholism has such poor outcomes. If you treat the symptom, rather than the underlying issue, you might succeed in alleviating the situation for a while, but sooner or later, the underlying issue will cause the symptom of alcoholism to erupt again.

The issues that lead to alcoholic drinking are many. It could be painful life events, poor thinking skills, emotional trauma, dealing with past pain, minor mental health issues such as social anxiety and overwhelm, or major ones like depression and schizophrenia. I could write a very long list, but let's look at some examples from my past caseload.

Simon was in his thirties and had recently left the army. He had a good life, a supportive wife and young children, and no money worries. He was also a fitness fanatic - except for his alcoholic binges, which were becoming so frequent there was hardly a break between them. He was panicking because he couldn't regain control. But only five minutes of talking to Simon revealed the underlying problem, as he talked about seeing his friends getting blown up in Afghanistan. He suffered with dreadful Post Traumatic Stress Disorder. He turned to alcohol when the mental and emotional pain was too much. I could help, but the main issue was his PTSD and counselling for that was the way he would control his excess drinking in the long term.

Amanda was in her early sixties and had drunk for most of her life without alcohol being a problem. But she had been caught in a perfect storm of events beyond her control. Two close family members had died in quick succession, her husband had been diagnosed with dementia and was showing distressing signs of deterioration, and she had to wind up her husband's business. Her drinking had escalated to help her cope with feelings of profound emotional pain and overwhelm. She came into treatment when she realized that she had lost control of her drinking. We could help in as much as teaching her some skills to control her drinking, and getting her a prescription for nalmefene to lessen the desire to drink. But clearly this was just treating the symptom. The cure came in her getting support around her life issues. Her life became less overwhelming as her grief lessened, she got support with her husband, and her husband's company was sold. Eventually, she stopped drinking altogether, not because she felt she had to, but simply because she lost interest in it. She had her life back.

Jeannine was in her forties and had been drinking to unconsciousness every day. At one time, she had been manager of a health foods store, but her self-neglect had become so acute that she had been admitted to hospital with malnutrition. She had lost almost all interest in eating. Her diet consisted mainly of cider and vodka. Her drinking had become heavy after her husband left her for another woman 10 years earlier. She had had time to get over losing him, but she could not let go of the sense of injustice, frequently saying how much she had done for him and how unfair it was. Jeannine's mind was constantly on the lookout for evidence of how unfair life was to her and for further outrages to fuel her sense of injustice, which in turn stoked her desire to drink to oblivion. Jeannine's mind was in a loop. The more she looked for outrages against her, the more she found them, which in turn encouraged her to look for yet more. Seeing that her drinking was a symptom of her self-defeating thinking, we set her on a course of intensive CBT. Jeannine started to identify that she could not prevent life being unfair, but she had, if she desired, total control over her responses to life's injustices. She also began to grasp that by constantly looking for what was wrong, she was not noticing what was right, such as the love of her grown-up son. It took time, but Jeannine began taking responsibility for herself, rather than looking to blame everyone else for her troubles. Her self-esteem grew, she started to take care of herself and she revived her interest in a healthy lifestyle. New people came into her life, attracted by her sunnier disposition, and opportunities started to open up for her. One day she announced she had stopped drinking, saying she didn't need it anymore. She didn't stay abstinent long term, but just drank on a very occasional basis. The compulsive urge to drink to oblivion had departed with her sense of outrage.

These examples are people who had all been drinking to levels diagnosable as dependent, but who had in different ways shown that they could move on, quite naturally, without having to be in life-long treatment. Dealing with their underlying problems had been how they had turned things around, rather than completely focusing on their drinking, which was merely the symptom.

These types of dependent drinkers are typical of the bulk of people who have alcohol problems. However, in order to give a complete picture, I should also talk about two client groups that are more complex and less likely to achieve alcoholism reversal.

The first group of drinkers are people who are physically dependent as well as psychologically dependent on alcohol. These are a minority, and it is interesting to contrast how different alcohol is to another very common drug in this respect, namely nicotine. Most people who smoke do so because they have a severe physical dependence, but not usually a strong psychological one. I have experienced first-hand just how severe nicotine addiction is, as I was a smoker for many years. The withdrawal I experienced when I stopped was horrific, and much of my motivation for never smoking since is that I never want to go through that again. Most smokers want to quit.

By contrast, the majority of alcoholic drinkers are not strongly physically dependent – we know this because they don't exhibit strong symptoms of withdrawal if they stop and don't require detox. They have what Alcoholics Anonymous calls the mental obsession, and I would agree with AA on that description. Most of the training I have done for working with drinkers has centred on physiological tools, whereas training I have done for smoking cessation has hardly mentioned this, focusing instead on dealing with cravings and nicotine replacement therapies. Also, in contrast to smokers who mostly want to quit, these drinkers mostly don't want to stop.

Drinkers who have both a strong physical dependence and the mental obsession have a much more difficult time than the majority, and may find that alcoholic reversal unachievable. For those who are physically dependent, stopping drinking without treatment is very dangerous. I do not think it is either sensible or ethical for me to suggest that every alcoholic can move on from alcohol dependence. For the minority, an abstinence-based strategy of containment is likely to be the safest option.

The classic signs of physical dependence are daily drinking, starting drinking early in the day, shaking in the morning before having the first drink, and heavy sweating, often waking up drenched in sweat. Physically dependent drinkers run the risk of seizure, which can be life-threatening, if they don't drink regularly, because their bodies have become so dependent on having a level of alcohol in the system, that the body starts to malfunction if that level isn't maintained. This is why some drinkers need to be detoxed under medical supervision. If you think this describes you, please go and see a physician or a counsellor at your local drug and alcohol service without delay.

The second group of drinkers who have a less optimistic prognosis are dual diagnosis clients. These are people with a mental health diagnosis that requires psychiatric support, in addition to alcohol dependence. In particular, paranoid schizophrenia and the more severe forms of depression can be challenging to work with, and these will usually come with other issues, such as severe anxiety, psychosis, and often poly-drug addiction. Progress can be made with this client group, but it requires a co-ordinated effort from medical, psychiatric and addiction services, and as such is beyond the scope of this book.

Case Study - Patricia

In this and the next chapter, we'll look at two real stories from people who have seen their alcoholism reversed. They are not following a program to keep the problem contained. They are not following any program at all. They are not in remission. They are fully recovered.

This is Patricia's story, told in her own words:

"My story goes way beyond a focus on alcohol. I truly believe the issues I had with drinking were related to how I dealt with my past.

My earliest memories were not happy ones. I spent the first few years of my life with a mother and father who fought regularly. The fights were usually during the episodes when my father drank to excess. There was shouting, physical fights and a wrecked house.

My mother and father divorced when I was five. The loss of my father affected me deeply. I did not see him again for 25 years.

My mother and siblings and I moved to another country. I felt different and became more isolated and withdrawn. Money was tight and I felt embarrassed by my poor clothes, sparsely furnished home, and basic food. I made no effort to make friends and kept people at a distance. My solace was books. I escaped my life through stories and imagination. I looked around and did not like the reality I saw. I sought escape.

I was a good student and did well at school. I arrived at university with good grades, but no experience or skills in dealing with people, life, or my own emotions. My sense of isolation increased. I was unable to relate to my peers who came from affluent, supportive families. I usually refused social engagements, feeling awkward and uncomfortable. Despite my social discomfort, I did manage to make some friends.

These friends took me out for my nineteenth birthday. The wine flowed and for the first time in my life I drank, and the lights came on and whistles went off. I was off - looking for the next party. Drinking took away the social discomfort; the sense of isolation - everyone was my friend. I felt part of the human race. I partied hard. I would go off for days, staying with friends, drinking, partying and generally having a good time. I lost interest in my studies and left the degree course. I took a job, but lived to get out and have a good time. On the bad nights, I would end up in hospital as a result of my drinking.

After a year of a basic job, drinking, and partying, I returned to university. I worked hard, studying and working to pay my way for the course. I obtained my degree and left home as soon as I could. My mother had always been difficult and I longed to escape. I left the country and got a good job in a field I enjoyed working in.

I had success in my life. I still enjoyed drinking but managed to avoid drinking during periods of study, exams and generally during the working week. However, come the weekends or social occasions, I drank a lot. Social situations without the crutch of alcohol made me feel uncomfortable. I always felt "less than". I felt uninteresting and boring. When I drank sometimes it was all jolly and a laugh, other times it was unpleasant. After a lot to drink I got argumentative and belligerent. I would even find ways to argue with people who were trying to agree with me.

In my late twenties, I had a nice house, a lovely healthy baby boy and was married. On the surface my life looked successful. However, I was unhappy in a marriage that lacked any closeness or warmth. I started to feel very low and drank more and more to feel better.

During this time, I became concerned about my drinking. I went to a counsellor who told me that I should drink glasses of water between alcoholic drinks - you can imagine, that didn't work. My problems continued. I drank frequently and felt lower and lower. But I always turned up for work. I cleaned my house, shopped, cooked and took care of my child. However, I felt more and more depressed.

The morning after another night of drinking and arguing with my husband I felt desperate for help. I flicked through the yellow pages and my eye was caught by the advertisement for Alcoholics Anonymous. Maybe if I contacted them, they could tell me where I could go for help. I needed some direction.

Within 24 hours I went to my first AA meeting. I loved it. I loved the openness and honesty of the participants. After a lifetime of feeling separate, isolated and socially awkward, I felt accepted and totally involved. People talked about their emotions, about feeling they had been born without an instruction manual for life - all concepts I could relate to.

I kept going back. I stopped drinking instantly and stayed stopped for many years. Alcoholics Anonymous became my social life, my spiritual centre and a focal point to make new friends in new places. I took on responsibilities in AA and usually enjoyed meetings. I rarely thought about drinking and had no craving or desire to drink. I did at times think I was not truly an alcoholic, after all I had never drunk in the morning, never been arrested, like the stories I heard in the rooms of AA. However, I was told "better to pretend you are an alcoholic and be in AA than pretend you are not an alcoholic and go out drinking." I could see the logic of this. So, I went to meetings - hundreds of meetings, over a period of many years.

As time went on, I felt bored by the drinking stories. I enjoyed stories of recovery. I enjoyed hearing about spiritual experiences and awakenings. However, I felt increasingly that my experiences were different. I felt a fraud.

I spoke to an alcohol counsellor, who carried out an assessment, retrospectively, on my previous drinking. I did not even come close to the score that someone would need to go into treatment. I stopped going to Alcoholics Anonymous. After some consideration, I decided to have an alcoholic drink. In AA, they tell you that a terrible relapse will happen if you pick up a drink. But in my case, nothing happened.

Nowadays, I enjoy wine. I can choose to drink it or not. I can have a couple of glasses and stop. If I have more than a few glasses, I want to stop. I don't want to drink to excess. I do not need or want to drink every day.

If I was an alcoholic, I am not now. I believe my previous difficulties were due to immaturity, particularly lack of emotional maturity, lack of social skills and self-confidence. I had an unhappy marriage. I lacked being able to process a difficult childhood.

I do not regret my time in Alcoholics Anonymous. I learned many, many valuable life lessons and skills. I learned how to cope with resentment and anger. I learned how to sit with uncomfortable emotions. I grew up.

Having a drink now is a totally different experience. I am happy to potter about with a glass of wine cooking dinner, but once I have eaten, the kettle is usually on. I like having a drink with friends, but the arguments and emotional intensity is in the past.

I was a young woman with some problems. Those problems are now in my past. Today I feel happy, relaxed, productive, and involved in life. Work colleagues, friends and acquaintances remark on my calm and positive attitude to life. I wouldn't swap my life today as a mature woman with that nineteen-year-old who really had no idea how to live life and found answers in a bottle all those years ago."

*****

Patricia has retrospectively diagnosed her problem herself. She realizes that her alcoholic drinking was her way of coping with immaturity and a lack of social skills caused by her isolating as a child in a difficult home environment.

Because of her behaviour when she was nineteen and through her twenties, it is easy to see why see thought she was an alcoholic and joined Alcoholics Anonymous. But while she was in AA, she matured as a person and matured out of her drinking problem. It wasn't immediately apparent to her that this had happened, as she wasn't drinking anyway. But she started to get an indication that something had changed when she began feeling a fraud in AA.

As she said herself, she grew up.

Case Study - Mike

As in the last chapter, here the story is told in his own words.

"I have no problem in saying I was an alcoholic. Looking back, it's obvious. I drank to excess almost every day for 20 years. I know now that I was typical of the most common kind of alcoholic, the daily drinker with a job, the so-called 'functioning alcoholic'.

Every day I would wake up, feeling the effects of the night before. I would drag myself together and get to work. I was never tempted to drink in the mornings, far from it. The idea of having another drink would make me feel sick. I often thought, "Maybe I should just give it a miss this evening." But I never did.

By the afternoon, the urge to drink would start creeping up on me, and by 5 p.m. I was dying for a drink. I was that regular: 5 p.m. was my drinking time. If I couldn't get to a drink at that time, I could just about hang on till 6 p.m. But past that, I would start to get desperate. My anxiety levels would start to shoot through the roof. All I could think about was getting that drink. If I didn't get a drink by 7 p.m., I would be like an emotional car crash, and my mind would be all over the place.

I didn't used to drink for a long time in the evening, but it would be intense for two or three hours. My favourite drink was strong beer. I would start by ordering two beers, because the first one would go down before the bartender had finished pouring the second. I drank fast. And when I was so bloated on beer that I couldn't drink any more quantity, I would switch to whiskey. When I felt I was on the edge of being unable to walk, I would head home, have something to eat, be short tempered with my long-suffering wife, and pass out on the sofa. I usually woke up covered in sweat in the early hours of the morning and would stagger off to bed. Then the cycle would begin again in the morning.

Inevitably, things got worse. Your mind and body can't take that sort of beating every day without the wheels starting to fall off. My reliability at work got worse and I became unemployable. I responded to this by becoming self-employed, which just made it easier for me to drink. My life started going downhill fast. It was getting scary. I realized my wife was going to leave me. I already had one failed marriage behind me. I didn't want to lose this one. Even in my inebriated state, I knew I loved her. But a stark reality was now staring me in the face. I would have to choose between the two great loves of my life: alcohol or her. Thankfully, I chose her.

I turned to my doctor for help. I told him I thought I was an alcoholic. I hoped he could prescribe me a pill to sort me out. Instead, he referred me to the drug and alcohol service in town. I hadn't known it was there. I'd never been anywhere like that. But I decided to give it a go. I had no choice. I had too much to lose if I kept on drinking.

My first impressions of the service weren't good. It looked a bit run down. There were a couple of very dodgy-looking characters smoking outside the front door. Inside was a reception with lots of dour posters warning of the perils of using various drugs.

I had an appointment to see a woman called Sharon who said she was recovery worker. Sharon looked more like a drug user than a recovery worker to me, but when we got talking, she was very business-like and obviously knew what she was talking about. There were lots of questions. It dragged up a lot of my past that I would have preferred to have forgotten. But the upshot of it all was that I agreed to start a program of reducing my drinking in stages.

My attempts to cut down my drinking were painful. I had a base level of alcohol I needed every day simply to feel normal, and if I tried to reduce below that, I became so erratic and anxious that I couldn't do anything but think about drink. After a couple of weeks of living in this painful place, another stark reality became clear. I couldn't reduce. I had to stop.

After 20 years of alcoholic drinking, this was the first time I had accepted that I had to stop, and it brought me an unexpected feeling of calmness. Then a couple of days later, while I was having my usual early evening drink with friends, I just thought 'I don't want any more,' and went home early. That was it. I had stopped drinking. The following day, I told my wife I had stopped. She was sceptical. I don't blame her. I was surprised myself.

The next few weeks were surprisingly okay. It seemed that for me the biggest obstacle to me stopping had simply been the fear of being without a drink. Once I had stopped, the fear was gone, and it wasn't as bad as I had imagined.

Obviously, I missed the drink, without doubt, and I also really missed my routine and my drinking friends. Life felt strange. I felt strange. It was like I had suddenly woken up as a child again, and was looking at the world as if it was for the first time. It all felt a bit dream-like, I would even go as far as to say that it felt magical at times.

I had also been fortunate in that I hadn't had any bad physical reactions to coming off the booze like some people do. I hadn't needed to be detoxed. My alcoholism was all in my head.

I had started going to recovery meetings at the drug and alcohol service, but I wasn't at all comfortable there. Most of the other people who attended were hard drug users. I felt out of place. I picked up a leaflet for Alcoholics Anonymous. I went to a meeting and I thought it was much more up my street, as at least they were all drinkers like me, or they had been. A whole new world with new people opened up. I went to meetings nearly every day. I was fascinated to hear people's stories.

I started reading the literature. I found some of the spiritual stuff a bit weird, and I found the Big Book a bit cheesy and dated, with all that folksy language of 1930s America. The one bit I really hated about the meetings was where everyone held hands in a circle at the end. But I was willing to put my doubts to one side because I was meeting people who had been sober for years.

One guy at a meeting said that h
years. I could hardly believe it
spoke to him after the meetir
came to meetings. He said i
sober for 26 years, which
Obviously, Alcoholics Anc
so I tried to go along with it.
the more semi-religious aspects of AA, ı...
prayer. Although I had tried to put my scepticism ı...
side, my doubts kept nagging at me.

Then I picked up a book on CBT (Cognitive Behavioural Therapy). It was a breakthrough. CBT is not about drinking, it's about thinking. The book described mind traps. These are the mixed-up ways of thinking that cause us problems. I could see me in all of these mind traps. I began to understand why I had been an alcoholic. It had been a way of coping with poor thinking skills. No one had ever taught me how to think before. I didn't realize it was something you can learn.

One thing that really hit the spot for me was the concept of Blame Shifting. This is where someone always blames someone else for everything that goes wrong in their life. That was me all over. Nothing that had gone wrong in my life was ever my fault. I had always been the victim. And

...m gave me an excuse to get off my head on

...could see now that by blaming everyone else for the ...ess I made of things made me the victim, and if I started to take responsibility for what happens in my life, I also take control. It was a tough lesson to learn, because my ego had to accept that something about me wasn't right. But I recognized that when I do take responsibility for myself, it empowers me.

I also learned about expectations. I looked back on my life and realized that even from an early age, I had had unrealistic expectations. In his song Train in the Distance, Paul Simon sings: "The thought that life could be better is woven indelibly into our hearts and our brains." That was how I was with my expectations. Ever since childhood, I'd had the expectation that my life should be better than it actually was, and the sense of disappointment that life wasn't better gave me a constant feeling of being down in the dumps, which was a great excuse for me to drink. There was no real reason for it. It was my expectation that good things should come to me simply because I thought they should, I shouldn't have to work for them. It was just ego again. It's crazy logic, but I drank on that for twenty years.

Sharon arranged for me to attend a course with a CBT therapist which really helped me get my thinking sorted out. In fairness to Alcoholics Anonymous, there are some good mental tools in the 12-Steps, too. But you have to work through all that 1930s spirituality stuff to get at them. CBT is much more direct and wide-ranging. Well, I think so.

I didn't have a drink for a couple of years. But I had the sense that my way of thinking had changed deep down, and I wanted to know if I had got rid of the obsession to drink to alcoholic levels. I didn't want to go through the rest of my life not knowing. The only way to find out was to try a drink. I looked upon this as a scientific experiment.

I admit, I was a bit nervous. It had been drummed into me that alcoholism was a progressive disease with no cure. But I believed that my alcoholism had in fact been the result of mixed up thinking, it wasn't a disease at all, and I knew my thinking was different now. If I was wrong and I ended up drunk, I promised myself I would never drink again.

I bought two cans of beer. I drank the first can. I had expected to get a feeling of relief after being abstinent for two years, and maybe my head would light up. It was all a bit of a damp squib. I didn't really feel anything, other than a slight fuzziness. I opened the second can. I realized that I didn't really want it. I had already had enough. This had never happened before. I had never experienced that feeling of having had enough alcohol previously. I drank half of the second can, and then poured the rest away. I just didn't want it. My alcoholism had gone.

Wind forward to today. I sometimes like a beer, but I don't drink much because I just get bored with it and wish I hadn't bothered. And if I don't have a drink, I'm not bothered either. I'm not using any drugs to control my drinking or any psychological tools. It's just different for me now.

I live in a small town and often bump into people I know from AA or from the drug and alcohol service meetings. They ask how I am. I know what they're thinking. They haven't seen me for a while and wonder if I've relapsed, but they're too polite to ask outright.

I just say I'm very well. I don't try to explain what's happened. I know they wouldn't believe it. They would be sure I was bang at the booze. And anyway, I know that what's happened to me wouldn't happen for a lot of people. There are lots of people I know who I think would probably go off the rails big time if they picked up a drink, and I don't want to say anything that would encourage them.

I sometimes wonder if I should stop altogether again. I know I don't need it. But if I did stop again, it would be a lifestyle choice for my health, like not eating meat, rather than something I was doing because I feel I have to. But in the meantime, I'm quite happy just to have the odd beer.

I never thought I would be able to say that."

****

Although Mike's drinking pattern was very different to Patricia's, there are obvious similarities. In both accounts, it was their thinking that needed to be sorted out. Once the thinking was straightened out, they realized that heavy drinking was just a symptom of their problem, not the cause.

Also, you notice that in both cases, they were not physically dependent, as they had no physical repercussions to stopping drinking. They had come to depend on alcohol to alleviate their distressed thinking.

In both cases, they went into treatment - both used AA, and Mike used a state alcohol service also. But to a large extent, they sorted out their own problems. In fact, if Mike had found that CBT book earlier, he might not have needed to go into treatment at all.

Another common point was that, although they both eventually drank again, they both had a long period of abstinence beforehand. I think this helps, because habitual behaviour is a powerful thing, even without a drug involved. So, a long a period away from alcohol helps to break both the habitual aspect as well as the psychological addiction.

I think the above points are ones I would expect to see in people who find they have reversed their alcoholism.

Book 3

Change Your Life Today

"You begin by always expecting

good things to happen."

Tom Hopkins

A User Guide to a Fabulous Life

The last chapter of "Alcohol and You" is called: "Now that the nightmare is over, what do you want the dream to be?"

When one of my first readers read that chapter, she said she found it really inspirational, and wished there was more. She felt that I should write another book that started where that one ended.

She was right, because most people who have a brush with alcohol addiction want to build a better life for themselves and their loved ones. Putting down the drink is just the start of the journey. And so was born "Change Your Life Today"

It's a book about the most exciting, awesome, mindblowingly amazing thing in your life: your future. It's your user guide to a fabulous life.

There are a couple of clear differences with this book compared to the two you have already read.

Firstly, when I started this book, I realized that the content was appropriate for anyone wanting positive change, not just ex-problem drinkers. And that's right, because you should no longer be treated as a special case, because of your drinking past. You have graduated. So this book is for everyone – and, naturally, everyone includes you.

Secondly, some sections of this book draw on my personal history. Again, I believe this is appropriate, as the core theme of this book is about embracing personal change, which is fundamental to the way I live my life.

But this book is not about me.

It's about you.

It's time to live your dream.

Change Your Life Today

Can you really change your life today?

Yes, you can. Today and every day, if you embrace change, rather than hide from it. This book is about how you can make change a force for good in your life, and achieve greater success and happiness.

You may want to get slimmer and fitter, find a better job, overcome an addiction, pass an exam, win the respect of your peers, start a business, stop self-destructive habits, live longer, win at a sport, move on from past pain, overcome anxiety, learn a language, find the perfect partner, or you might simply have a yearning for a more fulfilling life.

Whatever it is you want to achieve, you will find not only inspiration in these pages, but also effective techniques you can put into practice, right now, today.

As I write these words, it's winter. But where I am is not cold. I am sitting on my terrace in shorts and a tee shirt. Four hundred yards in front of me, the tranquil Atlantic Ocean glistens under a blue sky. I see herons and egrets in the fields. I see sand dunes backing onto a stunningly beautiful beach. It's peaceful, blissful. Inside the house, my wife is gracefully practicing yoga. All is well - I am a happy man.

But it hasn't always been this way.

As a young man, my life was chaotic. I dropped out of college. Work was a drudge that had to be done, as I drifted from job to job. I had no aim. There was a broken marriage. I smoked and drank, didn't exercise, had a poor diet and put on weight. Life became a battle, as I let change happen to me. The problems piled up higher and higher.

I became angry with the world for treating me so badly, for not putting me on the pedestal that I thought I should be on. Change was something I feared, as it always seemed to be bad and out of my control. I became desperate, thinking I would die of emotional exhaustion before I reached middle-age.

But desperation can sometimes be a blessing, and so it was for me, as desperation forced me to look for new solutions. Gradually I began to turn things around. I retrained as a therapist, learned Cognitive Behavioural Therapy and Motivational Therapy, and applied my new knowledge to myself. It was a revelation. My life changed from being harrowing and exhausting to being exciting and rewarding.

Since then, I have worked with thousands of clients in health centres, hospitals and in the community to help them experience positive change. Many of the original ideas in these pages were developed working with them, and I am grateful for their feedback.

In the course of this work, I have seen certain principles succeed time and again. These have worked with all kinds of people and in all sorts of different situations. The success rates have been phenomenal. Everyone who has stuck with the principles that you will discover in this book has succeeded – and I do mean everyone.

None of the concepts in this book are complicated. Mysticism or great leaps of faith are not required. You simply need to learn some principles that will give you a solid way to deal with your difficulties or achieve your ambitions, whatever they might be. All you have to do is apply these concepts and you will change your life for the better.

Looking back over the past few years, I can recall so many times when I have changed my own life for the better, sometimes in small ways, other times in major ways. I list below some of the changes I have made in the last few years that have been important to me, simply to demonstrate that I am not merely writing this book from theory.

I am no superman - I am a flawed human being. I have emotional ups-and-downs, fears and unhelpful thoughts. I do irrational things and make mistakes, just as we all do. But I have a set of cognitive tools now that limits my errors, cuts me some slack, and keeps me on track for whatever is my goal at any given time.

I have lived the ideas you will find in this book and continue to live them every day. They are vital to me – if I had not found them, my life would not be the joy it is today. They are a reliable and proven set of concepts and tools, which have allowed me to achieve diverse goals like these:

I have moved country three times, and have lived in some astonishingly beautiful places.

I quit smoking in 2012 and have stayed stopped.

I learned to speak Portuguese.

I monetized my hobby into a business with thousands of customers in multiple countries.

I found and married my ideal partner.

I lost 30 pounds without dieting.

I wrote a book, which became a bestseller in its genre, and am now able to work professionally as a writer.

I have found a way to eliminate colds and other minor illnesses from my life.

I am able to work when I want, and play when I want.

I created, with my wife, a two-centre lifestyle, dividing my time between two of the most stunning locations in the world. In the winter, I live in the sunshine of Portugal's Algarve coast. In the summer, I live in the gorgeous landscape of England's West Country.

I am living my dream.

None of the above happened by chance. It happened by choice.

You may want things that are very different to me. That's okay. The many clients I have worked with over the last few years all had different desires. They proved that the principles in this book can be applied to anything and used by anyone. Now it's your turn.

We will be discussing success and happiness. All humans want these things in their lives. But success and happiness will mean something different to everyone who reads this book.

Some people measure success in terms of money and material possessions, and that's great if that's what works for you. A mother or father might measure success by the application of their parenting skills. A single person could be looking for success in terms of finding a partner. For someone who is recovering from serious illness, getting through a day without unmanageable pain might be regarded as success. Similarly, everyone reading this book will have slightly different ideas about what happiness means to them. I have set out to write a book that caters for this diversity.

We will also be discussing our random world. You may believe that the world is part of a greater plan and everything has meaning. Equally, you may believe that the universe is chaotic. Either way, you will be aware that seemingly random events happen all the time – all the stuff you didn't see coming, whether it be good or bad, major or minor. This book will help you adapt and thrive with the unexpected.

As well as looking at ways you can get what you desire, we will also be looking at how to eliminate, as much as possible, any self-sabotaging behaviours that might blow you off course. This is a vital aspect of the book, and indeed many important concepts come in the later chapters - we will be covering a lot of ground.

Therefore, this book is rich with self-development material, some of which you might find challenging at times, while some you will find fun. But I hope you will find all of it enlightening and enriching. And if you stick with it and apply the principles, the success and happiness promised will be yours. No other outcome is possible.

So, please look upon reading this book as an adventure. You are about to discover much more about yourself, and what you are capable of.

And the adventure starts with your truest desires.

It All Begins with Desire

Have you ever wanted something, only to find out when you got it, that it failed to do for you what you thought it would?

Maybe you wanted a certain kind of relationship, but when you found it, you still felt unfulfilled. Perhaps it was a dream job, but when you got it, you found it unsatisfying and you wanted to do something else. Maybe you wanted a possession that you thought would make you feel happy, but by the time you got it, your mind had already moved on to the next thing you thought would make you feel better. Perhaps you heard of a drug that you thought might transform how you felt, but after you took it, life just seemed even worse. Maybe you wanted to live in a certain place, only to discover that when you moved there, you still felt empty inside.

If something like this has happened to you, then in all probability the reason was that what you thought you wanted was unaligned with your deep-down desires. So, when you got what you thought you wanted, it didn't light up your life as you thought it would. Instead, it was a disappointment, because your underlying desire was still unmet.

Or have you ever thought that you wanted something, but just somehow couldn't muster the motivation to go after it? You tried to use motivational techniques, but procrastinated anyway. You maybe even thought there was something wrong with you, that you were lacking in some way.

If this has happened, then it's likely that the same lack of alignment was the problem. You couldn't get the motivation to go for your goal, because, deep down inside of you, on an unconscious level, you knew it wouldn't meet your true desire.

This lack of alignment is an easy trap to fall into. It happens all the time. It has certainly happened to me. A common reason for this is that what we think we want is, in fact, what someone else wants. We are doing something to please other people. Or it may be that what you think you want is because of social conditioning: you are doing what you think society expects. You do things because that's the way it's always been done, without questioning if it's the right way for you.

People do things because they think they *should* do something. For instance, my wife once thought she should do a law degree. It seemed to make sense, as it was a good degree to have. But it wasn't her desire, her heart wasn't in it. After a year she abandoned it and studied history instead, which she enjoyed, and got that degree.

Some years ago, I thought I should get into IT work as the money seemed good, so I set up a business designing bespoke databases. The business made money right away. But I had to give it up after a year, because I became very unhappy in the work. It simply wasn't my desire at all. I really couldn't have cared less about databases - I was just doing it for the money, which rarely works out well in the long-term.

If that word "should" is involved, you can be pretty sure you are doing something that is unaligned with your true desire.

This can have disastrous outcomes. For example:

People end up in the wrong career because they are trying to fulfil their parents' ambitions for them, rather doing what would bring them joy and deep satisfaction.

Some find themselves trapped in unhappy marriages, because they think that they need a partner who fits certain stereotypes, rather than someone they truly love.

Others live a lifestyle which is not natural for them and brings them unhappiness, because they are afraid of stepping outside the social norms they were brought up with.

Some lose unhealthy amounts of weight, or even get surgery, trying to look like the models in airbrushed images they see in magazines, tragically not realizing that they looked great all along.

Still others turn to prescription or illicit drugs and, in the end, find they need to keep taking them just to feel normal.

So, before you begin the task of changing your life for the better, you need to know from the outset that your goal is aligned with your deep-down desire; otherwise disappointment or worse will surely follow. Achieving a goal that you never truly desired will sap your energy and resources and just leave you feeling empty, or perhaps even desperate.

However, you can use a simple technique to test your goal and check that it really is your true desire. I call it the "Why is that?" strategy. I have used this successfully with many of my therapy clients and I also use it on myself regularly. I suggest you use it yourself before you get deeper into this book. This is how it works.

Ask yourself, what do you want? Then ask yourself, why is that? When you have the answer, ask again, why is that? Keep asking the question for each answer you come up with, until you are sure you have drilled right down to your deepest desire.

I will illustrate how this works with a real-life example. I had a new client called Sam come to see me. Sam was a 27-year old self-employed builder, who lived with his wife and their young child. Things were going well. He was happy in his relationship. They lived in a fine apartment that Sam had lovingly refurbished himself. He had all the work he needed - the money was pouring in and he had taken on staff. There was, however, one big snag. Sam was spending all his spare income on his cocaine habit. He had come to me for counselling.

With this type of problem, the counsellor will usually try to help the client to focus on a positive activity to replace their addiction. So, when I initially spoke to Sam, I asked him to think about what he really wanted, then tell me what it was when we next met. This is what happened:

"So, Sam, have you chosen a positive goal for yourself?" I asked at the start of our next meeting.

Sam nodded and said: "I want to buy one of the white houses by the park." I knew the houses he meant. They were imposing, expensive and much bigger than Sam needed for his small family.

"Really? I thought you loved your apartment."

"I do," Sam replied. "But I want to move."

"Why is that?" I asked.

"It would be great to have a big place when my relatives come to visit," he said. "We have a family get-together at my place a couple of times a year. It would really impress them."

"You want a bigger house to impress your relatives? Why is that?"

"Well," he hesitated, "it's just that sometimes I think they look down on me."

"Really? Why is that?"

Sam started to open up: "My brother Darren was always the bright one in our family. He was the one who got the university degree. He went into banking and is doing really

293

well for himself. I guess if I got a house more like his, the family would see me more as his equal."

Now we were getting down to what Sam's real desire was. It wasn't the new house at all, he was happy in his apartment. What he really desired was to feel as valued as his brother.

"So," I responded, "what have people in your family said to make you think that they don't see you as equal?"

"Well, nothing really" he said, uncertainly. "But I guess with him being a banker and me a builder..."

I could see that the problem was not in the family's perception of Sam, but Sam's perception of his own status. Getting a bigger house was unlikely to change that. Over the next couple of sessions, we worked on Sam's feelings of self-worth. He was particularly helped by a technique I call Achievement Stacking, which I will be describing in a later chapter.

Sam began to see that what he had done as a builder was really to his credit, and the idea that his family looked down on him was an illusion of his own making. He turned his focus to expanding his business, which in turn built up his self-esteem, and his cocaine habit faded as it became irrelevant to his life.

You can see from Sam's story how simple but powerful the "Why is that?" strategy is. It really can be a revelation to people when they realize what they truly desire. In my exchange with Sam, I used "Why is that?" three times, and very quickly I was able to uncover what Sam's true desire really was, which on a conscious level, Sam hadn't seen himself.

Sam didn't realize I was using a technique to help him. But you can use it in a very conscious way with yourself. Keep asking "Why is that?" until you get to the truth. You might surprise yourself, as your unconscious mind gives up a secret it had been hiding from your conscious mind.

You can also use it in a caring way to help people in your life. It works on all levels. You can use it with your spouse or your parents. Equally, you can use it with your children as part of your parenting skills. It is also invaluable with work colleagues. If you are in any kind of management role, it will help you understand your employees' needs. But conversely, you can use it with your own manager to better understand what your organization requires of you.

However, I will add a couple of caveats to this strategy. Firstly, if you use "Why is that?" to drill down to your true desire, and it shows you something dark, something that could hurt you or other people, such as a desire to harm yourself in some way, then please get professional help.

Secondly, if you use it with other people, do so in a helpful and compassionate way, rather than try to catch people out.

But what if you are still unclear about what you really want? Let's look at that next.

But I Don't Know What I Want

Some people have found that using the "Why is that?" strategy doesn't work initially, because they can't answer the first "What do you want?" question. Most of the clients I have worked with in my professional life as a therapist have wanted change. But for many of them, they were constantly frustrated because they didn't know what the change was that they were looking for. They didn't know what they wanted - they just knew they wanted something better.

This can be a massive issue for people who pass from year to year without any sense of direction. They go around and around in circles in their minds, trying to find the answer. I have had clients in tears of frustration because they just can't decide what they want. Some people go through their entire lives in this miserable state.

I have come to realize that there can be differing reasons why people find themselves in this situation. The first reason is being overwhelmed. This happens when so much needs fixing in someone's life that they are mind-blown about where to start, and end up taking no action at all. They are bewildered about what to prioritize. Imagine having multiple fires burning in your life, but having only one bucket of water. Which fire should you put out? What about the rest?

I've found this is usually the case with people I have counselled for a self-destructive behaviour. Let's take excessive gambling as an example. They learn to stop the compulsion to gamble, but then find that they have to get on with dealing with the trouble the gambling had caused, like debts, broken relationships, lost housing, and ruptured careers. These clients often find they are frozen by indecision. They have ended their self-destructive behaviour, but they still have multiple fires burning in their lives.

Another situation might be where a client has already achieved a goal, and this has left them directionless. A common situation I have encountered, for example, is where someone has worked for years for retirement. This goal has kept them motivated and given their life meaning. Then the golden day comes when they can retire, and for a few weeks or months, it's wonderful – they can do what they like. But then they realize that they need a goal once more, but simply can't decide what. In the past, they didn't have to think about it. The goal was clear – retirement. Now they can't find anything which gives them that same compelling drive, and they miss that.

Other clients I have worked with have had their lives turned upside down by a sudden change in circumstances, such as unemployment, or relationship break-up, or a medical condition that has meant the person can no longer do what they used to. It leaves them feeling directionless and lost.

If you are one of those people waiting for that magical day when the clouds part and your true meaning is revealed to you like a blinding beam of sunlight, you might wait a long time. You might die waiting.

But there is a fix. In this chapter, I shall explain some different strategies that I have seen work for many clients. Take a look at these and see if there is one that can help you in your life.

Firstly, take a piece of paper and brainstorm with yourself (or maybe with the help of someone you trust) anything you might want to do. Don't worry about how crazy your ideas might be, just get writing. Make the longest list that you can. Keep going until you feel you have exhausted your mind of ideas.

Once you have done that, give each item on the list a score out of five for how important you think it is. Be careful that you are rating it as how important you think it is to you, not how important it is to someone else. You remember what we have already said about things you think you should do? Where that word "should" is involved, it usually means that you are doing something for someone else, or because of someone else's values. You are unlikely to get a good outcome, because it will be someone else's desire, rather than yours.

Having done that, go through your list again and give each item another score out of five, this time for how urgent it is to you. Be careful to understand that important and urgent mean two quite different things. For example, if I want my car to work, I would give putting fuel in the tank five for importance. But if I already have a full tank, I would only give it one for urgency. If I had half a tank, I would give it maybe three for urgency. If the indicator was on the red and the engine was running on fumes, I would give it five for urgency. Just because something is important doesn't mean it's urgent, and vice-versa.

Now go through your list again and add your scores for importance and urgency together for each item. You now have a total score out of ten for each item. The item that has the highest score out of ten would be a great place for you to be focusing your attention.

This system for prioritising works on many levels. It can be used to sort out major life priorities, or it works just as well for short term focusing, such as optimizing your work schedule. It's also really useful if you have a particular project happening, such as starting a business or buying a property. You start with addressing the item with the highest score then work down the list in order of the score.

The feedback clients have given me for this system has always been positive. It really cuts through confusion. As one client said to me, it gives "instant clarity."

Another system I have seen work well for people trying to get focus on the big issues in their lives is this: instead of asking yourself what you want, try asking yourself what you fear most.

We all have fears. The most successful person you know has fears. The most confident person you know has fears. Having rational fears is healthy; it keeps you safe from real dangers. Even irrational fears such as phobias can be quite harmless, unless they are extreme.

So, what do you fear? What do you desire not to happen? Maybe loneliness, ill health, business failure, old age, disease, whatever it is, put it to the "Why is that?" test to see if there is more going on than you consciously realised.

When you have your answer, you can start turning your fear to your advantage. To do this, ask yourself what you could realistically do to take you as far as possible away from what you fear. For example, if your fear is being overwhelmed by financial worries, your aim might be to downsize your commitments. If you fear ill health, your aim might be to change your eating and activity habits. If you fear loneliness, your aim might be to join an organization where you will meet like-minded people. And so on.

Finally, another way to address the problem of lack of focus is to start by looking at what you're good at, or have the potential to be good at. Everyone has some sort of talent. What's yours?

If nothing instantly springs to mind, think carefully, look at things you have done in the past that have gone okay, and get together a list. Maybe it could be something you have done before, but stopped doing, or something you do now, but not in a committed way. Is there something that you could be focusing on that you could get really good at?

The sub-title of this book talks about success and happiness. If there is something that you can focus on and enjoy success with, happiness will usually follow. We all like the feeling of doing something well, whatever that is.

Using the ideas that you have read about so far, you should be able to find out what, for you personally, is your desire.

Next, you need a path.

The Path

A few years ago, the hospital where I worked wanted me to run a series of therapeutic groups for some people who had been attending out-patient counselling. Although they had finished their program of counselling, the clients still needed some motivational support to help them move forward. As they had varying needs, it wasn't appropriate to focus on specific issues. Instead I needed to structure a program that would work for everyone. The program that evolved for these clients was super-successful.

It became known as: The Path.

I have since used The Path with many clients, who have all responded well to it. I have also used it on myself. Indeed, I am using it right now. I think the great strength of The Path is that it's clear and easy to understand and follow. Consequently, it doesn't get forgotten about in the hurly burly of daily life, which is the weakness of many self-development programs.

Having a carefully-crafted program is great, but it needs to be something that you can still remember when you are upset, or going through challenging times, or when you have just been hit by a seemingly random event. More than that, a successful program needs to be something you can fall back on when life is tough, as well as on good days. The Path achieves this. It's simple, but it's profound in what it can achieve.

This is how it works.

Imagine that what you want to achieve is on a distant hill. Between you and it, there are hills, valleys, forests and rivers. You don't know how to get to your goal on that distant hill. You can see it, but you fear you could get lost trying to get there, and maybe never reach it. The task is daunting.

But then, as if by magic, a path suddenly appears at your feet, and it runs through the countryside all the way to your goal on that distant hill. Suddenly the task is no longer daunting. You simply need to follow The Path and you will be alright. You will reach your goal. You feel motivated and inspired, because you realise that as long as you keep moving forwards and stay on The Path, you cannot fail.

That's right. You cannot fail. Stay on The Path and you simply have to reach your goal.

No other outcome is possible.

How good is that?

Path is an acronym. It stands for "Planning and Total Honesty". Let's start with your plan.

Planning

Your plan needs to contain a simple, achievable Daily Action that compounded over time will move you to your goal. This Daily Action is the minimum that you need to do to keep you moving forward every day. Think of this repeated Daily Action as being a step along The Path. When you have taken enough steps, you will have reached your goal. Let's look at some examples.

I mentioned that I am using The Path right now. In fact, I am applying The Path to writing the book that you are holding. The idea of writing a book can be overwhelming. It's a big undertaking. It would be very easy for me to procrastinate and never get around to finishing it. I could keep coming up with excuses. I could tell myself that something else needs to be done right now, or I need to do another thing first. But there is always stuff that needs to be done. So, I need to take that Daily Action to move me along my Path every day, or I will never finish this book.

My Daily Action is simply to get to my computer at 9.00 in the morning and before I do anything else, write at least 500 words. That's not a lot. I know I can achieve that, as I usually write far more. In fact, I have already written 500 words this morning in my first half hour at my computer. I'll probably go on to write much more today.

On another day, however, I might feel less inspired and writing those 500 words is hard work and might take a few hours. But to achieve my Daily Action, I must persist and do it. Then, even if I only ever achieved my minimum target of 500 words daily, I would write my book. It might take a few months, but I would get there. No other outcome is possible.

Let's take another example. Let's say you want to lose weight. You have realized that if you ditch all the junk food, and follow a low-fat, wholefood diet, you will lose weight. It's inevitable, because your caloric intake will drop significantly, even if you eat as much in terms of quantity as you do now (I'll be discussing this more in a later chapter on weight management). So, your Daily Action is to eat as much of that type of food as you wish. That doesn't sound too difficult.

If you want to become less anxious, your Daily Action could be to do 10 minutes of Mindfulness every day. It doesn't sound much, but the cumulative effect over a few weeks would be significant.

If you want to become more successful as a salesperson, committing to a Daily Action of starting work 15 minutes earlier and making 2 extra sales calls per day would inevitably increase your success rate. That's an extra 40 calls per month, which is likely to translate into more sales.

Total Honesty

Planning is only part of it. To stay on your Path, you must be totally honest with yourself. It's tempting to justify to ourselves why we should not do something we had planned to do today. Usually, this is just excusing procrastination.

So, next time you find yourself thinking this way, be totally honest and ask yourself: Is that the truth or just an excuse? For example, if your mind is talking you into not doing something because, let's say, you feel little unwell, ask yourself: truth or excuse? Am I really that unwell, or is it just an excuse to be lazy?

Focus on your Daily Action

Does your mind focus on the future? Are you prone to questioning your plans? Does your mind keep coming up with "what if?" scenarios that shake your confidence? I know my mind does, if I let it. The solution is just to focus on doing your Daily Action, and then you are done for the day. You don't need to project ahead. As long as you have taken your Daily Action, you know that you have advanced along your Path, and that's all that matters. You are closer to achieving your goal.

Check Were Your Feet Are.

Another way to make sure you're on your Path is to keep an eye on where your feet are. I am not talking figuratively here. I mean literally, what are your feet up to?

For instance, if you are on a diet and your feet are walking towards a pizza restaurant, are you about to step off your Path? If you have decided to stay out of the life of an ex-partner, why are your feet walking down the street where he lives? If you have resolved to go for a run every morning and your feet are still in bed 20 minutes after the alarm went off, are you still on your Path? If you have resolved to have a booze-free month, why are your feet walking down the alcohol aisle at the supermarket?

Rest Days

You should decide before you start on your Path, whether it is appropriate to take rest days, and if so, when. If you are following a fitness program, then rest days are usually part of the program. If your target is work or study related, then having days off would be healthy. I am giving myself weekends off from writing this book to keep my mind fresh, so I only do my Daily Action on weekdays. But if you are on a diet, you should decide whether you are going for it 100% or if you will have days off, and you need to do this in advance; otherwise you might be dishonest with yourself about your motives.

Now, let's look at how you can apply The Path to what you want in your own life

Following the Instructions

How many books in the self-development genre have you read? Is this the first? Probably not. More likely you have a little library of self-development on your shelf or downloaded onto your reading device. And from those books, how many have had a program that you have thoroughly followed? Any? Or have you simply started the next book?

Do you have books that promise you can achieve great things if you follow a particular plan for 7 days, or 21 days, or 30 days, or whatever the time scale might be? Have you ever faithfully followed those plans to the letter, for the specified time, and achieved the promised outcome?

No, me neither.

Until I did.

Then I found I could change my life - by choice, not by chance.

As a young man, I always tried to find my own way to do everything. I would always go for the short cut. I would try to achieve the most with the least amount of effort. No wonder my life became chaotic. I was constantly trying to think outside the box (as we used to say back then) for solutions, instead of just doing the obvious which worked.

I never followed instructions. I just couldn't be bothered. Anyway, I thought didn't need to. I thought I was clever. You can imagine what my attempts at self-assembly furniture were like. I always had lots of screws left over, and would wonder why the wardrobe I had just constructed fell apart when you hung your coat in it.

But over the years, I have gradually learnt that trying to do things my way might not always be the smart way. I struggled to make grades at school, because I didn't think I needed to do the work. I thought I could rely on my natural ability. I was wrong.

Later, when I trained to be a therapist, I discovered that if I actually turned up and did the work, I would get the qualification. This was a revelation to me. It wasn't painful, in fact it was quite fun.

I had finally discovered the power of putting my ego to one side and simply following a Path. It pained me to accept that I wasn't really the genius I thought I was, and that I just caused myself disappointment and frustration. But I discovered that life wasn't as complicated as I thought it was, because it had been me all along who had been making it complicated. I finally started following the instructions, and it changed my life.

Even now, when I'm faced with something new that I want to achieve, my mind tells me just to do it my own way. But at last, I finally know better. Instead of trying to be a genius, I use the genius of other people who have successfully trod the same path before me. In other words, I just look for a plan that has been proven to work.

Here's an example from my own life.

I had always detested running. When I was at school, the activity I hated most was cross-country running. I loathed feeling sweaty and breathless and, worst of all, being poor at doing it. That really didn't sit well with the high opinion I had of myself.

I convinced myself that I must be the wrong body type. All the runners I saw on sports programs were small and slightly built. I, on the other hand, am tall and broadly built. So that explained it. I was simply the wrong shape for running. So, I got good at sports where my long reach helped, like Badminton. I decided I would simply leave running to the fly-weights.

But then one day not that long ago, I read an article about a program called Couch to 5K. It stated that if you followed this program, in nine weeks you would go from being the proverbial couch potato to being able to run five kilometres (about three miles). At the time, I never even ran five metres, never mind five kilometres. But all you had to do was download the app onto your phone, then run three times a week, following the instructions on your ear buds while you were doing it.

Couch to 5K came from Public Health England, so I knew it would have been well researched and proven to work. It would be a quality plan that I could commit to.

It said that anyone could learn to run 5K.

Learn?

It had never occurred to me that you learned to run. I guess I had always assumed it was instinctive. That got me interested. At the time, I had been doing a lot of walking to keep fit, but felt that I needed to do something more to make progress. So, I decided to commit myself to the nine weeks.

The first session was mostly walking for half an hour, with a few 90 seconds bursts of running mixed in, but even that left me breathless. I felt unsure this was going to work. To go from struggling to run for 90 seconds to being able to run 5K, which would take about half an hour, didn't look likely to happen for me.

But I reminded myself that I had been told that anyone could learn this, and anyone includes me. I just needed to make the effort three times per week and put my faith in the program.

The little voice in my head that always wants me to put my feet up and procrastinate did its best to get me to abandon the plan. Every morning, it tried to talk me into an extra half-hour in bed. Every time there was a single cloud in the sky, it tried to persuade me that a deluge of Biblical proportions was bound to engulf me if I ventured out for my run. Nevertheless, I bought a good pair of running shoes and followed the instructions.

Nine weeks later I could run 5K.

Some people reading this will have always been good at running, and will be wondering why I am making a fuss about it. But I can't tell you how amazing it is to me that I can do this, and I go out for a run most days now. It seems like a miracle, but in fact it's just the power of following a

Path and doing the Daily Action (which in the case of Couch to 5K was to run three times a week with four rest days).

It also shows that when you are doing the planning for your Path, using well researched information that has been proven is the way to go. Don't just make it up yourself. Seek out what has been shown to work and do that.

Don't Wait until You're Ready

In the last chapter, I mentioned that little voice in your head. You know the one. It's the voice that tells you that you're wrong, that you are too slow, too fat, too lazy, too dumb, too clever, too young, too old, too tall, too short, too hairy, too bald, too underqualified, too overqualified, too experienced, too inexperienced, and so forth. It's the voice that beats you up when you make a mistake.

Psychologists often call this voice the Inner Critic. It sits in judgment of you all the time. But I think that gives it too much of a sense of authority, which is partly why people get pushed around by this inner voice. They think it's in charge.

I like to think of it as the little voice of your fears. It comes from past pain. It comes from all those times when life has hurt you. It's actually a voice of compassion, because it wants you to avoid feeling pain again. It associates change with pain, because you have experienced pain in the past when change has randomly been imposed upon you.

So, when you decide you want to make changes, it says, "Whoa, wait a minute. Are you sure about doing that? It would expose you to possible failure, and that hurts. Wouldn't it be better that you carry on doing what you're doing now? You know what that's like. It might not be what you desire, but at least you know what you're going to get."

Sometimes the voice will do a good job and keep you from getting into trouble. But it can also keep you in a situation that you would be best to move on from, because it tries to persuade you to stay with what you have, even if what you have is not what you want.

The voice tells you to stay in the same uninspiring job, stay at the same weight, stay with a partner who is hurting you, keep consuming things you know are bad for you, or stay in the same neighbourhood although you hate it. The voice argues the case for staying with what is familiar, rather than experience something new.

Working with clients, I find one of the biggest difficulties in my job is that I am competing with this voice of their Inner Critic. During the hour that I spend with a client, we can get a lot of things agreed, and the client goes away with a course of action to make positive changes to their life. But once the client leaves the room, the voice of the Inner Critic starts in their head, and it has all week, until the client next sees me, to sow the seeds of self-doubt in the client's mind.

A week is a long time for the voice to do its worst. And that's what the voice likes best, time to work with. So, it will intrude on your thoughts while you are at work, or when you are watching TV. Its favourite trick is to wake you up in the middle of the night and start you worrying.

Clearly, if you want to make changes in your life, you need to get the upper hand on the voice, or it will sabotage your plans every time. Here's how:

Take some action immediately. Don't wait until you think you're ready - that gives the voice time to sabotage you. You will never be 100% ready, anyway. Make a start. You will take the voice by surprise, because you will be taking yourself by surprise. And that will give you something very valuable:

Momentum.

And momentum will crush the voice of your fears.

So, if you were planning to study for a new qualification, get online and sign up now. If you intended to start a healthy eating plan on the first day of next month, start now instead, today. Clear out the cupboards of all your junk food and donate it to the food bank.

When I tried to give up smoking in the past, I always tried to start on a date and time I had decided in advance. It never worked. Then one day, at about eight o'clock in the evening, I suddenly decided to stop. It was so sudden, 10 seconds earlier I had no idea I going to quit. My Inner Critic was completely taken by surprise and kept quiet.

It was one of those random moments in life that I hadn't seen coming. I could have ignored it, and carried on smoking, but I decided to go with it. The following morning, when the cravings started to give me a hard time, my Inner Critic had had time to get over the shock of my sudden action, and it tried to persuade me to smoke. But, by that time, I had already gone 12 hours and I had momentum. I thought: let's get this done. I haven't smoked since, which shows the power of not waiting till you're ready and using randomness in your life to your advantage.

When I wrote my first book, a similar thing happened. At the time, I had been carrying out a lot of counselling work at a hospital out-patient facility with problem drinkers. The results had been excellent and I believed that I had valuable research that I should share with all drinkers in need of support, not just the ones in my town.

I decided to write an article about my work to submit to a magazine. But I quickly realized that I had so much information to share, that I was writing the introduction to a book instead of an article. I decided to carry on and get it done quickly. Three months later, my book "Alcohol and You" was selling on major online platforms, and I was receiving messaging from people about how life-changing they had found it.

If I had delayed, if I had thought, "I'll start when I have more time", I would probably never have written the book. The voice of my Inner Critic would have had chance to plant doubt in my mind. It would have said things like: "Who do you think you are? Are you sure you're qualified enough? Perhaps you should do another five years research? Why do you think you can write?" And so on.

But because I got on with it immediately, my voice of self-doubt got trampled as I ran down The Path to my goal.

A few years ago, my wife, Antonia, was very unhappy in her job. She was a teacher. She was working ridiculously long hours, had a long commute to her school, she was coming home late, exhausted, with work she still needed to do at home. Her doctor diagnosed her with stress.

Something had to change. It would have seemed sensible for her to start applying for other jobs, but it could have taken months to organize a suitable new post. She couldn't wait. Her happiness and health were on the line.

She quit her job, with no other job to go to. At this point, her Inner Critic could have gone crazy, beating her up for doing something so reckless. But it didn't have time, as she took immediate action.

Antonia had always loved animals. Where we lived at the time was in the countryside. Our garden backed onto hundreds of acres of quiet country lanes and fields. She loved nothing more than taking our dog on long walks, as it was perfect dog-walking country. She announced she was going to start a business looking after dogs.

Right away, she started putting out adverts on cheap or free web sites and social media. I designed a small, business web site for her. She bought business insurance. The phone started ringing. She had momentum. Within a few days, she was in business and the dogs started arriving. In her first month, she earned nearly as much as she had been earning as a teacher, doing something she loved.

The important thing to grasp is that change happened on the very first day. That's why the first chapter in this book was called Change Your Life Today.

But what happens after the initial rush of momentum slows? How do you keep going when self-doubt starts to creep back? How do you keep going on the bad days?

Let's look at that next.

Motivation on Demand

The concept of using The Path and taking your Daily Action makes it easy to overcome procrastination and feeling overwhelmed by your goals.

Using this valuable strategy for changing your life, most days you are likely to find that taking your Daily Action is not difficult, just so long as you are on a Path that is aligned with your deepest desire.

But even so, some days it can still feel almost impossible to get motivated. This is usually because that inner voice starts trying to stop you from changing. Change scares the voice, and it starts to kick up a fuss. That's when you need to be able to access motivation on demand, because the voice has a powerful ally – familiarity.

In my professional life, I have found that familiarity is a formidable foe for clients who want to change. Repetition hardwires our brains. In some ways this is useful. Having a positive daily routine is a powerful tool for getting things done and leaving time in your life for leisure. But negative routines get hardwired as well.

If you have started a fitness program, for instance, the voice will try its hardest to persuade you that the tiny twinge you just felt in your leg is a great reason to cancel your visit to the gym and get pizza delivered, just like you used to.

If you have given up smoking but associate having a cigarette with drinking coffee, you risk relapsing with every cappuccino, because your brain has hardwired the connection between coffee and nicotine through repetition.

So, we need a reliable way to call on motivation whenever we need it to overcome the allure of the familiar.

Motivation is misunderstood. People think getting motivated is arduous. I know I did when I was young. Procrastination seemed like the only thing I was good at. I thought I must have been born the laziest person on the planet. I can see now that wasn't true, because if something came into view that inspired me, I could be as motivated as anyone. But I ran into difficulties when I needed motivation to get things done that didn't inspire me. I thought I struggled to get motivated. I thought that it was something I lacked that other people had because they were born with it. I had just been born with a shortage of it.

What I didn't understand back then was that motivation is actually rather simple. It only requires a small movement. Think of rolling a ball down a hill. You only need a small amount of energy to get the ball moving, then momentum will take over and, before you know it, the ball is heading downhill at speed.

And that's the trick to understanding motivation. You don't need to make gigantic efforts or get wildly hyped up. You just need to take a little action to get something going, so that momentum can kick in, because momentum moves things on, momentum creates its own energy, like the ball rolling down the hill.

Take another analogy. Imagine you are going to start your car. Do you heave it out of the garage and start pushing down the road? No, of course not - you simply turn the key in the ignition. That's not a difficult thing to do, but it sets off a chain of events in the engine, and then you're off down the street.

Turning the key was like providing the motivation to start something. All you did was take the tiny action of turning the key, and moments later, half a ton of metal was on the move.

Motivation is a trick, a knack, a little technique. You just take the smallest action, and then let momentum provide the energy to keep things going.

Here's a simple motivational technique that I have recommended to my clients with great success, and it really works for me personally to keep me on my Path when I'm wavering.

Taking an Easy Action Right Now.

This involves just taking a small, easy action, such as thinking: "'I'll just get ready, then see how I feel."

So, if it's my day to go for a run, and the voice is trying to persuade me to stay home where it's cosy, I'll think, "Oh, I'll just get my running gear on and then decide." Putting my running shoes on is easy. I can't remember a time when I've got ready, then not gone for a run. I think, "Well, I'll just do it anyway." No iron will-power required. And by the time the voice in my head has realized what's going on, I'm half a mile down the road.

If I've had a busy day, but I still have client notes to type up, while the voice in my head is trying to persuade me to leave it till the morning, I'll think "I'll just make a start, I can always save it later." Of course, I will carry on and finish the task, and be pleased with myself that I did it when I come into work to a clear start the next day.

So, if you can't decide whether to go into town to your therapy meeting or stay home, try thinking: "I'll just get in the car and then decide." Or if you are a sales person, out on the road, and you know you should go back to the office and make five calls, but the voice is saying head home early, you could think: "Well, I'll just drop by the office and then decide."

If you don't feel in the mood to do the yoga practice you have scheduled, just try thinking, "Well, I'll go stand on my yoga mat and then decide." Then you might think, "While I'm here, I'll just do a few stretches." Before you know it, you've done your practice.

You just turned the key in your ignition.

If I'm working with a client on motivation, we'll start by working out when it is that they need to use this technique. We do this by identifying when are their habitual moments of self-sabotage – when the inner voice gets its way. What we then do is to work out a go-to action to use at that time which fits the "Easy Action Right Now" scenario. That way, you don't even need any thinking time, you just do it.

Open-Minded Outcomes

You need to be clear about the goal you are setting for yourself - the place you want to be when you reach the end of your Path. But it's worth being flexible about what the outcome will look like when you get there. That might initially seem a little contrary. We are used to the idea that we get a goal and go for it. Indeed, the concept of The Path might seem to re-enforce that view. But it isn't a rigid philosophy.

After you have set your goal, the focus then becomes the Daily Action. You can trust that if you take this step and don't move off your Path (keep being totally honest and checking where your feet are), you will reach the end of The Path. No other outcome is possible.

But the Path is an adaptable concept. Remember our random world. Between you deciding what your goal is and reaching that goal, many seemingly random events that you cannot currently foresee will occur. New information will come to light that you are presently totally unaware of.

This is a good thing, because, if you are open-minded, you might have the opportunity to achieve an outcome that is even better than the one you had originally intended. I can think of many times in my life where following a Path has led me to an outcome I hadn't imagined at the outset, but which was much better than I had expected. When that happens, you realise that instigating change is exciting and enriching. Here are some examples:

•   I know how long I want this book to be. But by being open minded about what I am doing, new ideas might come to me along the way that allow me to write a longer but better book.

•   The person who is quitting the drink for January might think it's rather cool and end up quitting for the whole year.

•   Someone learning Spanish might go to Madrid to do a course, and like it so much she decides to live there.

•   The dieter eating healthy food to lose weight might get the taste for it, make the change permanent and live a longer, fitter life as a result.

Here's a true story to illustrate this further. In the early days of the Internet, I became interested in web design and decided to try it myself. I was also interested in recreational travel, so I put the two together and came up with a web site that advertised lovely vacation properties in Italy. There was a new search engine that was just starting to gain market share called Google that picked up on my web site and I started getting enquiries.

Before I knew it, I had a little business going as an accommodation booking agent. When I look at how big and intense travel is on the internet now, and how huge Google has become, it seems like I was living in an age of innocence. This was even before broadband, and we had those clunky dial-up connections. Having broadband on your phone would have seemed like a miracle. It's amazing to think I'm only talking about the start of this century.

One little random event that happened to me was that I got an email from a travel agent in Portugal, asking if I wanted any Portuguese vacation properties on my web site. As you will know from the introduction to this book, I spend half my time in Portugal at present. But at that time, I had never been to Portugal. It wasn't on my radar at all. All I knew about it was that it was the little country next to Spain, the Portuguese had been the first Europeans to discover Brazil, and that they had invented Port wine. But that was about all I knew. I was shocked at my own ignorance.

My bookings in Italy were keeping me busy. I could have very easily just been closed-minded about the outcome I was looking for, and sent a polite "thanks-but-no-thanks" email back. But I was curious.

I had already started to find that the short season in Italy was a limitation – they take the covers off the swimming pools in Italy in May and put them back on in September. Portugal is further south and warmer, and I reasoned I could have a longer booking-season there. So, I decided to go and take a look with an open mind. I booked a flight from London to Faro.

A week later, I was on the flight. Although it was late in the season, I noted that the flight was full with British tourists wanting some sun. I saw the opportunity and a few days later started loading my website with Portuguese vacation properties to rent. The bookings poured in. By being open about my outcomes, I had ended up with a business that was fundamentally changed, the Path had led somewhere I had not expected at all – a different country - but it was a good outcome from the business point-of-view.

But there was more. I discovered when I got to Portugal that I loved being there – so much so that I stayed for 7 years. As a write these words, I am back again. By being flexible about my outcomes, I have enriched my life and experienced a country and culture that had never been in my plans, but I'm really glad my Path has led me here.

When I make a goal for a new project nowadays, I am always open about the outcome. I regard setting the goal as a statement of intent, and indeed, that might well be exactly where I end up at the end of that particular Path. But I'm always open to the idea that the Path might take me to an even better outcome.

This might sound a little mystic, but it's not anything of the kind. When you take your Daily Action, you will set off a chain-reaction of events. This is simply cause and effect in action. But where that chain of events leads you can be surprising, because all around you every day, change is happening, so you can take the same action on two consecutive days, but the result might vary.

This is how you can find success and happiness in a random world.

Recording the Stats

If you go into a sales office at, say, a motor dealer, insurance, or an office equipment company, in all probability you will see a board on the wall showing the sales of the individual sales people. The reason for this is clear. Simply seeing the numbers is motivating. If you are at the top of the sales league, you want to stay there. If you are in the middle, you want to get to the top. If you are at the bottom, you will desperately want to move up. The sales management know this, which is why the board is there.

You can use this simple technique to help yourself along your Path. It can be applied to most things we do – there is always a way of recording the stats.

When I gave up smoking, I put up a monthly planner on the wall of the kitchen, where I couldn't help but see it many times per day. At the end of every day when I hadn't

335

smoked, I would put a sticker on that date. I made getting to the end of the day and putting my sticker on the chart the most important thing in my life for a month, because I knew how beneficial stopping smoking would be. My goal was to reach the end of that month, with a sticker on my chart every day. I was simply recording the number of days, one by one, in a very graphic way.

Does this sound too simple? Surely there must be more to it than that? Well, I had tried more complicated ways. I had spent a fortune on nicotine replacement products. I spend a couple of years smothered in nicotine patches. I forced myself to chew that vile-tasting nicotine gum. I had used nicotine inhalers. Then there was hypnotism. Did that make a difference? No. I had wanted to smoke as soon as the session was finished. I read Alan Carr's book, which told me that I could stop smoking "the easy way". Did it work? No, it didn't make the slightest difference. I'm sure it has worked for many people, but for me, there was no easy way.

But there was a simple way. Simple and easy don't mean the same thing, as I would discover. But I found the way.

I had a Path, to get to the end of the month. I had a Daily Action, to be able to put my no-smoking sticker up at the end of the day. I had the monthly planner as motivation, I was recording the stats.

All my previous attempts to stop smoking had ended in total failure – and I had made countless attempts. But this simple method worked first time.

If you have ever been addicted to nicotine, as I had been for decades, you will know just how difficult giving up is. Research shows that 40% of smokers try to give up every year, yet the number of smokers only comes down by 1% per year. That means there is a huge failure rate. I can understand why. Nicotine withdrawal is horrible. Your head is spinning for days, you cannot concentrate, and you have cravings hitting you all the time. I was even hallucinating on the first couple of days of giving up. But this uncomplicated method got me through to the end of the month. Then, I knew there was no going back. It had been so painful; there was no way I was ever going to endure that again. I haven't smoked at all since.

Another example of the power of recording the stats happened only yesterday. I have an app on my phone that records the number of paces I take every day. It's a great little app. It can tell the difference between when I'm running or walking, it tells me how far I have gone, and it tells me how many calories I have burned.

But the most important stat for me is simply the total number of paces. I set myself a minimum daily target of 8,000 paces. I can go over the minimum as much as I like, but I have made a deal with myself that I will do that minimum every day. It's non-negotiable. Whatever is going on that day, however busy I am, or whatever the weather is like, I will find a way to reach that minimum.

Yesterday, when I got home late afternoon, I checked my app and realized that I was about a thousand steps short of the minimum. That immediately motivated me. I didn't need to stop and think. I went straight out again. I took a brisk walk down to my local beach, and explored part of it I don't usually go on. It was fun. By going after those steps, I had enhanced my day. In the end, I was a couple of thousand steps over my minimum. But if I hadn't been keeping the stats on my app, I probably would have just sat down at home and turned on the PC.

Another use I have found for that particular app is in helping me sleep. I have a recurring problem with sleeping. I can get to sleep easily enough. The problem is that I will wake up in the night, my mind will be busy, and I find it difficult to get back to sleep. I tried various remedies. The pharmacy recommended an antihistamine-based pill, but that didn't help me sleep and I felt a bit woozy in the morning. My doctor prescribed me low dosage Amitriptyline, which did help me sleep, but turned me into a drooling zombie in the morning – thank goodness he didn't prescribe a higher dose. I tried listening to hypnotherapy at bedtime, but no result there either. I tried various recommendations for sleep hygiene, but again no luck. I tried meditation techniques, which had some success, but usually my busy mind took control and I was wide awake. I also experimented with what I ate or drank to see if that make a difference. I couldn't find any.

But then I started analysing the data from my walking app. I realized there seemed to be a direct connection between the distance I had walked in the course of the day and having a good night's sleep. It had to be brisk walking or running. The magic number I came up with was four miles. If I briskly walked four miles in the day, I would probably sleep well. Four miles for me is about 8,000 paces, which is why I have put that in my app as my daily minimum.

Curiously, that four miles figure seems quite exact for me - it's the sweet spot I need to hit. If I fall short by just half a mile, I will probably be awake in the night. If I walk a longer distance, I don't sleep for any longer. I don't have a problem with motivation, as I know I won't sleep if I miss my target. Of course, there are all sorts of other health benefits in walking that distance every day, so come what may, I need to make time for it.

I also use an app currently to record what I eat to ensure that I have eaten enough high-nutrient foods every day. I have realized that this is also where I need to record the stats. It is easy to read up a subject like nutrition and think, "Yes, I'll do that - I'll eat all that good stuff." But then you go and get on with your busy day, and you simply forget - but not if you are keeping a record. What's more, it's really satisfying at the end of the day to see my record of all the good stuff I have eaten. If you're interested, the app is called The Daily Dozen, and it was created by Dr. Michael Greger.

I had a manager once who had a saying: "What gets recorded gets done." He used to annoy me with that phrase and all the ways he made me record what I was doing. I got a bit resentful. Surely, he could trust me to get on with my job? But my productivity went up. I got more done. The quality of my work got better. I have to admit he was right.

Finding Your People

You might have noticed there is a quote at the start of this book from Tom Hopkins, who you might be familiar with if you work in sales, as Hopkins is a legend in the world of sales training.

When I was in my twenties, before I retrained as a therapist, I got into sales work. The reason was money – with my first child on the way, I needed to earn more, and sales seemed to be the way that I could. I wasn't very good at it. That's not surprising. Doing something just for the money is rarely a happy arrangement, because it isn't your true desire. But I needed the stuff.

Then I discovered a book called How to Master the Art of Selling by Tom Hopkins. I don't think I ever really mastered the art of selling, it wasn't my calling, but I got a lot better. As I remember, the book had lots of handy sales techniques. But what really sticks with me now, decades later, is the bit that changed my life.

Hopkins talks in his book about a character called Jack Bumyears. This is the person hanging around the office who is a perennial under-achiever. He hates to see new people coming in and doing well, because they show up his own shortcomings. He is the person who won't take on new ideas. He is the person who gossips behind people's backs and likes to talk everything down. He is the voice of negativity that drains the enthusiasm and joy out of those around him.

So why did Jack Bumyears change my life? Well, two reasons:

Firstly, after reading that book, if I ever find myself being negative and talking things down, I will think: "Oh my God, I'm being like Jack Bumyears", and that will snap me out of it.

Secondly, it alerted me to all the Bumyears-like people in my life. We all have them. If you are totally honest, you will probably admit that you go into Bumyears-mode from time to time yourself. We are all prone to griping and moaning sometimes.

But plenty of people live in a world of fault-finding and complaining. Indeed, some people seem to need it, like it is their default setting to seek out the worst in any situation.

For such people, social media must have been like a gift from Heaven. Do you belong to any Facebook groups, or similar on other platforms? I do, as they have their uses. I am on groups for authors and also for expats in Portugal, for instance. Being able to share information with like-minded people can be really valuable. But amazingly, some people seem to be on these groups just to be sarcastic and nasty, while hiding behind the anonymity of a profile page.

Just recently I saw a post on an expat group from a lady, who lived in a remote area of the Portugal, wanting to know where she could source some ingredients for cake-making. Not a contentious post, you would think. But no, the trolls were out making snide comments accompanied by laughing emojis. The thread was really long, and when you scanned down towards the end, people were having the social media equivalent of fisticuffs with each other over politics – cake making had been forgotten and the post was being used as an excuse to vent hate for people with different views. Unbelievable, but sadly true.

People like this are just a drain on your mental and emotional resources, whether you encounter them in your home environment, at work, or online. They have a knack of being able to wake up the voice of self-doubt in your head and generally make you feel that life is a drudge.

So, what can you do?

Well, you can start by setting an example, and not behaving like a Bumyears yourself. You can also do your best to avoid such people, but this is not always easy. Online, you can just block someone, but if the Bumyears in your life is a close member of your family or your boss, that's a different matter. Realistically, you can't purge your life of every Bumyears, they are everywhere. Even inside the best of us, there is a Bumyears trying to get out.

What you can do, however, is to counter all this negativity with your own supporters. Who agrees with what you are trying to do? Who would offer you words of encouragement on a challenging day? Who would love to cheer you on, across the finishing line of your Path? These are the people you would be wise to hang out with, whether it be people in your day-to-day life or online. These are the people who will help you find success and happiness in a random world.

I think it is a good exercise to take a sheet of paper and brainstorm with yourself exactly who these people are. Some will be obvious - if you have a supportive partner or parent, for example. Others might be less obvious, maybe a cheerful person on the front desk at work, or someone who shares a particular interest with you.

When you consciously recognize who these wonderful people are, you can cultivate your relationship with them, and they are there for you to tap into when the forces of negativity are trying to sap your strength.

Next, it's time to look at the super-powerful strategy of Achievement Stacking.

Achievement Stacking

You read earlier about how Antonia started her dog care business and achieved immediate success. She didn't wait until she was ready, she just went for it, and it worked right away.

Her success continued. She was getting plenty of work. Her marketing costs were virtually zero. The phone was ringing. She was even being able to pick and choose which dogs she took on. The owners were happy. Some were becoming regular customers, which is what any business wants - repeat business. They had confidence in Antonia – she was clearly doing a great job. This was not surprising as she was very organised, and had previous experience of working with dogs from being a volunteer in an animal rescue centre. She was insured and had taken an animal first aid course. She was prepared. She had faith in her own ability.

But, despite her obvious ability to run her business, a curious thing happened. About eight weeks into the business, she had bookings and money coming in fast. Yet, she started to worry that someone would challenge her and say things like "Who do you think you are? What right have you to run a business like this?"

It seemed she had an attack of Impostor Syndrome. This is where self-doubt leads someone to feel they could get exposed as a fraud, despite obvious evidence to the contrary. It's a tactic that your Inner Critic loves to exploit to halt your desire for change.

Ironically, Impostor Syndrome is often a sign that things are going right. It follows an achievement. For example, someone who lands their dream job might find that they feel in over their head, that they aren't up to the work and aren't equal to their peers, even though there is no evidence to support that view.

In Antonia's case, that little voice of her Inner Critic, which had been swept aside by her initial burst of activity and success, had enough time to recover and was starting to undermine her. It could have led her away from her Path.

These attacks of self-doubt have no logic. I have experienced it many times. In my work, I have run hundreds of therapeutic groups in out-patient services.

This is where I have anything up to 20 people, who are in treatment, come in for a structured discussion, and led by me and usually another colleague, on a certain topic.

I have a good reputation among my colleagues for facilitating these groups – it's one of my strengths. I usually feel totally comfortable. But sometimes, for no reason, I will see the room filling up with clients and suddenly start feeling that I'm not up to the job today. I will feel a fraud. The feeling usually goes as soon as the group starts and I get into my stride. But it's unsettling.

I helped one client who had previously been in the military, and during that time, he had flown thousands of miles and made dozens of parachute jumps. Then one day after he left the military, he was flying home from a vacation on a short-haul flight. With no warning, he felt himself starting to breathe erratically and sweat. He felt light-headed and frightened. Out of nowhere, he had suddenly developed a fear of flying. He was unable to fly for years afterwards.

Confidence comes and goes with us all. Fear can come and tap you on the shoulder at the most inconvenient times, and you can be sure it will happen often while you are changing your life for the better. So how do you find confidence when you need it?

If you are using The Path, try reminding yourself that as long as you do your Daily Action and don't allow yourself to be dragged off The Path, you will reach your goal – no other outcome is possible. Repeat this to yourself as often as you like.

But if self-doubt still troubles you, try a technique I have used successfully many times with clients and also myself. I call it Achievement Stacking. There are two variants I use – the lifetime version and the daily version.

We'll start with the lifetime version, which you do only once. Take a notebook. Then, think about your life so far. Think about its different aspects and give them different category names. What you choose is up to you, it's your life. But you might choose, for instance, Childhood, School, College, Relationships, Work, Parenting, Helping Others, Playing Sports, and so on.

Now, for each part of your life, I want you to think of achievements you have made, and for each category, make a vertical list, starting at the bottom of the page and moving up a line each time write down an achievement. This is your stack. Make your stack as high as you can.

Think of ten categories in your life, and then keep digging down into your memory for each category until you have a stack of at least ten achievements for each category. So, you are aiming for a hundred in total.

Does a hundred sound too many? No, it isn't. This is a lifetime inventory of your achievements you are creating. You will have to tailor it to yourself. Clearly if you are sixty years old, you have a lot more material to work with than someone who is twenty.

Certain categories will be easier for some people than others. If you did well at school and went on to do a degree, then getting a high stack for Education will be a breeze. If you dropped out of school, it will be more difficult. But don't give up. If you dig down, you will find those achievements.

What you call an achievement will also be personal to you. What is routine to one person, would be an achievement to another. Most of us wouldn't regard buying the groceries as an achievement. But for someone who is trying to overcome chronic agoraphobia, going out to buy a can of beans would be a genuine achievement.

If you are career-oriented, then you might break down the work category into several sub-categories. Someone focused on bringing up a family might sub-categorize parenting. If I were doing this exercise, I would think of the names of clients whose lives I feel I have greatly impacted for the better, and turn that into a stack. I might also list all the training courses I have completed for another stack. Both of these would be tall stacks and I would be up to 100 in no time.

If you are struggling, when you have identified one achievement in a particular stack, try asking yourself "What else?" Keep asking yourself "What else?" until you are really sure you've built up that stack as high as you can.

I have had clients, whose lives were highly challenged, look at me in disbelief when I have asked them to do an Achievement Stack. People have said things like "You must be joking, my life is a mess, and I've never achieved anything!" But once they have made a start, and kept asking themselves "What else?" they have amazed themselves with what they have achieved.

Remember, this is a big inventory. Take your time. Do it over a few days, as old achievements will start popping up in your head that your conscious mind had forgotten about. Enjoy the process. This is all about you.

When you feel sure that you have completed the inventory and can look with satisfaction at a number of tall stacks in your notebook, keep it somewhere safe. Every time you feel self-doubt creeping in, look at your stacks. Take heart from your own past achievements.

You might like to highlight the ten or twenty achievements that give you most satisfaction. Perhaps keep them on a note on your phone, so you can refer to them and take strength from them any time you're feeling challenged or unsure of yourself.

You might like to recite them to yourself every morning when you wake up, or when you take the dog for a walk. It's a great way to build self-belief. If you have achieved all these things in the past, surely taking your Daily Action along your Path is easy.

The above version of Achievement Stacking is a one-off tactic. The shorter version will help maintain self-belief on a daily basis. This is how it works.

At the end of the day, take a couple of minutes to think about your day. Pick out your achievements that day. They are likely to be much smaller things than on your lifetime achievement inventory. They are things that if you hadn't done this exercise, you might have forgotten about.

It could be a telephone conversation where you have said something that really helped a client or a friend. It could be an email you wrote that you thought communicated a point particularly well. It could have been an act of kindness to your partner. Maybe you had to be especially patient with your child. You might have faced up to making a call you had been putting off to an authority figure. You filed your tax return. Or maybe you just made a great sandwich for lunch.

Create your stack for the day. Some days it will be easy. But where you might find it really helpful is on a bad day. You know the sort of day. It's the day your boss gives you a hard time for no obvious reason. You get a parking ticket. You have a huge bust-up with your partner. You dent your car. Dinner is a disaster. You smell cigarette smoke on your 14-year-old's clothes. Your head feels like a sack of worries and your stomach is churning like a washing machine.

On days like these, it's difficult to find the achievements, but all the more reason to look hard for them. Even if they are just small, find at least three. It will give you faith that even when things seemed to be going badly, there are still good things going on. And if you have done your Daily Action, you will still be on The Path to your goal.

At the end of your week, take a look at your daily stacks from the week. Pick out your favourites. Take a few moments to enjoy again some satisfaction from your achievements. It will give you momentum to do more next week.

When you have finished your Achievement Stacks, it's time to move up a level. It's time to look at Super Empowerment.

Super Empowerment

Stephanie was a well presented, articulate woman in her thirties who regularly attended one of my therapeutic groups. The group was themed around self-management. The format was that I would begin by asking the participants if they had any current life issues they would like to discuss with the group, and from that I would draw up an agenda for discussion.

Stephanie always wanted to discuss her mother. They had a volatile relationship. She would frequently be in tears about something her mother had said. It sounded like her mother was very judgmental and had a way of saying things that really hit Stephanie's weak spots.

Stephanie's story was that she had regular rage-attacks, which were invariably triggered by an argument with her mother. She didn't normally drink, but on these occasions, she would hit the vodka and completely go off the rails. She would become uncontrollable; she would break up the house, and give a verbal mauling to anyone who got in her way. It had all got too much for her husband, Mike, who had moved out and taken the children with him.

Not surprisingly, members of the group suggested she should attend anger management, but Stephanie would not. "It's not me that's the problem, it's my mother. She's the one who needs treatment, not me," she insisted.

Then one week, she came to group, her eyes puffed up and red, in floods of tears. She had had another outburst of rage. She wanted to talk to me alone, so one of my colleagues took the group, while I made Stephanie some tea, and then we talked.

"It was my mother again. She says it's just as well Mike's got the kids, she says I'm not fit to be a mother". Remarks like that hurt Stephanie the most. Not being under the same roof as her children was an open wound which, for some reason, her mother couldn't resist poking.

"I went home, but I bought some vodka on the way. Then I started messaging people. I was so upset. My best friend came over to try to help," she said. "But I just totally lost it. I was so angry. I thought she was just trying to interfere and I got really abusive. She won't speak to me now. I'm so sorry. I don't know what came over me. I've lost my husband. My kids aren't speaking to me. Now I've lost my best friend. And it's all my mother's fault. What can I do about her?"

"You may not be able to do anything about her." I said. "You can't change her, and you don't have power over the horrible things that she says. But you can change the way you react to her. You actually have the power to stop these events that are causing you pain."

We discussed that as long as she reacted instinctively to her mother's jibes, she would be her mother's victim. But if she took responsibility for how she reacted, and accepted some anger management training, she could stop her rage-attacks, and that would turn her from being a victim to being empowered.

"That's not fair. It's her that should get treatment, not me", she reiterated.

"I see your point," I said, "and I understand why you think it's unfair. But it's not a question of whether it's fair or not. It's about you moving the power in your relationship from her to you. It's about stopping you damaging your own interests. It's about you getting the life that you want. It's about you being empowered."

As children, we learn to shift the blame onto others. How many times have you heard children exclaiming something like, "It was her fault, not mine." Children will deny their actions, even when it's blatantly untrue. But they will do it with such passion that they will believe it's true.

As adults, most of us do the same. It becomes our go-to response to blame anyone else but ourselves for things that go wrong in our lives. And we do it with such a passion that we believe it ourselves. It's what's often referred to as being in denial, and it comes from the reflex to blame others.

But while it might feel good to blame someone else, you are in fact making a victim of yourself. You are effectively saying that your happiness and security are in the hands of other people. That's asking for trouble, because you have no power over other people, yet you have handed all the power to them. If they let you down – which they probably will, even if unintentionally - you are the one who suffers, and you blame them to vent your frustration.

In the end, Stephanie did accept help. She learnt some techniques to control her reactions to her mother. She learnt to call a counselling service rather than reach for the vodka – she could let off steam safely on the phone to a counsellor and diffuse the situation. Having an outlet for her feelings was vital. Feelings of outrage and injustice are exceptionally painful, and can blow a massive hole through your ability to think rationally. Having a safe way to vent those feelings is much more sensible than just trying to bottle them up, as that risks an even bigger explosion at a later point.

Stephanie worked at her reactions and it paid off. She came to understand that if she waited for her mother to change her ways, she could wait forever. But she had the power to change her side of the relationship immediately. No one got hurt anymore, especially Stephanie herself. She still thought it was unfair, but the benefits of gaining control of her life outweighed the feeling of resentment. Her friend forgave her. The last time I saw her, her children were talking to her and she was hopeful Mike would move back in with her.

Another client, Gwenda, was dependent on social media. Every time I saw her in the waiting room before a group workshop, she was on Facebook or some other site on her phone. Even during the group sessions, I could see her taking sneaky looks at her phone.

Her moods would swing dramatically and were dependant on the reactions she got to her posts. Her happiness was in the hands of other people, many of them strangers she had never met, but with whom she was "friends". People can be cruel on social media, and one harsh word would bring Gwenda's world crashing down. They were not being fair, she said. They had misunderstood what she meant. There were often tears.

For most people, it is human nature to want to be liked. But Gwenda had an addiction to approval, and it made her unhappy. She could have a dozen people saying nice things about her, but if there was one disapproving comment, she would focus on that, and ignore all the nice stuff. And it wasn't just social media. In a group, she was always fishing for complements, and you could see her expression drop if she didn't get them.

It took Gwenda a long time to grasp that she had made herself a victim, and that the power to change that was in her hands. As far as social media was concerned, she could simply turn it off, take the apps off her phone, and it was gone, just like that, in an instant. But she couldn't just turn off meeting people face-to-face. We worked on this, and she started to understand that the problem wasn't other people's reactions, it was her expectations.

Gwenda would expect people, often strangers, to react positively to her. But there was no basis for her expectations. Other people could not live up to Gwenda's expectations, because they had no idea what her expectations were. She had not communicated her expectations to them and they weren't mind-readers. Gwenda was being illogical. But she was also being very human.

Once Gwenda realized that her expectations of other people came from her being judgmental of how other people should behave, she could start to let go and take responsibility for her own thinking. It was that word "should" causing trouble again.

Taking responsibility for what happens to you is genuinely life-changing. You can try it yourself now. Is there an area of your life where you feel outraged by someone else's behaviour? If you can put aside your emotion, can you see a way you can take control by managing your reactions?

You need to be really honest with yourself. Remember that Path is an acronym of Planning and Total Honesty. Without the honesty, you might fall off your Path and never reach your goal.

It might feel unfair. It might feel that the other person should behave differently. But rather than be resentful, which will only make you unhappy, try to get some acceptance that they are just like that, you can't change them, and you have a part to play in what's happened yourself. It is not totally their fault.

Acceptance doesn't mean you have lost. Acceptance is not the same as resignation. Acceptance is a jumping off point to something better. Once you have acceptance, you can then take action to change your reactions to what whatever is happening. And that will allow you to breathe easier and allow some contentment to come into your life.

Another benefit of changing how you react is that it might encourage the other person to behave better towards you. We tend to get our own behaviour reflected back to us. To take a simple example, if you approach someone you are about to meet for the first time with a smile, it's likely you will get a smile back. But if you have a face like thunder, it's unlikely you will get a smile.

I can't guarantee that the person who has been causing you pain will change to reflect your behaviour. Some people are so self-absorbed they don't notice. But it's worth a shot, you don't know until you try.

You might like to take a little time to reflect on this chapter. My clients who have absorbed this concept have found it deeply life-changing; I know it was for me.

Then, when you are ready, let's move on and discover the magic of living life with a lighter touch.

Living with A Lighter Touch

Three years ago, Antonia and I decided on a life change. We were living in a house in the idyllic county of Dorset in England. Dorset is a place of outrageously stunning villages with thatched-roofed cottages, rolling hillsides, and spectacular coastline, the sort of place the English Tourist Board might put on the cover of its brochure. It would be many people's dream to live somewhere like that, and we were living the dream.

But it didn't feel like a happy dream. We like to be outdoors a lot, and frankly the weather in England is pretty dreary for six or seven months of the year. Also, we were working in demanding, stressful jobs, just to pay for the mortgage, bills and vacations.

I was working in an out-patient unit. Being a therapist probably might sound quite easy. You might imagine clients turning up on-time, ready for their weekly chat with the therapist, it all sounds rather cosy. But the reality of working with people who are often in crisis is not like that at all. It can be seriously demanding, with clients pitching up on the doorstep in all states of distress.

At the same time, Antonia was working in a special unit for children with severe emotional disorders, often working long shifts and anti-social hours. We were taking three or four vacations a year to warm, sunny places, just to keep a feeling of balance in our lives.

We realized we had dug ourselves into a stressful hole. It can happen to anyone. You are so busy day-to-day that you don't realize that you are digging, until one day you look up and suddenly see how deep you have got yourself in. We needed change, and we knew it was up to us to instigate that change. Simply wishing for something better wouldn't work. We needed to take action.

We started by taking stock of where we were. Our lives were full, and we needed to clear the decks to be able to start making changes. Changing your life becomes more difficult if unnecessary commitments and possessions are weighing you down, and we had got ourselves into that position.

It's so easy to fill your life with clutter, both physical and mental. It's easy to overburden yourself with commitments that you don't need any more, and possessions that are doing nothing for you.

We all need to accept some commitments. But few of them are life-long. And life isn't about having a house full of miscellaneous stuff. You can have possessions that are like a weight tied around your neck, or alternatively you can use possessions to facilitate your happiness, and when they have served their purpose, you can let them go and move on. Possessions can be very temporary, like a hire car or a hotel room. You don't need permanent ownership to get pleasure from them, just a short-term lease on their time.

It was on one of our vacations that we began to take stock. We had returned to Portugal's sunny Algarve region for a visit. In the past, we had lived there for seven years, but hadn't been back for almost as long. It felt strange going back; I wasn't sure how I would react. I needn't have been concerned. It immediately felt like home. On the first night, we decided we wanted to return there to live, if not all the time, then at least during the months that are wet and gloomy in England.

It sounded a great idea. Live in a gorgeous part of England in the summer, and then Portugal the rest of the year. But how could we achieve this? Surely, we would need to be rich to do that? How about our jobs? Surely, we would have to take on even greater financial commitments and the stress that comes with that? How about all our possessions?

We had our goal, but we needed a plan so that The Path would reveal itself.

And it did.

We called it living with a lighter touch.

Rather than take on more expense and commitments to realize our dream of a two-centre lifestyle, we decided to go the opposite way.

We would cut our commitments and outgoings, be able to save money, be happier, stop working so hard, and live a life that really was a dream.

Sound impossible? We've done it. Here's how.

We looked at our situation. We lived in a family house. But there was only the two of us and the dog. The youngest of our children had left home. In fact, we only regularly used about half the house. We didn't need all the space. So why were we living there? Why were we working ourselves into the ground to pay for it?

The rest of the house, the half we didn't use, was only useful as somewhere to keep all our possessions. But why did we have all this stuff? Most of it we didn't need. I mean, why did we have hundreds of CDs that we had acquired over decades, when we didn't play them anymore? So, we turned the ones we really liked into MP3s, which we store on a cloud somewhere, and got rid of all the discs.

All the books we never read went as well. We can store hundreds of books on a reading device and then just have a small bookshelf for the ones we really wanted to keep in print format.

Antonia had a lot of items of sentimental value, but she realized that most of them she rarely looked at, so she took photos of them, so she could remind herself of the sentiment, and let the physical objects go.

I went through my wardrobe. About half the clothes in there had been unused for at least a year. I was keeping clothes on the basis that I might wear them one day, but if that day hadn't come in over a year, it probably was never going to arrive, so half my wardrobe went to charity.

I found it hard to part with my fly-fishing gear. I had a bond with it. But I hadn't fished in six years. There was no reason to keep it. It was just taking up space in a storage room. So, I closed my eyes and let it go one morning at a car boot sale.

Then the furniture started to go. Why did we have three sets of tables and chairs just for us two? We never watched the television, so we gave it to someone who was grateful for it. Gradually the house started to empty.

Over the next few months, we sold what we could on websites like Gumtree. We were frequent visitors to car boot sales. The local charity shops started to bulge at the seams with all our donated items.

The point of all this was so we could downsize. I had worked out how much all those vacations had been costing us. We had been spending a lot of money, just so we could spend about 30 days of the year in sunny places and recharge ourselves.

I ran a calculator over how much we had been spending and compared it to what we would be spending in our ideal new lifestyle. The figures were amazing.

If we downsized and had a smaller place as our summer home in England, we would lose the mortgage. Then we could rent an apartment on the Algarve coast of Portugal for eight months of the year, which would cost less than the vacations had been costing us.

We would no longer need the vacations, as we would be living in a sunny place. At the same time, we would feel the relief of having fewer commitments, be less stressed and happier. And our wonderful new lifestyle would actually cost us less than our stressful lifestyle had been.

Brilliant!

There was just one snag. We would still need income while we were in Portugal - we would still need to work. But we didn't want to put ourselves in the situation that we were working all hours in the Portugal, find ourselves back under pressure, and lose the benefits of having a good lifestyle.

But I believe that if The Path you are on is the right one for you, solutions will appear. There are always going to be obstructions in your way, but on a right Path, getting past these will feel like opening doors, not like breaking through brick walls, it will flow. As long as you continue to take action, you will reach your goal.

When my first book became a success, I realized the potential of using my professional training in another way. I now had an alternative to being employed. I could publish some more of my writing. I could also build a small caseload of private clients, and see them via Skype when a face-to-face meeting wasn't practical. In short, I could free myself up from the need to be in one location all the time.

As for Antonia's work, she found a job which is ideal for her at an English-speaking school in Portugal. In order that she wouldn't have the daily grind of commuting, we found an apartment in a seaside town 10 minutes from her work, with sea view, beach, and palm trees included. Then, during the school's summer break, we could enjoy the summer in England.

We transformed our lives by taking Daily Actions over a period of time until eventually we found ourselves at the end of our Path and living our dream. No mysticism, no so-called Law of Attraction, no walking across hot coals on motivational training courses. We had simply harnessed the compounding power of action leading to outcome, repeatedly, over time.

The first time we moved to Portugal, which was back in 2003, we arrived in two cars, which were packed to the roof with stuff we thought was essential. Then we had a container of more things we thought we couldn't leave behind delivered from England. As it turned out, most of the stuff we had had delivered at great expense wasn't of much use at all. We had just moved a load of clutter across Europe.

The second time we moved to Portugal, in 2018, we had learned from our previous experience and it was different. We had set ourselves the target of moving in one car, and we wouldn't get anything delivered. It sounds far too little, moving to a different country, with just a few bags in the car. But we had become really ruthless at working out what we really needed. What would be the point in bringing lots of kitchen equipment, for instance, when there would be equipment in the new place we would be renting? So, we just took clothes, work items like laptops, and a few personal items. There was even room for my golf clubs. We moved country in one saloon car.

Back in England, we now have a mortgage-free loft apartment to return to when we choose. The location is wonderful, with stunning views over the West Country. A management company looks after the building maintenance. The bills are low. We can just lock up and leave for as long as we like, whenever it suits us.

So, we are now in Portugal, and plan to return to our home in England to enjoy next summer, and catch up with family and friends.

Living life with a lighter touch has become fundamental to our view of the world. It means that we are not stressed. We have what we need to keep us happy, and discard things when they no longer serve us.

This could mean discarding physical things like clothes or books that can go to a charity shop, where they can serve someone else. It could mean discarding our current apartment in Portugal, if we decide we want to live somewhere else - which will be a simple matter, as we don't own it - and then someone else will have the opportunity to enjoy it.

It means not holding on to ideas that no longer serve us. It means having the flexibility to make our lives a rolling creation. Maybe after next summer in England, we will come back to Portugal. But maybe we will go to live for a while in Spain or Italy or Florida.

We don't need to think about that now. Our next Path will reveal itself if we continue to take Daily Action and live in accordance with our beliefs and values. Action always leads to outcome.

We have that freedom now. By downsizing on what we don't need, we have a bigger life.

So, could living life with a lighter touch benefit you? True, you might not want to move around as we do, you might be happy living where you are. But are you weighed down by ideas, commitments and possessions that no longer serve you? Do you get stressed-out working all hours just to pay the bills so you can keep working? Is changing your life for the better so difficult because you don't have the mental or physical space to work with? Do you spend your time doing things that you think you should do, rather than what you desire?

There are some commitments we make that we want to be permanent, such as to the people we love. These commitments are a joy, not a burden. But commitments to paying for things that don't serve you any more, or to ideas you don't believe in any more, are just clutter in your life.

You can take the first step to living with a lighter touch right now, today.

Have a look around you. What can you see that no longer serves you? What can you let go of? It may be a physical thing. It may be an attitude that keeps causing you problems. It may be a habit.

Let go of something now. When you let go of physical or mental clutter, you make space for something better. You make space for a little magic to come in to your life.

One thing you might want to make space for is more success. Let's talk about that next.

Serving up Success

A few years ago, I was working in a government-funded counselling service. It so happened that I was transferred to a new location. I was unimpressed by my new place of work. It was seriously underfunded, leading to a lack of adequately-qualified staff. This meant that everyone was under pressure with ridiculously heavy workloads. Staff morale had sunk so far, all the talk in the office was of leaving. Some staff were on long-term sick leave with stress. The management seemed to have lost direction and had almost given up.

The atmosphere transmitted itself to the clients, who were losing faith in the service, and numbers of engagements with the service were dropping. I wondered what on earth I had gotten myself into.

My job was to carry out clinical assessments, one-to-one counselling, and run group workshops. The workshops were a part of my job I had always enjoyed – it was great to have a roomful of people to work with. I was given two workshops per week to run at the new location. They were based around personal development. There was a dedicated meeting room I could use, which could seat twenty people.

But there was a big snag. Because client numbers were dropping, I was only getting two or three clients attending, and sometimes no one turned up at all, which was very dispiriting. I couldn't see me staying in the job for long.

As luck would have it, I had a vacation booked a couple of weeks after I started at the new location, so I had an opportunity to take stock. When I arrived at my vacation location – a lovely resort in the Canary Islands – life seemed better and the sun was shining, but the thought of going back to my job hung over me like a dark cloud.

But, have you ever found that when you are looking for a solution, something that you hadn't really thought about will keep cropping up until you take notice? I think what is going on is that when you have a problem, your subconscious mind starts scanning for solutions, and if it thinks it has found something, it will keep dropping hints.

In this instance, the word "service" kept coming to my attention. I had brought my reading device with me to use by the swimming pool; so, I downloaded a couple of books and read about service. It changed my working life.

I realized that all my life up until that point, I had been thinking about work backwards. I had always looked at work in terms of what I could gain. But I needed to look instead at what I could give. How could I better serve my clients, co-workers and employers?

The logic ran that if I focused on providing great service, then I didn't need to concern myself with how I would be rewarded, because great service gets rewarded.

It's a simple enough concept. If you are a waiter and give your guests great service, you will have more fun in your job, your guests will have a more enjoyable dining experience, and also you will be the one who gets the best tips. Everyone wins. I thought a lot about how I could apply all this to my work.

I resolved that when I got back to work, I would commit to delivering great service. And I did. I didn't wait until I was ready - I threw myself into it from the moment I walked through the door on my return to work. I felt motivated and excited to apply the concept of serving.

It seemed to me that the best way of making a difference quickly was through the group workshops, because that was where you could engage with the largest number of people. When I started thinking in terms of what other people wanted, rather than what I wanted, I realized that I needed to run workshops based around what was truly relevant to the clients, not what I thought they should hear.

So, the first thing I did when I got back to work was to move my desk from a private office to the reception area. That way, I would see all the clients when they turned up for appointments or to make enquiries, and I canvassed them about what they would like to cover in the workshops.

People got curious and started turning up for the workshops. They got engaged in the content, because it was what they wanted, I just had to gently guide the discussion. I made it more interactive and fun. We had videos, quizzes, I got people moving around rather than being rooted to the chair, I brought in advisers to speak on subjects the clients had requested. I got the meeting room spruced up, looking more welcoming, I put fresh fruit out for clients to graze on, and got the best quality coffee we could afford. In the good weather, we ran workshops down on the beach. In short, I was focused on serving my clients as best I could, rather than focusing on what I could get out of the job.

It worked. The numbers attending grew rapidly. We ran out of chairs and had people standing or sitting on the floor in the meeting room, so I started designing extra workshops to cope with the demand. The whole place started to get a buzz about it. We attracted some new staff with a positive mind-set who enjoyed the re-invented atmosphere.

We had momentum.

Word started to get around the county, and workers in other counselling facilities started to get in touch. They had heard what was happening and wanted to find out more. The turnaround was huge.

I was rewarded in several ways. My job got a whole lot more fun. I had the pleasure of seeing more clients responding to treatment. I was given an improved work contract.

Moreover, serving others became my go-to. When I felt a bit low or tired, I would go and find someone to serve, because if I was focused on someone else, my own little troubles would go away, and I would feel better. It's impossible to be self-absorbed and focused on someone else at the same time. You can try this yourself. If you're feeling a bit down, find someone to serve, even if in just a small way, and you will probably feel better.

Another aspect to this story is that I was trying to innovate in the way that I was serving. The interactivity of my workshops was new to the clients. They liked it and felt more engaged. I gave the workshops catchy names. I had a leaflet printed up with info on the workshops and, crucially, I didn't just write a dry description of what the workshop contained, instead I listed the benefits the client would get from attending to make it real and relevant for people.

Everyone who entered the building had a leaflet given to them. It sounds just a small thing, but no one had done that before. And I thanked the clients for attending. Even though they were coming to us with their troubles, they felt wanted.

So, can you use service to enhance your life and those around you? Can you better serve employers or customers? Can you even apply it to your private life? If you do, you will surely attract benefits.

Now that you know about the power of serving, let's look further at how it can pay off in your life.

Creating Something out of Nothing

I find being able to create something out of nothing really exciting. It shows the power of your mind, to be able to look at an empty space, and armed with nothing but your imagination and a notepad, you can design the most amazing things. Then by following a Path, you can bring it into reality.

In the early days of the Internet, I found web design amazing. I bought a book on the subject and shut myself off in a room for a month, while I designed my first web site. It was about travel. There have been two quite different strands to my working life, being a therapist and creating projects in travel business. I feel the diversity has enriched my life.

My first web site was a travel information site that would look very basic compared with what we have today. But almost as soon as I put it online, the page visit counter started to move. People were looking at my site and the repeat hits showed they liked it. Eventually, a big company bought my site, and I was financially rewarded for serving travellers in an innovative way. As the internet grew, big money moved in and it became much more difficult to do what I had done. But I was hooked on creation.

I find it thrilling to think that in just a few weeks' time, people around the world will be reading this paragraph. Readers will be downloading the e-book from all the major online stores. The paperback version will be shipping from warehouses in the United States and Europe. The technology is awesome, and embracing it is something else that has changed my life.

In this chapter, I'm going to explore ways in which you can create and make things happen in the physical world from your imagination, if that is your desire. This could be a business, charity, club, or society. It could be for profit, for the wellbeing of your town, for your family and friends, or simply for the fun of turning your thoughts into reality.

When I am looking at the creative process to bring into being some sort of enterprise, then I look for three key elements.

Service. Who are you going to serve?

Innovation. What can you bring to your client that makes you different?

Specialist Knowledge. Why should anyone listen to you?

If you look at the story of my workshops in the previous chapter, you can see that it had all three of these elements. I had a specific group of clients I wanted to serve, I had innovated in how to present the workshops, and I had specialist knowledge from all my training and previous experience.

When Antonia started her dog care business, she knew who she wanted to serve: dog owners who wanted their pets to have personalized care. She was innovative in only ever accepting a small number of dogs at any time, so she could attend to their individual needs in a homely and domestic setting. Antonia had specialist knowledge, having worked with large numbers dogs before in an animal rescue centre. It was an act of pure creation. She hadn't taken over an existing business, it was entirely the product of her own imagination, and it all came into existence in a matter of days.

My first book had all the elements. I knew exactly the readers I wanted to serve: problem drinkers who wanted help. I was innovating, because I knew there wasn't another book on the market like it. I had an important story to tell. I had specialist knowledge in heaps from having counselled this client group for years.

When you put together these three elements – service, innovation, and specialist knowledge – what you create is your product. If this is a commercial venture with those three magic elements, people will want to buy your goods or services. If it's a club, people will want to join. If it's a charity, people will want to donate.

There is a mega-zillion of businesses who want to sell you food. Many come and go. The ones that succeed are the ones who have clearly defined the three elements. They have a clear type of client in mind, whether it's a steak-lover, or a vegan, or someone wanting a snack on the run, or someone wanting haute cuisine - whatever the client group is, they will lay out their stall to attract that type of eater. They will innovate in terms of their pricing, offers, and types of meals on offer. Their specialist knowledge is in the preparation of the food itself. True, there will be other considerations, such as location, but without those three elements, the restaurant will struggle in even the greatest location.

Technology is an area where the top companies demonstrate their knowledge of the three elements on a grand scale. The founders of these companies changed their lives by changing ours. When I was young, my only experience of using PCs was where you had to start it up in the old DOS operating system. If you are too young to know what I'm talking about, trust me, it was pre-historic.

Then one day I was in a computer store, and the guy who ran it called me over. "See what you think of this," he said. I looked. It was amazing. I had to have it. "I think this is going to be popular," he said.

That was an understatement. I was looking at a Windows operating system for the first time. No wonder Microsoft became the biggest company on the planet. They knew who they wanted to serve: all those frustrated DOS users, millions of them. They innovated in a big way. They had specialist knowledge from having one of the best R&Ds on the planet.

Some might question why I don't mention marketing in the three elements. Surely, marketing is critical? Well, yes and no. Marketing isn't part of the product. The product has to come first. 80% of your effort needs to go into the product. Without a great product, you can market all you like, but you will get found out.

If you have a successfully-marketed restaurant drawing in the crowds but the food isn't up to scratch, people will leave bad reviews on Trip Adviser and other platforms, and the crowds will start going elsewhere. If you have a restaurant with great food but your marketing isn't up to scratch, you might still thrive, as word of mouth and positive reviews do the work for you.

Yet, it seems so many people spend the 80% of their time on the marketing. It's so easy to fall into this trap. If you think you need to be on every social media platform, blogging like a person possessed all day, where's your time for being creative, improving your product and listening to your customers? Who are you serving? Are you focusing on income or service? If you aren't focusing on serving, you are less likely to get the income.

You will also need to have good systems backing you up. The money needs to be collected, the bills paid, the computers serviced, and so on. It is tragic if a great product doesn't make it because the admin is a disaster. If this is not your strong point, outsource it, so you can focus on your product.

Realizing that you can create an enterprise from your imagination is life-changing. It was for me. It has allowed me to have more than one career, which has enhanced my life. It has allowed me to react to opportunities. Here's an example.

I used to be crazy for playing golf. I couldn't get enough of it. I loved the look of an ocean-side course, the smell of the cut grass, cleaning up my clubs, browsing in golf stores - it had me in its spell. So, when I saw an opportunity to live in one of the world's major golf centres - the Algarve - I went for it. I played every course. I became an expert on the area.

I became fascinated by the phenomenon of golf tourism. Although my local courses were in Portugal, hardly any of the golfers were Portuguese. The majority were from northern Europe and were on golf breaks. I started posting information on a website for these visitors, an insider's view of playing in the area. People started asking for help in booking their golf breaks.

I had an idea that I could serve these golfers, my innovation was that I was telling people the unvarnished truth about playing there, rather than a lot of sales gloss, and my specialist knowledge came from being a local. I didn't wait until I was ready; I just got on with it. It was just as well I didn't wait, if I had procrastinated and told myself I needed to do more research, I would have discovered just how good the competition was, and might have never gone ahead. Sometimes a little ignorance can be strength.

I was a blur of activity. I got on the phone to the golf courses, and started to sign contracts to re-sell tee times. Some golf courses were reluctant, saying they had enough agents, which was probably true, but I was persistent. I did the same thing with hotels, as my golfers would need somewhere to sleep. I signed up with car hire companies and airport transfer companies. I set up a Portuguese company and got an accountancy firm to look after all the legal stuff.

Within days, the first bookings started coming in. Within a couple of weeks, the first customers arrived at the airport. It was hard work, but it was amazing, it was fun. I was playing some of the best golf courses in Europe with my customers. I had momentum and I was living the dream.

I received requests from golfers wanting to play other areas. So, I expanded the operation. Soon, I had customers arriving in the Algarve, Lisbon, and southern Spain. I had reps meeting them at the airports. I had transfer companies moving them from one course to another. I had clients from all over Europe, the United States and Canada. I even taught myself basic German so I could respond to emails in that language. What had started off just as an idea in my head had become an operation with thousands of golfers arriving annually.

I would, however, like to put in a caveat. You can't escape motivational slogans nowadays. Motivational memes are everywhere online. People wear clothes with motivational messages. Some even have motivational tattoos. One such slogan you must have seen says: Do what you love and you will never work again – or something similar, there are many variations around. We are advised to monetize our passion. It seems to make sense. If you do something you enjoy and the money will follow.

It would seem that I had done exactly that. Surely there can't be a downside?

Well, maybe.

I loved golf because it had been my release from the day-to-day. It was magical for me. When it became my job, I started to lose that. Imagine a boy who loves watching magic tricks. He grows up and learns to be a magician. He now knows how it works, and he loses the sense of magic, it becomes a job. In the end for me, turning up at a golf course became just like turning up at the office.

So, if you are looking to turn something you love into your work, it's worth considering that you might succeed in a business sense, but lose what you love at the same time. And besides, just because you have a passion for something, it doesn't necessarily follow that you will be able to turn it into a successful enterprise. You could be passionate about tennis, but that doesn't mean you're good, and if you play like a person with two left arms, you will never make it as a tennis coach, no matter how passionate you are.

I suggest that instead of following what it says in memes and soundbites, that instead of thinking about yourself and what you want, I suggest instead that you think of the kind of people you have a passion to serve. Don't think about yourself, go and serve them.

In my golf business, I had succeeded in creating a business out of nothing more than my imagination. I had reached the end of my Path. I realized that I needed a new Path, a new challenge, new people to serve.

I realized that serving golfers was no longer my passion. Golf and golfers could get along absolutely fine without me. I was just there for the money, and as discussed before in this book, being there just for the money rarely works in the long-term. I left my business.

I find that every few years, the time comes to hit the reset button, and I had reached that point. I needed someone new to serve. I found those people. I brought my counselling skills up-to-date and went to work in part of the health service in the UK. I wrote earlier about being open-minded about outcomes. When I started on the Path of counselling in the UK, I had no idea that the Path would take me to writing and becoming a bestselling author. I just took my Daily Action (turning up for work with a sense of curiosity and enthusiasm) and this is where the Path has taken me.

Life is amazing.

Next, let's remove a major obstacle from your Path to success and happiness.

Taking Off the Filter

Imagine that you had a headset, like one of those virtual reality headsets. But this headset is a little different. How it works is that it filters out anything that you don't want to see, and it covers your ears, so it also filters out what you don't want to hear

It doesn't exactly show you virtual reality. Rather, it shows you the version of reality that you would like to be true. It shows you how you think the world should be. (That word "should" is causing trouble yet again.)

It feels good, though. There you are in your own little world where everyone and everything agrees with you. It takes away cognitive dissonance – that uncomfortable state of mind when a truth is impinging on what we would prefer to believe. Your mind is at peace. But this headset is a danger to your happiness.

Let's say you have a new love in your life. You think she (we'll assume it's a woman) is wonderful. You're in love. You want to think that your feelings are being reciprocated. But you can't help notice that she seems to get a lot of messages and she won't say who they're from, and some nights she disappears and won't answer your call. Your head hurts, because reality is suggesting that something is wrong. But you don't want it to be that way. So you put on your headset and you see and hear only what you want to be true. Isn't that better? No more of that horrible cognitive dissonance. You can relax......Until she dumps you, and your headset gets ripped off.

These headsets don't really exist, of course. But they don't need to, because your mind creates them for you without you realizing. In Cognitive Behavioural Therapy, we call them mental filters. They let in what you want to see, not what is necessarily true, and filter out the rest.

They are a menace. However, they are alluring because they seem to make sense to the individual. A mental filter offers a comforting point of reference in our random world, because it gives you a fixed viewpoint, it feels like you have something solid in your life. It's easier to have a fixed view than have to consider a whole bunch of variables.

Our modern world encourages mental filters. It's so easy to find chat rooms and Facebook groups for people who have the same mental filter as you do. It could be people with the same political beliefs, religious beliefs, or maybe just people who like the same football team as you - whatever it might be. What happens is that you keep reinforcing each other's filters. You come to believe that you must be right and that anyone who disagrees is wrong, so the filter conveniently keeps out other views.

The trouble is that beliefs based on mental filters are spurious and do not serve us. They cause a huge amount of trouble. Mental filters stand between you and total honesty, and if you are not being totally honest with yourself, your success and happiness are at risk. It's like living in a shack in an earthquake zone, assuming nothing could go wrong.

I had a client who opened a little boutique fashion store, specialising in one particular label that she adored. She believed that because she felt that way, so would other people and the store would be a success. This belief had become a mental filter, and her mind had filtered out evidence that shoppers in the area of her store tended to be price-sensitive, and that her label was expensive.

What happened was that shoppers would come in and make positive comments, and her filter would let these comments through, as they reinforced her beliefs about the label. But when the same people left the store without spending any money, her filter rejected that piece of vital information, as it didn't sit well with her. If the filter had not been in place, she would have seen what was happening and been able to adapt to the client group. But inevitably, the business failed.

Despite the failure, her filter stayed in place, and rather than think of a new, more suitable enterprise, she just became bitter about the shoppers in her area. She called them fools. In fact, they were simply behaving perfectly normally for price-sensitive shoppers. They would look at the clothes in the boutique and make flattering comments, because the garments were lovely. But then they would take a look at the price and go and buy at the bargain store around the corner.

By preventing her from seeing the truth about the incompatibility of her products with the local clientele, the filter had undermined both the success and happiness of the boutique owner.

Another client was a great computer salesperson, frequently being the top-seller at his dealership. He was bright, articulate, and was seen as good management material. This was the route he wanted his career to go down. But he had a very common problem: he had a fear of public speaking, which meant he got really distressed about doing sales presentations within his company, an essential for a manager. His problem wasn't in doing the presentations themselves. He was very professional. But he dreaded feedback. He had a deep fear that one day he would say something ridiculous in front of his management and peers that would make him look like an idiot and wreck his career. He was scared of humiliation.

His filter worked in two ways. Firstly, for days before a presentation, it would let through all the fears about things that could possibly go wrong, while filtering out thoughts of everything that could go right. Secondly, if he got a slight criticism of a presentation, his filter would let that through and magnify it, but if he got praise heaped on him, his filter would shut that out as being irrelevant.

Do you have a filter at work in your life, blocking your way to success and happiness?

The difficulty with filters is seeing that they exist in the first place, as people can believe in them passionately. To see this in action, you only have to watch a political debate on television to see mental filters being used full-on. Participants will totally ignore arguments that would undermine their beliefs, as unwanted truths just bounce off the filter.

However, if you have a belief that you suspect might be holding you back, try to prove it. This is what worked with the computer salesperson. I asked him to prove that his fear had a basis in reality. I asked him to pretend he had to present evidence in a court of law to prove his fear had a basis in fact. He could not, and that came as a great relief to him. His fear evaporated. Instead, he worked on achievement stacking, which is much more constructive.

If you can't prove it, that's probably because it's a filter at work. Once you can see through a filter, they lose their power completely. It's like taking off a headset.

Now, let's look at a massive, self-defeating behaviour that could be limiting your access to success and happiness.

This Time will be Different

I believe in cause and effect. I believe in actions leading to outcomes. That's science. I also believe that lack of action will have an outcome also, and usually an undesirable one. That's why this book is about embracing change.

Change works if you have a Path, with a realistic plan, and you take action in the form of a Daily Action. That keeps you persistently on the Path, and, as they say, persistence pays. And it does pay, as long as the plan is realistic. But what if it isn't? What if you are persistently pursuing a misguided goal? How do you know?

In my job as a therapist, I have worked a lot in addiction services, and something that I was up against all the time was the cycle of recovery followed by relapse followed by recovery and so on. It was tragic to watch. My job was about trying to help people break that cycle once and for all. But it wasn't easy.

Time and time again, you would see people go through the pain of coming off a drug, only to repeat the behaviours that had caused them to relapse previously, such as hanging out with their old friends and going to their old haunts, which would invariably lead to another relapse.

It seems obvious that if you know that doing X always causes Y to happen, and you don't want Y to happen, then you should stop doing X, shouldn't you? It makes total sense. We can all intellectually grasp that.

But we are humans, not machines, and we don't always do what we know intellectually to be true. Frequently, we will work out what to do with our brains, but then act on the basis of our emotions, and go and do something different. We go and do X all over again.

This is because we want to believe that this time it will be different. We kid ourselves that this time, when we do X that Z will happen instead. But it doesn't. As usual, Y happens, and we're back to where we started.

It's not just people in addiction that have this tendency, it's all of us. It's the power of familiarity. We are attracted to doing what we have done before. It makes doing X seem somehow comforting, even though we know deep down that it's a bad idea to do it, and that it will hurt us. We just end up with Y all over again, and start beating ourselves up for doing X once more.

What's going on here is that voice in our head is at work - that voice that doesn't want us to make changes, because it's scared of change. It's telling us that it's okay to do X again, because this time it will be different. Even though we know that it isn't true, we end up believing the voice because we want to believe it - it's telling us what we want to hear. It's telling us that we can get a desirable outcome without going through the scariness of change. It's telling us a lie because it doesn't want us to change, because it knows that change has hurt us in the past. But that was when we let change happen to us, rather than instigating change, so the voice is misguided.

There is a way out of this cycle. It's a method I have used with a lot of success with clients. It's also a method I use with myself all the time, because, even with my training, I am still a human being and make frequent errors of thinking. You can't stop it entirely, but you can minimise it, and in that way help you experience more success in your life, and we all want that, do we not?

The method I use is called Solution Focused Thinking, or SFT. This has its origins in a form of therapy that psychologists in Milwaukee pioneered towards the end of the last century called Solution Focused Brief Therapy. A brief therapy is one that is used for quick results. It has become one of the key tools for people in my line of work.

But you don't need to be working with a therapist to use SFT. In fact, the basic concept, like others in this book, draws strength from being really simple. Solution Focused Thinking can be summed up in two sentences:

Do more of what works for you.

Stop doing what doesn't work.

It sounds so obvious when you look at it. Of course, if you do more of what works and stop doing what doesn't work, you are bound to be more successful. I have managed to achieve much more in my life since I started applying those two sentences to what I'm working on. It's powerful.

In my early days as a therapist, I would reveal this simple concept to clients with a kind of "Ta Da!" note of triumph. There you go, work these two sentences and your troubles will be over. Yet, I was disappointed with some of my early results.

Solution Focused Thinking is indeed simple, but there is a big difference between simple and easy. Simple concepts still need to be applied. It only works if you actually use it.

If you programmed a computer to apply SFT principals, it would work brilliantly. But we humans have a way of sabotaging ourselves without even realising we are doing it. That voice in our head starts undermining our best ideas. It's when the mental filter gets in the way. Instead of doing more of what works and stopping what doesn't work, we fall for the old "This time will be different" trick, and repeat our old errors yet again. Let me give you an example.

As you know already, I had a lot of difficulty in giving up smoking. I become physically dependent on nicotine very easily and once it gets me in its grip, it doesn't let go without a big fight. Every time I stopped smoking, it was painful, and the voice in my head would convince me that it would be okay to smoke just a little bit again, that this time it would be different and I would be able to smoke on just a casual basis, whenever I chose.

But the voice is a liar. Deep down, I knew it was, yet I wanted to believe it. So, I would pick up something to smoke and become instantly hooked again. And again and again. I was doing X and expecting something other than Y to result. But I always got Y. I was breaking the rules of Solution Focused Thinking, because I was repeating what I knew didn't work.

Then, some years ago, I managed to give up. In fact, I gave up for six months. I was convinced I had beaten nicotine. But one day, I was in a bar waiting for a friend who was late, and I noticed individual cigars for sale behind the bar. I thought, I could buy one and smoke it while I was waiting. I hadn't smoked in 6 months, what could possibly go wrong?

Well, you're probably ahead of me already. I smoked one cigar, and by the next day, I was back to smoking as much as ever. I had done X and, sure enough, Y followed. The old "This time it will be different" trick had made a fool of me yet again.

It took another 10 years until I finally gave up forever. What a waste of money and how risky for my health. But this time I know it is forever, because I finally understand that, when it comes to nicotine and me, X will always produce Y, no exceptions, it will never be different next time.

Solution Focused Thinking invites you to turn all this to your advantage. It invites you to look at your life and see the things that work for you, and to do more.

Some people reading this book will be having difficulties right now, and might think that nothing is working for them. But if you are having a difficult time, start looking anyway. You will find some things that are going okay. Maybe just little things, but if you start doing more of them, your life will get better.

I'm not talking here about trying to kid yourself into thinking that things are better than they are. I'm not going to suggest that you start putting on a smile when you're dying inside (although it might help). I'm not going to suggest that you recite affirmations that you know you don't mean. This is not kidology. This is looking for the building blocks you can work with to find greater success and happiness. You can turn the whole X and Y argument to your advantage. If Y is an outcome you want, keep doing more of X!

One of my clients was a street musician. Life was tough. He was couch-surfing. He had very little money, his music wasn't going well. Yet, he was a good musician, he had real talent. So, we put together a plan, based on Solution Focused Thinking, to try to turn his fortunes around.

First of all, we looked at where he played. He targeted the train station. It made sense, because there was plenty of footfall morning and evening. But, looking at the commuters, you could see why he wasn't doing well with them. People went past him, hands in pockets, looking at their feet, clearly wrapped up in their own world, probably thinking about work and other life issues. They were mostly oblivious to the man with the guitar.

SFT tells us to stop what doesn't work. So, he tried a change. Instead, he targeted the town centre at lunchtime, in the area where the restaurants and take-away food outlets were. His takings went up. I could see why. At lunchtime, people were more relaxed, as they had gotten out of work for half an hour. Also, they were out to buy food, so they were already in spending mode, hands on wallets and purses, and more receptive to getting out a coin for the musician. Things were looking up.

Then we looked at what he played. He usually played his own compositions, which were good, but people didn't know them and didn't connect to them. So, he experimented with playing music from different genres. What he found worked best was old pop and rock classics, the sort of stuff that people knew from childhood, and in particular songs that were cheerful or inspiring. So, if he played the Beatles' "Here Comes the Sun" or Bon Jovi's "It's My Life" the money poured in. So, he played more of that. He did more of what worked.

Finally, he tried putting some information about himself on a board. It was just things like his name, where he came from, and how old he was. He noticed that people who stopped to read that would leave money. You can see why.

Passers-by were now able to connect with him on a human level; he was no longer just another anonymous street musician. So, he made his board bigger and had more personal information. It worked. He got together enough money for a rental deposit on somewhere to live, and his life was taking off. He has simply applied the SFT principals to his situation.

I have realised from working with clients that the main difficulty people face in applying Solution Focused Thinking in their lives is that what really works for them is not what they want it to be. A great example of this is the work I have done with problem drinkers. For 90% of them, stopping drinking, at least for a while, is the action they need to do more of, in order to break the cycle of recovery followed by relapse. But they almost always want to cut down, although it has never worked for them before. They cling onto the belief that it will be different this time, and that this time X will result in Z. But that never happens. The drinkers who succeed are the ones who ignore the voice in their head, throw away the filter, and are totally honest with themselves about what works.

Being totally honest with yourself, even when the truth is not what you think you want, is hugely empowering. What we think we want and what we truly need are often very different. So, how do we get totally honest with ourselves, when our own minds are playing tricks on us to persuade us to take a different path?

Here is an experiment you can run with yourself right now that will help you to be totally honest with yourself and see clearly where you need to put your efforts in life.

For the rest of today (or from tomorrow morning, if you are reading this late in the day) try to be aware of every time an opinion comes into your mind. It doesn't matter what it's an opinion on. You might be surprised by just how many opinions you have. Then look at your opinion, and ask yourself "Is this really true? Could I prove this under oath? Or is this just an illusion or wishful thinking?"

This is an exercise that will teach you a lot about how your own mind works. If you do this just for one day, you will strengthen your decision-making skills for ever, and will make it easier for you to get more success and happiness into your life.

I imagine that most people reading this won't try it. It's human nature. Readers will think, "I must try that sometime," but sometime never comes. That's your prerogative. You paid for this book (thank you!) and it's up to you to use as you see fit. But for those of you who try this experiment, you will change your life today.

Obsessed with Addiction

You have already discovered that I have done a lot of work in the field of addiction – indeed you might even have read books I have written on the subject. I would include obsessions in with this. The difference is really just the choice of words. Addiction carries with it some very negative associations – obsession just doesn't sound quite as bad.

But this is not a book about addiction, you might think, so why am I writing about it here?

The answer is that this is a book about success and happiness, and addictions and obsessive behaviours are major blocks to your personal development. If an obsession or addiction gets out-of-hand, it can be like a wrecking ball, smashing up your life.

If you say the word addict to most people, the first thing that comes to their mind is a drug-user. But this is misleading. We are all addicts to some extent. It's part of being human.

In fact, it's amazing just how many things we human beings can get addicted to. Here are some that spring to mind:

Gambling

Sex

Drinking

Sugar

Shopping

Approval

Video games

Smart phones

Cigarettes

People

Social media

Prescription drugs

Exercising

Watching television

Body building

Shoplifting

Salt

Work

Speed

Coffee

Arson

Tattoos

Praise

Dieting

Binge eating

Taking risks

Plastic surgery

Hoarding

That's a long list, and you could add to it almost endlessly, because there will be someone, somewhere addicted to just about anything you can think of.

So, what exactly is an addict or an addiction? After all, some of the things on the list above seem perfectly fine. What could possibly be wrong with watching television or exercising, for instance?

It's a question of degree. If you have an activity or interest in your life that you take to an extent where it's harming you, then you have reached the point where your happiness is being eroded.

Take, for example, collecting. We humans like to collect things. Most people have a little collection of something. Children in particular love to collect. If you are a parent, you will know what I mean. Your child comes home in a state of uncontrollable excitement about some new thing that the kids at school are collecting, and won't be able to rest until he or she has some, too. They badger you for money and to take them to the store or go online to get some of whatever it might be. Then a few weeks later, another collecting craze will sweep the school. Do you remember Pokémon cards and Cabbage Patch Dolls? Kids went crazy for those.

411

When I was a boy, I was the same. Like most boys I knew, I went through phases of collecting football cards and stamps. At one point, I got really interested in Roman coins. I spent my pocket money on mail ordering the more common coins that I could afford. I got really involved. I learned a lot about Roman history. Then I lost interest. I can't remember what distracted me, probably girls or playing guitar. I guess I was a pretty ordinary boy.

Clearly, there was nothing wrong with my collecting Roman coins. It did no harm, and I learned some history. But what if it had got out-of-hand? What if I had got so obsessed that my school work had suffered? What if I had started stealing money from my parents, so I could buy more coins? What if I had started lying to cover up the extent of my obsession? What if it had let me into hoarding?

When I was working in counselling, I was approached about working with hoarders. I must admit that my first reaction was negative. I didn't see hoarding as being something that needed professional help. But Sonia changed my mind about that.

If you saw Sonia in the street, you might think she was a bag lady. In fact, she had quite a large house where she lived alone. Her concerned family had referred her. They said her hoarding had taken over her life and she was neglecting herself. Our first approaches to Sonia were rebuffed. She didn't want anyone around her house. She was covering up. After several counselling sessions with a patient worker, however, she relented and agreed to let workers in.

The house was full of just about anything you can imagine. And I do mean full. There was nowhere to sit and hardly anywhere to stand. There were piles of magazines that were taller than Sonia herself. And it didn't stop at the house. Sonia had run out of space in the house, so she had started burying things in the garden. It was then that she had begun questioning what she was doing; she had begun seeing through her filter, which was why she had decided to accept help.

Some people would just write Sonia off as being a crazy old lady. But that would be wrong. She was addicted to collecting. She would collect anything. Far from being crazy, she was mentally very sharp in certain ways. She had an amazing memory. To someone coming into her house, it would just look like a huge mess - but not to Sonia. She knew everything she had and where everything was. It was incredible. Her brain was like a huge library where she stored the locations of all her items.

Sonia is, admittedly, an extreme example, but I use her story to make a point. The difference between my collecting Roman coins and Sonia being a self-neglecting obsessive is just a question of degree.

My definition of an addiction is thus:

The pursuit of one particular source of pleasure to the detriment of other vital aspects of life.

By vital aspects of life, I mean things like having healthy relationships, maintaining personal standards, health, career, and finances. If these things start to suffer because someone is pursuing an obsession with drinking or gambling or eating or travelling or buying things they can't afford, or whatever it might be, then you have found an addict, and the pleasure they are pursuing is their addiction.

Does this describe someone in your life? Indeed, does it describe you?

It certainly describes me. I've already written about my nicotine addiction. But there have been others, some worse than others. At one time, my obsession with golf would come close to meeting my definition of an addiction. At another time, I was just as obsessed with fly fishing. That might sound harmless enough, but at one point I was spending all my money and neglecting my career and family just so I could catch trout. It sounds crazy now, but I was obsessed.

You might look at some of the items in the list above and wonder how they could be harmful. Can watching television, for instance, really be classed as an addiction? Again, it's that question of degree. If you watch an hour in the evening to unwind, no it isn't an addiction, but if you spend half your life watching television to the detriment of your relationships and profession, if your health is suffering because you get no exercise and spend most of your time on the couch in front of the television munching pizza, then it meets my definition of an addiction.

So, how come we can get obsessed or addicted to such a wide variety of things? And how come some people get addicted to substances they put in their bodies, anything from caffeine to cocaine, whereas other people get addicted to an action, such as running?

The science isn't totally conclusive on addictions; it really is a challenging thing to analyse. But one theory that has widespread acceptance in science and makes sense to me is that it has a lot to do with neurotransmitters. These are chemical messengers in the brain. There are several of these, but when it comes to obsessional or addictive behaviour, it seems the important one is dopamine.

When released in your brain, dopamine makes you feel good, which is why it can create addictions. Quite why different things cause dopamine release with different people is unclear. It just seems to be human diversity. But it explains why some people can get addicted to certain behaviours, such as gambling, whereas others get addicted to substances, such as alcohol. The common factor is that they produce a burst of dopamine in some people, and the person feels good, so they want to do it again, and end up with a compulsive behaviour.

It even explains why people can get obsessed with other people. If you get a dopamine rush when you see a person, you might get obsessed with them. In fact, there is a lot of similarity between addiction and love, which is where co-dependence comes from.

The downside with dopamine is that it is short-term. It might seem nice because it makes you feel good, but it doesn't produce long term happiness (serotonin does that, which we'll discuss later). An extreme example is crack cocaine, which apparently sends dopamine levels up to 70 times normal, but only for a few minutes, which is why people can spend a fortune on crack, because they want to get that feeling back again and again. But you don't have to take hard drugs to get a dopamine rush. Some people might get that rush from eating ice cream – but just not to the same extent as crack, or Ben and Jerry's would be the biggest company on the planet.

If you have an obsession or addiction holding you back from achieving success or happiness in your life, what can you do about it?

You can start by using the "Why is that?" technique we learned early in this book. Put your obsession to the test. Taking the example of the television addict, ask "Why is that?" The answer might be that the person is bored. But then ask "Why is that?" again, and keep digging down to the real reason, and find the desire that is hidden.

Once you have done that, you can start constructing your Path to your true desire. The key to overcoming an obsession or addiction is usually in finding something you want more, and something that is good for you that will produce that success and happiness. If you have an addiction problem and don't know what that something you want more could be, you might like to revisit the chapter It All Starts with Desire.

But first, I want you to meet Terry.

A Taste to Die For

I had a new client called Terry. His wife referred him to me, as she was worried about his health and, in particular, his weight. This was an unusual referral for me, as I am not a doctor or nutritionist, I am a therapist. But she felt I was the right person for him to see, as she believed his problem was more in his head than his stomach.

I invited Terry to attend one of my cognitive therapy-based groups, but he was horrified at this. In fact, he said he would like to come and see me when there was no one around – an unusual request. So, I met Terry at the end of the day, when most people had already left the building.

Terry was a pleasant and well-mannered 59-year-old. But he was obviously obese, he wore capacious track-suit bottoms as he would have difficulty with normal trousers, and he wore oversize Croc sandals, because his feet were swollen.

He told me that he had been able to retire at 50. Since then, he had piled on weight. He said he had a holiday home on the coast that he often visited with his wife. I knew where he was referring to – it was a beautiful area where I often used to go walking myself. But he didn't like to go out during the day, because he was embarrassed about his weight. This was why he had asked to see me when the building was quiet. It caused problems for his wife, who often had to go out alone, because he didn't want to be seen.

I had met his wife. She was trim and liked walking. She dearly wished her husband would join her on walks out in the countryside. But his social embarrassment, coupled with lack of mobility due to his size, meant that this wasn't possible. This just added to Terry's embarrassment out himself.

Terry talked about his fears for the future. He was worried that because of his weight, he wouldn't live much longer. He was worried his wife would leave him, as he didn't participate fully in their life together. He had a lot of motivation to take action. Yet he did not.

It started to become clear why, when he described his typical day's eating. He said he loved meat with rich sauces and all the trimmings. He loved eating out, the shiny cutlery, gleaming glasses, and chatting to the waiter. He loved to wash it all down with copious amounts of alcohol. He ate eye-watering amounts.

But it wasn't so much what he said, as the way he said it that caught my attention. Although his eating was the root cause of all his problems and he knew it was killing him, he spoke of it with such passion. When he said he loved his food, he really meant he loved it. His wife wished he spoke about her with so much passion.

When we talked about taking action about his eating, Terry became very defensive. This might seem odd, as this was exactly what he said he wanted to do. But when we spoke about reduction, there was a look of panic on his face. I knew that look from my work in addiction services. It was the same look of panic you see if you suggest coming off a methadone prescription to an opiate user. It was the same look of panic you see if you suggest giving up the booze to an alcoholic.

Terry didn't just love his food; he was addicted to it.

Terry's passion for food fitted my definition of an addiction: The pursuit of one particular source of pleasure to the detriment of other vital aspects of life. Although Terry intellectually understood the danger his eating was putting him in, his addiction was over-riding his common sense. He just couldn't stop himself. He was dying because of the tastes he loved so much.

When a chef designs a dish for his customers, he chooses a combination of ingredients that will please them. He wants their business. What he is really doing is selecting a combination of tastes that will light up the pleasure centres in the brain and release the neurotransmitters that give us a feeling of pleasure.

Within food manufacturing companies, creating the tastes that will release those neurotransmitters gets even more technical. It's not only chefs that are involved, food scientists are, too. The complex combinations of salts, fats, sugars and other additives are tested and thoroughly market-researched. When you are making product-release decisions in big food companies or restaurant chains, billions of dollars are at stake.

Companies try to get just the right amount of salt, fat and sugar in products to create something called the Bliss Point. This is where the taste lights up your pleasure senses, but without totally satisfying the desire for salt, fats and sugar, so you crave more, and a desire to overeat is created. Small wonder that so many of us in the West struggle with our weight when food manufacturers are deliberately trying to turn us into addicts. The food industry has a word for making food addictive: optimizing.

I can relate to the addictive nature of processed food. Put a packet of some kind of potato chips in my hand and I have to finish the packet. The safest thing for my waistline is not to lift the packet in the first place.

Terry's conversation went between extremes. Sometimes lamenting what his eating was doing to himself, then, often in the next breath, defending his eating. This seems illogical. It was like Terry was arguing with himself. In fact, he was arguing with his addiction, and much of the time I felt like a bystander, cheering on Terry when he started to win the argument.

You always knew when the addiction was winning, because Terry would start worrying about protein. "Where will I get my protein from if I stop eating sausage?" he would exclaim. I explained that Terry's main problem with protein is that he ate far too much of it, he ate enough protein to keep an army platoon going on manoeuvres. But he couldn't accept that.

So, Terry would use this as defence of his eating, even though he knew the damage it was doing to him. This conflict of logic, cognitive dissonance, is common in people with addictions, and it drives people crazy, until they can see through the filter. In Terry's case, the filter was filtering out the truth of what his eating was doing, and letting in all the wishful-thinking arguments for carrying on as he was.

Terry was caught in a classic addiction trap. He ate because it made him happy in the short-term - the dopamine released by the tastes did that. But it was conversely destroying his long-term happiness, because he hated looking in the mirror and seeing what it was doing to him.

A direct link exists between good health and happiness. To an extent, you have to play with the cards that genetics has dealt you. Also, you cannot go back in time and undo any damage you might have done to yourself. Your health might have been compromised by sheer bad luck, if you have caught an infectious disease or been the victim of an accident. But you can accept where you are now, and make a start to change your life today.

Terry's solution was to commit to a long-term Path of change and take the Daily Action of cutting out all the high-calorie fatty foods that gave him the short-term dopamine buzz. As his overall happiness increased, he found that it became more important than tastes that were killing him.

Let's look at how Terry or anyone can achieve that.

Weighing Up Success

In doing my research for this book, I found that diet and weight maintenance were related issues people particularly wanted to address. I feel this is an important area for this book, as successful change in this area leads to more happiness, for three reasons:

What you eat and drink constantly sets off chemical cause and effect in your body and your brain. It can take your mood up or down and also cause your mood to change with more or less volatility. In other words, it affects the chemistry that controls your happiness.

If you eat a diet that is good for you, then you will have far less anxiety about suffering with sickness and disease. This peace of mind helps facilitate contentment and happiness.

We all like to approve of what we see in the mirror. I'm not saying you should conform to some stereotypical view of what is attractive – that's really setting yourself to fail. But if you look a way that you are comfortable with, that will add to your feeling of confidence, enhancing success and happiness.

So, in this chapter, we'll look at applying the concepts in this book to losing weight, or keeping your weight in balance if you are happy as you are.

Fortunately, I have found a single plan that achieves both aims. I have confidence in what you are about to read, as it's not just theory, I have proved it on myself.

Passions can run high when we talk about food, as you will see if you join a few food-related Facebook groups. People end up trading insults from their entrenched, dogmatic positions on food. It can get political and for some people even religion can come into food.

Personally, I'm a pragmatist with a background of working in healthcare. I look for what actually works, not what fits a political agenda. I look for what is backed up by quality scientific research. The following is what I discovered, and I share it with you now in the hope it can change your life for the better.

When I was in my early twenties, I had a naturally active lifestyle. I lived in London and got around the city on the underground train system. That meant I did a lot of walking, either between home and the local station, or between other stations and my destinations. I also used to be on my feet most of the time at work. I remember I ate reasonably healthily at home – I didn't earn that much, so I ate at home, rather than buying food on-the-go. I can see from photos from back then that I didn't have a weight problem – in fact, I was a stick.

That changed in my mid-twenties. I moved out of London, got a car and started driving everywhere. I got an office-based job and spent much of my day in a chair. I also had the money to buy fast food. Almost without my noticing, the weight started to pile on. Pretty soon, I was going up in trouser-sizes. My life got busy with work and a young family. I neglected my health in favour of a convenience-food lifestyle, eating in the car on-the-go, instead of just eating at proper meal times. I thought that I must do something about my weight, but before I knew it, years had gone by, and the weight stayed on.

Then a few years ago, I tried to get a grip on the problem. I realized that as I was getting older, I needed to take action, or I would be over-weight all my life. I looked into various ways of losing weight. There's no shortage of people out there willing to give advice, but as anyone reading this that has been in the same position will know, there is so much conflicting advice – it can't all be correct.

Big money can be made from selling diet books or supplements or special foods or diet drinks to people hungry for weight-loss. The search for health seems to have gotten trampled underfoot by the stampede of companies wanting to make money from dieting. People lose weight, then put it back on, try one diet then another, buy this product then that, and overall few people achieve long-term weight balance.

The failure of the dieting industry is, ironically, great news for the dieting industry, as it means the customers keep coming back to try again, and any business likes repeat customers.

I was as confused as everyone else. So, I set out to look at the whole business of controlling my weight from scratch, trying to use Solution Focused Thinking to help me. I started by looking at cutting out sugar. Many people have success in weight management by cutting out sweet things. But I realized that wasn't my problem. Cutting out sugar didn't make much of a difference, because I've never had much of a sweet tooth. I love savoury things. I loved sausages, bacon, chorizo, cheese, pastry-covered savouries, and my favourite meat was pork, especially the fattier cuts. It's not surprising weight was a problem. I tried various ways to cut down my calorie intake, but I just got hungry and would blow it.

Then I read up on low-carb style diets. Book shops and blogs were bursting with advice on this subject, and still are. I tried the Atkins and other similar diets that have followed it, like the low-carb, high-meat Keto and Paleo diets. I liked the idea of a diet that would appeal to my savoury tastes. I had a few goes at this type of dieting, and it worked a bit, but then I would just put the weight back on. One thing that really puzzled me was that I would eat enough to feel full, yet I still craved food. Why was that? I couldn't figure it out.

Also, I found this kind of diet seemed counter-intuitive; I couldn't help feeling that a diet that was high in fat must be bad for me. It seems I was right to be suspicious, as since then I have looked into what major scientific studies have concluded, which is that these low-carb diets are really quite dangerous, with an elevated risk of premature death. For instance, research on data from 24,825 participants in the U.S. National Health and Examination Survey showed that people with the lowest intake of carbs had a 50% higher risk of death from heart attack or stroke than those consuming the most carbs. It sounded like a low-carb diet is something I should be avoiding! But there are so many people making money out of these kinds of diets, I doubt they will go away any time soon.

But if I was to avoid the low-carb route, this left me without a plan. In terms of working a Path, I could not get going. Remember the "P" in Path stands for planning, but I could not find the right plan. I had tried working things out for myself and simply counting calories, but I constantly came up against the problem of bingeing when I got hungry. Bingeing is a flaw I have that I have to work around. I rarely eat chocolate, for instance, but give me a box of chocolates, and I will want to eat the lot in one sitting. I am also the kind of person who finds it hard to leave food on the plate, even when I know I'm full. So, my attempts at controlling calories always ended up in a binge.

If controlling calories didn't work and diets like the Keto were downright dangerous, then I couldn't work a Path, until I found a plan that was binge-proof. My breakthrough came when I discovered the writings of Dr John McDougall.

McDougall is an American physician who went to work at a sugar plantation in Hawaii when he was first qualified to practice. His patients were immigrants from Asia who had come to work there. They had brought with them their traditional way of eating, based around grains, vegetables and fruit. McDougall realized that the older people, who stuck to their traditional diet, were generally slim, fit and healthy, avoiding common western diseases, including obesity, and living to an active old age.

By contrast, their children and grandchildren had started eating the usual western diet of processed foods, based on refined carbohydrates, meat, and dairy. These younger people were fatter than their elders and suffered from all the diseases common diseases that plague the west, like diabetes, heart disease and various cancers.

McDougall saw that, as these people had the same genes, it must be the western diet that that was making the younger people fatter and less healthy. So, he set about learning how he could treat patients using diet, rather than prescribing drugs.

Inspired by the traditional diet of the fit older generation he had encountered, he encouraged patients to eat foods that were high in nutrients but low in fat. He was seen as a maverick at the time, but since then science has increasingly supported his views about diet to the extent that it is now becoming mainstream. This has taken time; his first book on the subject was published in 1983. His work is no fad. It has stood the test of time.

The health benefits of the diet-based treatment that McDougall had trail-blazed were impressive, and we'll look more at health in the next chapter. But what caught my attention was that McDougall's original recommendations had been for general health, not weight-loss. Yet his patients found they lost weight as a by-product of adopting McDougall's healthy eating program. Then, by making the change in their eating habits permanent, rather than going on a short-term weight-loss program, they could manage their weight for good.

Up to that point, I had gleaned my knowledge of diet in a haphazard way, reading an article here and there. The same is probably true of most people. Which is how I had picked up on the idea that somehow carbs were bad and fat and protein were good, as the proponents of Paleo and Keto say. But McDougall explained that an adult man like me needs only 20 grams of protein and 3 grams of fat daily. These are not large amounts. Most people already consume far more than this.

To put that into perspective, a single cheeseburger without the bun, weighing 100 grams, would give you 15 grams of protein and a whopping 14 grams of fat. I also discovered that you can get as much protein as you need from vegetables alone. In fact, plants make protein molecules, not animals. The reason why there is so much protein in the cheeseburger is that the animals that were used for the meat and cheese ate plants. The protein you get from animals is recycled by the animal. If you eat plants, you get protein direct from the source.

The idea that we lack protein is one of the most successful pieces of disinformation in history, and started out from marketing done by the livestock industry in the 1950s. Not only don't you need protein from meat, but there is increasing evidence from science that protein from meat could cause cancer, whereas plant-based protein is totally safe. Moreover, just about everyone gets more than enough protein already.

Do you know the name for severe protein deficiency? It's actually kwashiorkor. The reason why you've probably never heard of it is because it's almost unknown in the west. I mean, do you know anyone with kwashiorkor?

No, me neither.

The fact is that excess protein is more likely to be a concern in the West than lack of protein. This is what the US government agency the National Centre for Biotechnology Information says: *"Extra protein is not used efficiently by the body and may impose a metabolic burden on the bones, kidneys, and liver. Moreover, high-protein/high-meat diets may also be associated with increased risk for coronary heart disease due to intakes of saturated fat and cholesterol or even cancer."*

Yet the myth that we need more protein is deeply engrained into popular culture. The food industry takes advantage of this by putting labels on food saying things like "good source of protein", knowing this will help sales, because the consumer associates eating protein with being healthy, which it is, up to a point, as we need protein. But given that most of us eat too much protein already, and the very stark warning about excess protein above from a US Government agency, perhaps we should start seeing labels like "good source of protein" as being a health warning, rather than a reason to buy.

By contrast to fat and protein, that same average male we were discussing needs 700 grams of carbohydrates to meet his energy requirements, according to McDougall.

However, it's vital to understand that not all carbs are equal and healthy. Carbohydrate from wholegrains and vegetables are really good for your health and help you feel full, while being naturally low in calories, and as they take a while to digest, they keep you satisfied for longer.

The so-called refined carbs are a different matter. These are carbohydrates stripped of all their goodness and these are the types of carbs that are found in white bread, pastries, cakes, and most fast food products made with white flour. Refined carbs are poor in nutrient content and are digested quicker, so you feel hungry again sooner.

Wholegrain carbs are better for your mood. As they release slower, you get less insulin-spiking in your bloodstream, which will help you stay feeling calmer and more balanced.

As a therapist, I have found this knowledge really useful in helping me to serve my clients better. My training was all about using cognitive therapy, essentially looking at how people think and how this could be adjusted to help them lead better lives. This is great, it does work. But it isn't always the thinking skills that are the total problem.

In recent times, I have asked questions about the client's diet during the initial assessment. The reason is that if the client's mood problems are because of their diet causing wild insulin spikes, rather than their cognitive skills, then using cognitive therapy is going to be a waste of time.

In short, what you put in your body affects your mental health as well as your physical health.

So, I got into the idea of wholefoods rather than processed foods. For a lot of people, the word wholefood has kind of hippy, cranky overtones. But it's not like that at all. Again, it's just common sense. A useful definition of a wholefood is something that has had nothing bad added and nothing good taken away.

Take, for instance, an apple. If you eat an apple, you are clearly eating the whole food. But if you drink apple juice, that is not a wholefood, as something good had been taken away – in throwing away the pulp of the apple, you are also throwing away the important dietary fibre. If you turn your apple into an apple pie, you are probably going to be adding sugar and also refined carbs in the pastry, so it's no longer a wholefood.

Sometimes the difference is less obvious. Peanut butter, for example, by definition has been processed to turn it from a solid nut to a spreadable paste. Many brands of peanut butter contain lots of oils and other additives and are clearly a processed food. But if you make your peanut butter from 100% peanuts, which some brands are, then you have not added anything bad or taken away anything good, so it still fits the definition of a wholefood.

McDougall cleared up for me the mystery of why I would still want to eat on a low-carb diet, even though my stomach felt full. He explained that if your body was short of carbohydrate, you would get cravings for it, even though your stomach might be full. That explained why I could eat my fill of chicken, for example, but still want more to eat. It wasn't that I simply wanted more food per se; my body was telling me it needed more carbohydrate for my energy needs, and meat doesn't give you that.

I did some more research, reading the writings of other important writers that have come along since McDougall began his work, like Dr Joel Fuhrman and Dr Michael Greger. If nutrition interests you, I would recommend reading their work.

These writers disagree on a few points, but on the overall thrust of their work, there is great agreement. Eat a nutrient-rich, plant-based, wholefood diet and you will get healthier, and if you need to lose weight, that will happen without the need to go on a calorie-restricted diet. In fact, as long as you stick to vegetables, legumes and wholegrains, cut out oils and processed foods, eat nuts and fruit in small but regular amounts, and greatly limit your intake of animal products, you can eat as much as you like.

Eat as much as you like? That sounded like the diet for me!

It's easy to see why this works. That cheeseburger we were looking at earlier contains 303 calories per 100 grams. If you imagine how big a single cheeseburger is without the bun and imagine how much space it would take up in your stomach, you can see that it would not fill you up. That's why you need the bun as well. If you add to that a portion of fries and maybe a milkshake to wash it down, before you know it, you're over 1,000 calories.

Compare that to a vegetable - let's say spinach - which contains 27 calories per 100 grams, and you see why you can eat a heck of a lot of plant-based foods and feel full without racking up lots of calories. Obviously, you wouldn't just eat spinach, but you can see that just a few hundred calories of any combination of vegetables is going to fill you. It simply makes sense.

So, at last I had my plan: I was going to commit to a high-nutrient, low-fat diet. My Daily Action was to eat this way every day. I decided in advance that I would allow myself a bit of slack – I wasn't going to beat myself up if I ate a slice of white bread occasionally, for example – but it was important for me to be totally honest with myself, so any exceptions I made to my new way of eating were few in number. I also decided to be open about my outcomes. I wasn't going to set myself a target date to get to a certain weight. Instead I would focus on my Daily Action of eating healthily and let nature do its thing.

I had some decisions to make first, though. Firstly, was I going to eat meat? In McDougall's writing, he suggests eating meat just on special occasions, what he calls feast days. Joel Fuhrman suggests using meat as a garnish, rather than the main part of the meal, if you just can't get along without the taste of it.

The decision to cut out processed foods that contained meat was easy when I looked at the facts. There is now a big body of scientific research that shows that processed foods made with red meat could be as harmful to your heath as smoking. That's frightening. I didn't go through the pain of giving up smoking just to kill myself with sausages. Okay, that meant I would have to give up sausages and bacon, and I did like the taste, just like Terry in the last chapter. But I asked myself, which would I prefer: a life without the taste of processed meat or a fatal disease?

Easy choice.

I decided the simplest thing to do was to just stay off red meat altogether, and maybe have a little lean poultry occasionally, if I got desperate for the taste of something that wasn't vegetable-based.

I also decided to keep a little fish and seafood in my diet, especially the small stuff at the bottom of the food-chain, like prawns, sardines and mackerel. These little items are big on important nutrients, notably certain types of omega 3s, and are also less likely to be affected by marine pollutants than fish higher up the food chain. Moreover, I can get a great supply of super-fresh fish where I am currently living, in a village on the Atlantic coast of Portugal. In fact, from where I am sitting now, I can see the fishing fleet of small, traditional wooden boats on the beach. Many of the seafood restaurants are within a matter of yards of where the fish are landed. You can't get fresher than that. It would seem perverse not to include some in my diet.

But I still had to decide whether to include any dairy in my diet. I was a big consumer of dairy. I drank a lot of milk. I loved cheese. My default snack at home was a thick layer of mature cheddar melted onto toasted white bread. No wonder I was over-weight and unhealthy. Cheese really is a high-fat, unhealthy processed food, even the so-called low-fat cheeses are bulging with fat. But I loved dairy. How was I going to kick that?

The answer came in the writings of Dr Michael Greger. He runs a not-for-profit web site called nutritionfacts.org, which analyses and compares scientific studies on nutrition. It's a mine of information, and you can read up on the science that backs up this chapter on that site. He also wrote the book "How Not to Die", an amazing book on nutrition and health.

Greger pointed out that we humans are the only species that drinks milk when we are no longer babies, and that we are also the only species that drinks the baby milk of another species, or foods made from it, like cheese.

I had never considered that before. I suddenly saw through the filter and realized just quite how bizarre it is that we drink milk at all. It was a real moment of insight for me, and now I can't watch someone putting milk in coffee without thinking how weird it is. Once you've had a moment of insight like that, you can't go back to how you used to think.

Moreover, by drinking milk, I had been drinking something that contains bovine hormones that nature designed to turn a calf into a 900-pound bull. Common sense told me that was not a good idea if I wanted to manage my weight. I was brought up with the idea that dairy farming was some sort of charming bucolic activity with cheerful country folk lovingly milking happy cows. But it's just a romantic illusion. I looked into how milk is produced to industrial quantities. It's not pretty. Taking all the above into account, I was put off dairy for good. I had no difficulty in giving up cheese afterwards.

When you look at leaving things out of your diet, you could feel that you're depriving yourself, which is a major reason why diets fail. We don't like to feel we are missing out. But in changing in my diet, I had a lot of eating to do just to consume all the things that were recommended, so I was never hungry and had few cravings for things I had cut out.

The last difficulty I had to plan around was being able to stick to my new eating plan during busy times. It was easy enough at home. But during the day, I was working in a busy out-patients wing of a hospital, and I didn't have time to prepare food at work. I had been in the habit of going out to grab something for lunch from local stores in the town.

I quickly saw that it was not going to be easy to find ready-to-eat food that fitted my new eating plan. Shelf after shelf was stacked with processed food snacks, most containing meat or dairy. Even the ones that didn't contain meat or dairy weren't great choices – a processed food snack that doesn't contain animal products might be better than one that does, but it's still processed food with added salt, oil, sugar or whatever, so not ideal. I even found I had to be wary of pre-prepared salads, as they usually came with dressings that pushed the calorie-count up dramatically.

The difficulty in finding non-processed healthy food in convenient form brought home to me just how processed-food manufacturers dominate our lives and our health - small wonder that we in the West are getting heavier every year.

So, as part of my plan, my Daily Action included preparing food at home to take to work. I discovered I enjoyed foods that I would previously never have dreamed of eating. My

442

default snack to take to work was spinach, rocket, spicy salsa and low-fat hummus, rolled up together in a whole-wheat wrap, burrito-style – a far cry from the pastry-covered meaty snacks I used to live on.

Finally, to keep my motivation going, I kept reading books by the previously-mentioned authors and watched videos by them. There are lots on You Tube and Nutritionfacts.org.

I had done my research and my planning. Next, I just needed to keep doing the Daily Actions to take me down my Path.

So, did it work?

Yes, it did. I lost thirty pounds. It took a few months, but as I was never hungry, I was never at serious risk of blowing it and bingeing, which is what had always happened when I had tried to lose weight in the past. What's more, I've been happy to make permanent changes to my way of eating. It's easy, because over time your tastes change anyway, and also the health benefits of this way of eating are massively motivating.

On the subject of which, let's look at staying healthy.

Healthy Ever After

If I told you I had a substance that, if you took enough of it daily, would greatly reduce your chances of having a heart attack, stroke, or getting type-2 diabetes, would you take it? You might be a bit sceptical. You might be concerned that it would be hugely expensive or have side effects. In fact, if a drug company could come up with a pill that would do that, they would charge big money for it and it would make them billions. It would become one of the most successful drugs of all time.

But how about if I told you it was not a drug, it was totally safe, not expensive, and had no side effects, would you take it now? You might still be a little sceptical, you might think I'm a crank, because it sounds too good to be true. But how about if I told you that world-class science supports the effectiveness of the substance, now would you take it? Does this miracle substance really exist?

Yes, it does.

A research team at the University of Otago in New Zealand announced the results of a major study in early 2019. And I do mean a major study. We see research studies reported all the time in the press, often contradictory and confusing. But Otago was a real benchmark study - commissioned by the World Health Organization - that will no doubt influence nutritional advice we will be given over the coming years.

The researchers analysed 40 years of information on this substance and the results of 243 studies and clinical trials using thousands of people. This showed "a 15 to 30 per cent decrease in deaths and incidence of coronary heart disease, stroke, type 2 diabetes and colorectal cancer" in people who took sufficient quantities of the substance. That is massively impressive. No drug can come even close to producing such amazing results.

So, what is this magic substance that could save your life? In fact, you eat it already, but if you eat a typical western diet, you probably don't eat anywhere near enough of it. According to the renowned medical journal The Lancet, in the United Kingdom, for example, only 9% of the population eat enough. We are talking about nothing more than humble dietary fibre.

Fibre-rich foods pack a big nutritional punch, because they also tend to be the kinds of foods that are high in all the other good stuff your body needs, like vitamins, minerals, anti-oxidants, and phytochemicals. So, by taking the easy step of just focusing on getting more fibre in your diet, you can make a huge overall difference to the quality of your diet and your health. It's an easy-to-follow, low-maintenance, high-reward strategy that you can put in place right now and change your life today. It's a no-brainer.

The research recommends at least 25 grams of fibre daily, and 30 grams would be better. Fibre comes from those good carbohydrates we discussed in the last chapter. Sources include wholegrain bread and pasta, vegetables of all descriptions, fruits, beans, peas, lentils, oats, and nuts.

To give you an idea of what this means, here are some examples. A medium potato in its skin would give you 4 grams of fibre; a pear would give you 5 grams; a cup of whole-wheat pasta would give you 6 grams; a cup of baked beans would give you 10 grams; a cup of split peas would give you 16 grams. By comparison, the cheeseburger we talked about in the last chapter would give you just one pathetic gram of fibre. These are just a few examples. You can find many lists of fibre-rich foods online. The Mayo

Clinic's web site has a good list, just type "mayo clinic fibre" into Google.

Foods that are poor in fibre and other nutrients are carbohydrates that have been stripped of their nutrients, like white bread and white pasta. It's important to look for wholegrains.

Another easy health-hack is boosting your intake of antioxidants, which help to slow down aging and combat major diseases. Fruit and vegetables are again the main source of these, but the hack is to go for fruit and vegetables that are darker in colour. The reason is that antioxidants add colour to food, so the darker colours will contain larger amounts of antioxidants.

Therefore, dark purple romaine lettuce will be more beneficial than pale green iceberg lettuce; dark red grapes are better than light green grapes; red potatoes are better than white potatoes, and so on. Colourful beans and peas of all types are great. Berries are fantastic, and bright red strawberries are bursting with antioxidants, but the dark colour rule still applies, so darker blueberries will trump strawberries.

Pale fruits are still worth eating, of course, as they have other nutrients. I wouldn't want to stop eating apples or bananas. But the reason why apples start to go a rusty colour if you cut one open and leave it exposed to the air is that it is oxidising due to its lower antioxidant content. That wouldn't happen with an orange or a mango. So, if you eat an apple, eat the skin, which is where there will be more antioxidants.

Following a diet based on wholegrains, vegetables, pulses, fruit and nuts is healthy. But how exactly do you know that it's working? A healthy diet reduces the chance of you contracting a horrible disease. But on a day to day basis, if you stay disease-free, you don't know if it has worked or not. You might not have got a disease anyway. So how do you know healthy eating works?

I know it works. I have been following this style of eating for several years. I'm not a saint. I love my food. I eat some processed food, for instance, but I limit it, and I never eat processed meat products. I think 90% of my diet could be classed as healthy.

The reason I know that my high-nutrient, low-fat diet works is that in the last three or four years, I haven't had any illnesses: no colds, sore throats, coughs, or cold sores on my lips. I always used to get these things on a regular basis. But I haven't had any since I changed my diet. The only logical explanation for this is the food I eat. Nothing else is different. I am not taking any medication. I don't take supplements. It must be diet.

This makes sense, because the food I eat is constantly releasing high levels of nutrients into my body that boost my immune system, and that's what fights off illness. Sometimes I feel I have a cold or sore throat coming on, but then the symptoms vanish again before the illness develops. That's my immune system kicking in. And logically, if it keeps off the small illnesses, it will help keep the big diseases at bay as well.

I have also been able to measure the effects of my change in diet. Since making the change, my blood pressure and cholesterol readings have fallen to reassuringly safe levels.

Cholesterol in particular has become a target for me. The government recommends that adults have a cholesterol level of less than 5 mmo/L (millimoles per litre). But three out of five people are above this, and the average level is 5.7. In other words, based on cholesterol readings, 60% of the population have an elevated risk of coronary heart disease. My cholesterol reading used to be high, so much so I had a warning from my doctor about it. But now it is an impressively low 3.9 mmo/L. (Note that cholesterol levels are often quoted in mg/dL, milligrams per decilitre, and if you see that, the level you are looking for should ideally be below 200 mg/dL, which equates to 5 mmo/L.)

The difference in my cholesterol is entirely due to diet-change. I take no drugs to control it. In fact, it seems ridiculous to me that drug companies make mega-billions out of selling statins, when simple changes in diet are far more effective, cheap, and have no side effects.

The benefits of changing to a healthy diet are vast. Recent research shows that all of the common diseases that we suffer from in the western world can be treated, and even reversed, through diet change. It's not difficult to do, either. This begs the question, why doesn't everyone do it?

Partly, this is due to lack of information – the word is still getting out there. But many people are enormously resistant to changing from the junk-food diet that is killing us in the west. We saw in the chapter about Terry why this is. As we discussed in the last chapter, processed foods in particular are addictive. They are designed to be so. The companies who make them want you to be hooked on the tastes. It's all about profit. And, as you now know, addicted people see their information through a filter – they see what they want to see, and the rest is filtered out.

But you don't need to be addicted, to this or anything else, because you know the power of having a Path.

The other main hack for health that I focus on is building incidental exercise into my day. Only this morning, Britain's Guardian newspaper, which isn't known for being sensationalist, ran a story headlined: Sitting down for too long may be causing 70,000 UK deaths a year.

What I mean by incidental exercise is keeping on the move as much as possible as part of your normal day, rather than, say, going to the gym occasionally, or doing all your exercise all in one go, once a week. In the study of longevity known as the Blue Zones, researchers looked for similarities in the lifestyles of societies around the world who live the longest. One of their findings was that in long-lived societies, people had naturally active lives. They walked a lot as part of their normal day and had routine manual activities that kept that their bodies moving.

This is an issue for me, as writing is a sedentary business. So, I look for little opportunities to get some more movement in my day. Nowadays, I avoid using my car as much as possible. If I can walk, I walk. There are all sorts of little hacks you can build into your life. For instance, if you can do your food shopping in bits and pieces every day, walking to the supermarket, you will get a lot more incidental exercise than loading up the car once a week.

One other thing that the Blue Zones researchers found was that all the longest-lived societies on earth had diets that were high in nutrient-rich, plant-based foods, just like we have been discussing over the last couple of chapters. So put that way of eating together with incidental exercise, you have a winning combination that will keep you healthy.

A lifestyle like this will also result in your feeling happier. We all want happiness. So, next we'll look at how to get more.

Happiness by Design

Wouldn't it be great if you knew the secret of happiness? Then you could use it to design a happy life. Sounds idyllic, doesn't it? But surely, it's not possible. If you Google happiness, you will come up will a huge variance on what people believe it is. What makes one person happy doesn't cut it for someone else. There is no common denominator. We are all so different. So, there can't be just one secret.

But maybe there is, and science can point us in the right direction.

We discussed neurotransmitters in the chapter on addiction, and in particular dopamine. Neurotransmitters are chemical messengers that whizz around your brain all the time, taking information from one place to another. Dopamine gives you a short-term feeling of pleasure. It's the source of the feeling of pleasure that Terry got when he experienced a favourite taste. Dopamine encourages you to want more, which is why it has a link to addiction.

But it's not the only neurotransmitter. Serotonin is another, and it's rather like the other side of coin to dopamine. Serotonin also feels good, but it isn't short-term and addictive, it gives a longer-lasting feeling of happiness. Perhaps, indeed, serotonin is happiness.

Therefore, if serotonin makes you happy and you knew how to generate it, you could be happy by design.

Sounds good, let's look deeper.

Serotonin is associated with positive moods, social behaviour, good appetite, digestion, sleep, and sexual desire. Lack of serotonin, however, is associated with anxiety, poor sleeping patterns, low self-esteem, and even depression. In fact, the most common drugs for treating low mood and depression are called Selective Serotonin Reuptake Inhibitors, or SSRIs, which work by boosting your serotonin levels. These include well known drugs such as Citalopram, Fluoxetine and Sertraline. If you've ever been prescribed Prozac, you were taking an SSRI.

But you don't need to take a drug to boost your serotonin and your happiness. There are simple actions you can take that will achieve the same result.

Exposure to natural light is up there at the top of the list. It's no co-incidence that people are more likely to suffer from low mood and depression in the winter. So, making the most of the available daylight is the place to start if it's in short supply where you are right now.

Exercise is a big serotonin-booster. As an extra bonus, exercise also releases another neurotransmitter, endorphins, which is like a natural morphine − it helps reduce pain and also prevents anxiety.

Meditation also boosts serotonin. If you think meditation is some sort of mystic voodoo, it's time to take off the filter and look again. I know you've probably been bombarded with articles about Mindful meditation over the last few years, and if you've never tried it, you might be sick of hearing about it. But it works and science backs it up.

Mindfulness, as it is used nowadays in the West, was pioneered in the 1980s at the University of Massachusetts Medical School for stress reduction and chronic pain management. In the United Kingdom, the National Health Service has recommended Mindfulness for anxiety relief since 2005, saying it is at least as effective as medication (like SSRIs). If you haven't used Mindfulness before and would like to have a go, I can recommend the books written or co-written by Dr. Danny Penman.

I had a first-hand opportunity to put all this to the test a few years ago. I was back in England after several years away, and was suddenly hit by low mood at the start of the winter. My doctor diagnosed Seasonally Adjusted Disorder; a kind of depression brought on by lack of sunlight. It's really weird, it's like a switch has been flipped in your head in November, then turns off again just as suddenly in the spring.

Winter days in England are short and there's a lot of cloudy weather, so you can go days without even seeing the sun. At the time, I was working in a hospital. The sun was only just getting up as I arrived at work, and by the time I left, it was already dark.

Never having had any kind of depression before, it was a shock. My doctor prescribed a low-dosage SSRI. I am reluctant to take meds, but I felt I couldn't work with clients who were suffering with mood disorders themselves if I was, too. So, I took the medication. It worked, and then as soon as the sun came out three months later, I was absolutely fine and stopped taking them.

The following winter, it happened again. I took the medication again, but this time it didn't work. I don't know why. I felt awful, worse than ever. My doctor suggested trying something else, till we found a drug that suited me. But I decided to take a whole new approach, with no meds.

I did my research, got a plan, and then started on a Path for the winter, taking Daily Action.

Firstly, I maximised the amount of time I spent in the daylight. Every lunchtime, I got out of the hospital and went walking to soak up whatever light was available.

Secondly, I got exercise. I parked a mile from the hospital on my way to work and walked the rest of the way. That way, combined with the lunchtime walking, I was walking several miles a day. At the weekend I got out as much as I could.

Thirdly, I listened to Mindful recordings in the morning and evening. I also attended Mindfulness groups, and took part in an eight-week course.

It worked. The combination of the above activities kept the seasonal depression at bay until the sun returned in the spring. True, it would have been much easier to have simply taken a pill. Doing it my way was a lot of effort. But I feel that I changed my life for the better. I have never suffered with Seasonally Adjusted Disorder since then. And if life starts throwing those unwanted random events at me and it all gets a bit demanding; I now have Mindfulness to fall back on.

There are other ways to boost your happiness by design.

Serotonin likes you to feel valued. If you don't feel that way, I suggest going back to the chapter Achievement Stacking. That's a great way to boost your feelings of confidence and self-esteem.

Serotonin rewards you for being sociable. Dopamine will give you a short-term buzz for doing something on your own – eating a crafty slice of cake while no one's looking, for instance. But serotonin will give you long term feelings of satisfaction for being part of a group and participating in your society.

Serotonin will reward you for giving. Dopamine will give you a short-term hit for grabbing something for yourself. But for long-lasting feelings of wellness, try giving of yourself. Take another look at what we were saying about being of service to others. I get a great feeling of warmth and pride looking back on work I've done to help people and serve them to the best of my ability.

Serotonin will work its magic for you if you have a belief you can follow. This could be a secular philosophy, a religion, a lifestyle choice like yoga, a political calling, anything that helps you to make sense of your world in those moments when your mind starts ruminating on the big life questions that none of us can answer.

And Serotonin will also reward you for having a Path, focusing on your Daily Action, and being open about the outcomes. You will be calm and assured, if you take this approach to our random world.

Dreams by Choice

Early in this book, I wrote that I was living my dream, not by chance, but by choice.

Now it's your turn.

You have learned how to see clearly what your greatest desires are. You now know the simple power of creating a Path and using a Daily Action to take you to your goal. You have learned how to defeat procrastination by not waiting till you're ready, and can call up motivation anytime through taking a small action to create momentum. You now understand that you can achieve even greater things than you planned by being open about your outcomes. You know that recording the stats and cultivating cheerleaders will help you onwards, and you can empower yourself through achievement stacking and taking responsibility for your reactions to other people and events. You've discovered how to succeed through giving service and using your imagination to create something out of nothing. You have learned how to overcome addictions, anxiety and self-defeating thought-traps like mental filters and thinking that doing the same thing will give a different result. You know how to have a healthy mind and body, and you can create happiness by taking simple actions.

You have everything you need to turn your dreams into a reality - except for one thing.

You need to take some action. Right now.

None of what you have read will help you if you don't use it, and if you wait, you will give that voice in your head a chance to undermine you. It will try to convince you that you don't need to act today. It will suggest that perhaps you had better wait until Monday, or until your birthday, or until New Year, or until Jupiter is in your birth sign, or whatever excuse it can think of, to prevent your embracing change. It will tell you that you don't know enough yet, that you need to do more research and read more books. But you don't. You are already holding the book that you needed all along.

Take an action, take yourself by surprise, and trample that voice of self-doubt underfoot as you run down the Path that leads to your dream.

Thank You

Thank you so much for joining me on the journey through this book. If you have enjoyed it, I would be massively grateful if you could take a couple of minutes to leave a review on Amazon.

I wish you well.

Printed in Great Britain
by Amazon